THE BEST AMERICAN HISTORY ESSAYS ON LINCOLN

Edited by Sean Wilentz
for the Organization of American Historians

THE BEST AMERICAN HISTORY ESSAYS ON LINCOLN
Copyright © Organization of American Historians, 2009.

All rights reserved.

First published in 2009 by
PALGRAVE MACMILLAN®
in the United States—a division of St. Martin's Press LLC, .
175 Fifth Avenue, New York, NY 10010.

Where this book is distributed in the UK, Europe and the rest of the world,
this is by Palgrave Macmillan, a division of Macmillan Publishers Limited,
registered in England, company number 785998, of Houndmills, Basingstoke,
Hampshire RG21 6XS.

Palgrave Macmillan is the global academic imprint of the above companies
and has companies and representatives throughout the world.

Palgrave® and Macmillan® are registered trademarks in the United States,
the United Kingdom, Europe and other countries.

ISBN-13: 978–0–230–60914–3 (pbk)   ISBN-10: 0–230–60914–7 (pbk)
ISBN-13: 978–0–230–60915–0 (cloth)   ISBN-10: 0–230–60915–5 (cloth)

Library of Congress Cataloging-in-Publication Data

The best American history essays on Lincoln / [edited by] Sean
Wilentz; for the Organization of American Historians.
    p. cm.
Includes bibliographical references and index.
ISBN 0–230–60915–5—ISBN 0–230–60914–7
    1. Lincoln, Abraham, 1809–1865. 2. Lincoln, Abraham, 1809–1865—
Political and social views. 3. Political leadership—United States—
History—19th century. 4. United States—Politics and government—
1861–1865. 5. United States—History—Civil War, 1861–1865.
6. Presidents—United States—Biography. I. Wilentz, Sean. II.
Organization of American Historians.

E457.8.B47 2008
973.7092—dc22   2008035164

A catalogue record of the book is available from the British Library.

Design by Newgen Imaging Systems (P) Ltd., Chennai, India.

First edition: January 2009

THE BEST AMERICAN HISTORY ESSAYS ON LINCOLN

CONTENTS

III LINCOLN THE POLITICIAN

IV LINCOLN, THE PRESIDENCY, AND THE CIVIL WAR

ACKNOWLEDGMENTS

For this special bicentennial year of Abraham Lincoln's birth, we focus our *Best American History Essays* volume on the sixteenth, and arguably greatest, U.S. president. We are indebted to editor Sean Wilentz and thank his stellar editorial board—Richard J. Carwardine, James Oliver Horton, James McPherson, Mark F. Neely, Jr., and Joan Waugh—whose vision and wise counsel contributed to this selection of the very best scholarship in American history written on Lincoln in the last sixty years.

A lot of behind-the-scenes work at the OAH executive office made this book possible. We thank Publications Director Michael Regoli, as well as Annette Windhorn, Ashley Howdeshell, Jason Groth, Phillip Guerty, Chad Parker, Amy Stark, and Indiana University editorial intern, Emily Deal.

We are also very grateful to our colleagues at Palgrave Macmillan, especially editor Christopher Chappell, and production editor Erica Warren, whose efforts were essential in pulling together all the strands that made this book a reality.

—Lee W. Formwalt
Executive Director,
Organization of American Historians

First, I wish to thank the distinguished historians who, without hesitation, agreed to serve on the advisory board for this volume. Each of them knows far more about Abraham Lincoln and the Civil War era than I (as evidenced, in part, by how often many of their articles and essays appeared, independently, on each others' lists of suggested titles, as well as my own list). They made my job, which was to forge some sort of rough consensus by my own lights, much easier than it might have been.

I am grateful to Pete Daniel, the president of the Organization of American Historians, for having faith in me to edit this volume in the continuing series of collected essays sponsored by the organization. Lee

Formwalt, the executive director of the OAH, did an excellent job of getting the project started, and then kept it on track to the end. Michael Regoli, the OAH's director of publications, provided important additional help as the book began taking shape. We all owe gratitude to Christopher Chappell at Palgrave Macmillan for his unflagging support.

—Sean Wilentz

PERMISSIONS

"Abraham Lincoln and the Self-Made Myth," from *The American Political Tradition* by Richard Hofstadter, copyright 1948, 1973 by Alfred A. Knopf, a division of Random House, Inc. and renewed 1976 by Beatrice Hofstadter. Used by permission of Alfred A. Knopf, a division of Random House, Inc.

"Abraham Lincoln," from *Patriotic Gore: Studies in the Literature of the American Civil War* by Edmund Wilson, 1962. Used by permission of Oxford University Press, Inc.

"Naturally Antislavery: Lincoln, Race, and the Complexity of American Liberty" by James Oliver Horton was first presented as the 27th Annual R. Gerald McMurty Lecture at The Lincoln Museum in Fort Wayne, Indiana.

"A Strange, Friendless, Uneducated, Penniless Boy" reprinted with permission of Simon & Schuster Adult Publishing Group from *"We Are Lincoln Men": Abraham Lincoln and His Friends* by David Herbert Donald. Copyright © 1995 by David Herbert Donald.

"Mary and Abraham: A Marriage" by Jean H. Baker from *Lincoln Enigma: The Changing Faces of an American Icon*, 2001. Used by permission of Oxford University Press, Inc.

"The Master Politician" from *The Lincoln Nobody Knows*. Copyright © 1977 Richard N. Current. Reprinted with permission of The McGraw-Hill Companies.

"The Origins and Purpose of Lincoln's House Divided Speech" by Don. E. Fehrenbacher from *Mississippi Valley Historical Review* 46 (March 1960). Copyright © Organization of American Historians. All rights reserved. Reprinted with permission.

"Why the Republicans Rejected both Compromise and Secession" by David M. Potter reprinted with permission of Louisiana State University

INTRODUCTION

Sean Wilentz

No president of the United States—and probably no figure in all of American history—is as widely revered as Abraham Lincoln. For several decades, scholars and the general public alike have uniformly ranked Lincoln, George Washington, and Franklin D. Roosevelt as the three greatest presidents, and Lincoln almost always heads the list. The number of biographies and commentaries written in the United States about Lincoln is exceeded only by those written about Jesus Christ. As emancipator, commander-in-chief, orator, and martyr, Lincoln—or the image of Lincoln—stands for the nation's highest values.

Yet as historians know, this is not the whole story. Before he was murdered, Lincoln was the butt of ridicule and worse from all across the political spectrum—in the North as well as the South. Since then, scholars have continually disagreed, sometimes sharply, about whether Lincoln truly earned the accolades he has received—and, if he did, what has made him so deserving.

This volume, sponsored by the Organization of American Historians, marks the bicentenary of Lincoln's birth by assembling some of the very best historical writings on Lincoln, dating from the end of World War II to the present. With interest in Lincoln bound to reach a new peak, it seems an excellent occasion to present to the wide reading public what might be called the historical Lincoln—including the work of scholars and critics who have devoted their lives to learning, writing, and teaching about Lincoln and his times.

Professional historians have recently acquired a reputation for producing abstruse, narrow works, written in a heavy prose that is meant to impress only fellow academics and that scares off most readers. The reputation is not completely undeserved. But as the essays collected here show, historical scholarship of the highest order has literary merit as well, and sometimes great merit. Anyone with even a passing interest in Lincoln and his place in history ought to find these essays engrossing as well as illuminating—more so, on both counts, than most of the picturesque costume dramas that commonly appear under the heading of popular history and biography. The essays are provocative as well, and sometimes startling. They offer penetrating appraisals of a complex man—and, by doing so, challenge those iconic accounts of Lincoln that, in trying to render him larger than life, unwittingly diminish his stature. Diverse in their perspectives on Lincoln and on American history generally, the authors of these essays pierce through accumulated heroic legends and try to comprehend the intensely human politician and statesman that lay beneath them. Taken together, the essays also convey how historians' approaches to Lincoln have evolved in recent decades.

In the late 1930s and early 1940s, four influential works, none of them by a professional historian, best conveyed the prevailing impression of Abraham Lincoln in Americans' minds. The poet and folklorist Carl Sandburg's two-part, six-volume life of Lincoln (*The Prairie Years* and *The War Years*) completed in 1939, mixed fact, fancy, sentimentalism, and self-consciously poetic prose to create a mythic Lincoln who was at once a homespun American and a spiritual titan—the flawed common man as epic hero, the rail-splitter as democratic avatar.[1] John Ford's film *Young Mr. Lincoln* (1939), starring Henry Fonda, offered a different mythic Lincoln in its portrait of the Emancipator as a young man—freely adapting the true story of Lincoln's clever defense, in his early days as a lawyer, of two men unjustly accused of murder. A year later, Raymond Massey's portrayal of Lincoln in the more comprehensive film *Abe Lincoln in Illinois* (directed by John Crowell and based on the stage-play by Robert E. Sherwood) displayed the conflicted and even passive sides of the hero's personality, but left no doubt about his emerging greatness.

Finally, there was Aaron Copland's orchestral *Lincoln Portrait*, completed in 1942 as part of the patriotic war effort (and soon followed by Copland's "Fanfare for the Common Man"). Copland's work included passages of folk music while it paid homage, in spoken interludes, to the most stirring passages in Lincoln's major writings, including the Gettysburg Address—all in the leftist Popular Front Americana style of which Copland was the musical master.

These idealizations of Lincoln as Father Abraham have never completely lost their purchase on Americans' imaginations, but for some writers, they were always too lofty to be true. Among academic historians the interpretations of the so-called revisionist school, including Avery O. Craven and James G. Randall, held sway from the 1930s until the early

1950s. These revisionists rejected what had become the accepted view, advocated by the historian Charles A. Beard and others, that the Civil War was an irrepressible conflict between an industrial North and an agrarian South. On the contrary, they thought the war could well have been avoided but for the errors and extremism of a blundering generation of national politicians who came to the fore around 1850. Lincoln, by these lights, was very much a member of that unfortunate generation—although his moderate politics helped him escape the worst of the revisionists' censures. Indeed, Randall's monumental four-volume work, *Lincoln the President,* criticized him for, among other things, allegedly mishandling the secession crisis of 1861—yet also praised him as a courageous, tough-minded "liberal statesman," who "favored human rights above property rights."[2]

Harsher criticisms, directed chiefly at the Lincoln mythmakers, came from other quarters. The omnivorous young critic Edmund Wilson, after reading the biography by Lincoln's law partner, William Herndon, in the 1930s, praised it as "one of the few truly great American books of its kind," unlike "the sentimentalities of Sandburg and the ladies who write Christmas stories."[3] Wilson thought that Lincoln's personal miseries had burdened his grandeur, and he admired him as "agonizing" in his genius; yet Wilson never bought the modern Lincoln legend, and went on to call Sandburg "the worst thing that has happened to Lincoln since Booth shot him."[4] In his massive study of the literature of the Civil War, *Patriotic Gore,* which appeared in 1962, Wilson wrote a powerfully moving essay (included here in chapter 2) on Lincoln's profound spirituality, but also condemned him, in the book's cranky introduction, as a ruthless centralizer of state power, on a par with Lenin and Bismarck.

Wilson's resistance to the Lincoln myth originated in the disillusionment with nationalist and military pieties that gripped the rising generation in the aftermath of World War I. In 1948, the young historian Richard Hofstadter registered another kind of dissent. Hofstadter's thinking, at that point in his career, was rooted in the Marxism of the 1930s, but he was also deeply alienated from of the sort of populist radicalism that portrayed Lincoln as a rough-hewn forerunner of the proletarian Left. To Hofstadter, Lincoln was actually an intensely ambitious striver, fully in the unheroic mainstream of American politics, whose career ratified the middle-class myth of the self-made man. Hofstadter was skeptical even when he interpreted Lincoln's most revered statements and achievements, including the Emancipation Proclamation—a document, he wrote, that contained "all the moral grandeur of a bill of lading."[5]

The civil rights movement and reforms of the 1950s and 1960s, described by the eminent historian C. Vann Woodward as "the Second Reconstruction," unquestionably influenced what became a full-scale historical reevaluation of the institution of slavery, the origins of the Civil War—and in time, Abraham Lincoln.[6] Traditional and revisionist historians alike had generally denigrated slavery's role in causing the war. Some had portrayed the institution in the apologetic, even benevolent tones associated with the pro-Confederate myth of "the lost cause." (In these studies, Lincoln's reputation escaped calumny only because he seemed to be charitable to the South compared with the supposedly vicious radicals inside the Republican Party.) Others subsumed slavery under the broader heading of "agrarianism," and interpreted the clash between an aggressive northern industrialism and southern rural society as the basic cause of the war. But beginning in the mid-1950s, two generations of historians, including Kenneth M. Stampp, John Hope Franklin, Stanley Elkins, Eugene Genovese, Robert Fogel, Stanley Engerman, Herbert Gutman, Ira Berlin, and Eric Foner, ended the great academic evasion of slavery's evils, even as they strenuously debated how the slaveholders' regime—and the slaves' activities under it—ought to be understood. Their work put the causes of the war and, in time, Lincoln's political and presidential career, in a fresh light.

Much of this new scholarship had been presaged by the work of black historians, including W. E. B. Du Bois and Carter Woodson, whose writings the mainstream academy had marginalized. Most of the new scholarship, moreover, dealt with the social, cultural, and economic history of slavery, in keeping with a new wave of interest in social history and the lives of ordinary Americans. The politics of the 1850s and after, and Lincoln's place within it, received proportionally less attention—but not for long. On issues crucial to the new literature on slavery, ranging from the rise of the Republican Party to the promulgation of the Emancipation Proclamation, Lincoln and the larger political world could not be evaded. And because Lincoln still loomed so large in Americans' imaginations, he became the subject of numerous studies reflecting the preoccupations of the new social and cultural historians. What was Lincoln's family life like, and how much did it reflect emerging Victorian middle-class norms? How much did Lincoln's views on race temper, and even vitiate, his professed anti-slavery? Books appeared on Lincoln's melancholic psychology, his Illinois home county's place in settling the West, even on his sexuality (including one study purporting, sympathetically, that he may have been homosexual).

Some social historians, to be sure, were apt to take up Lincoln chiefly in order to take him down, once again, from the pedestal he enjoyed in American lore. One group of scholars suggested that a large part of the credit for emancipation ought to go not to Lincoln, but to the slaves who freed themselves by running off the Union lines—and who thereby, in effect, forced Lincoln to sign the Emancipation Proclamation. Other writers went much further to condemn Lincoln as a thoroughgoing racist who as president was initially interested only in saving the Union, not in ending slavery. Lincoln issued the Emancipation Proclamation, these historians say, entirely as a matter of military expediency; finally, they claim, he aimed to turn the United States into a lily-white nation as quickly as possible by carting the freedmen off to Africa. Still other writers agreed that Lincoln was indifferent to the slaves' plight, but insisted he was driven by his dark pursuit of a new, unconstitutional federal autocracy—a dream, these writers claimed, that Franklin Delano Roosevelt eventually fulfilled with his New Deal. Here, Lincoln reappeared as a decisive force, but for tyranny, not liberty.

Still, Lincoln hardly disappeared into the folds of the social history vogue, let alone into the morass of historical polemic. Through the 1950s, '60s, and '70s, a great deal of careful scholarship reclaimed Lincoln's reputation without resorting to the familiar hero-worship, more alert to nuance and paradox than even the best earlier writing on Lincoln. Much more appeared about the free-labor ideology that Lincoln expounded, what the Lincoln scholar Gabor Boritt called "the economics of the self-made man"—an outlook that, though full of homiletics about hard work and social mobility that later generations hear as clichés, had genuinely revolutionary features in its clash with slavery.[7] Using some of the insights of the new social and cultural historians, Lincoln scholars reassessed the evolution of his thinking—and his actions—on subjects ranging from civil liberties to military strategy and tactics.

Beginning in the 1980s, historians renewed their understanding of the Civil War as the central event in the nation's history since the American Revolution. The general public may have understood this point implicitly; at any rate, the public had always been fascinated by the war, as shown by the proliferation of Civil War reading groups, roundtables, and battle reenactment associations around the country. With the publication in 1988 of James M. McPherson's best-selling and highly acclaimed *Battle Cry of Freedom: The Civil War Era*, university scholars began tapping into a public historical imagination and consciousness that many of them hardly knew existed. The Ken Burns television documentary *The Civil War*, broadcast a few years later, tightened the connection. And since then, academic study of every facet of the Civil War has boomed, including study of Abraham Lincoln.

Trying to choose some of the best examples of this scholarship, as well as earlier scholarship dating back to 1945, has proved a daunting task even with the generous advice and counsel of some of the finest living Lincoln scholars. Numerous questions arose about the standards for selection. Should priority be given to the very latest writings, or should older classic essays be included as well? Which of the many sides of Lincoln's life should be treated, and which deemphasized? Should the book stick to Lincoln's public career or delve into his domestic life as well?

There was universal agreement on one point: No book of this length could possibly include all of the writing that deserves to be ranked among the best on Lincoln. Many superb articles, essays, and book chapters suggested to me by the advisory board had to be laid aside for lack of space; and even then, painful publishing realities forced me to compress further the proposed table of contents. Consequently, readers should be aware that this collection is hardly a definitive presentation of all of the absolutely essential reading about Lincoln. At the same time, I am confident that all of the essays here would make any extended list of the most rewarding.

Instead of presenting the selections strictly in the chronological order of their original publication, I grouped them under headings that cover the length and breadth of Lincoln's career. Arranging the selections this way suggests something about the arc of Lincoln's development, from his early days as the son of an unextraordinary farming family through his harrowing and abbreviated presidency. (I would have liked to include something on Lincoln's assassination and on what the historian Merrill Peterson has called his "apotheosis"—but, again, space limitations got in the way.)[8] The book commences with three essays that cover broad themes in Lincoln's life, as preparation for the more specific studies that follow.

Above all, the book is intended as a spur to further reading and research, with the firm conviction that there will always be a great deal to learn and understand about Abraham Lincoln. Writing in the *American Historical Review* in 1936, James G. Randall addressed the question, "Has the Lincoln theme been exhausted?"[9] Randall's own subsequent work, that of his students, and succeeding decades of scholarship have all affirmed that he was correct when he insisted that the theme was as rich as ever. So it remains more than seventy years later, in the bicentennial year of Lincoln's birth. Insofar as his life incorporated and touched upon so many central themes of our history, the perennial changes in historians' views of America will always prompt fresh reflection about Abraham Lincoln. Here, then, is some of the best Lincoln scholarship of the last several decades, offered with the happy assurance that it does not represent anything close to the last word.

NOTES

1. Carl Sandburg, *Abraham Lincoln: The Prairie Years* (2 vols., New York: Harcourt Brace & Company, 1926); Sandburg, *Abraham Lincoln: The War Years* (4 vols., New York: Harcourt Brace & Company, 1939).
2. James G. Randall, *Lincoln the Liberal Statesman* (New York: Dodd, Mead, 1947); Randall, *Lincoln the President* (4 vols., New York: Dodd, Mead, 1945–55), i, 24.
3. Edmund Wilson, "The Old Stone House," in *Travels in Two Democracies* (1936), reprinted in Lewis M. Dabney, ed., *The Edmund Wilson Reader* (New York: Da Capo, 1997), 18.
4. Ibid.; Wilson to John Dos Passos, April 30, 1953, in Edmund Wilson, *Letters on Literature and Politics, 1912–1972* (New York: Farrar, Straus & Giroux, 1977), 610.
5. Richard Hofstadter, *The American Political Tradition and the Men Who Made It* (1948; New York: Vintage, 1973), 169.
6. C. Vann Woodward, "From the First Reconstruction to the Second," *Harper's*, 230 (April, 1965), 127–33.
7. Gabor Boritt, *Abraham Lincoln and the Economics of the American Dream* (Memphis, TN: Memphis State University Press, 1978).
8. Merrill Peterson, *Lincoln in American Memory* (New York: Oxford University Press, 1994), 3–35.
9. James G. Randall, "Has the Lincoln Theme Been Exhausted?," *American Historical Review*, 41, 2 (1936): 270–294.

I

GENERAL APPRAISALS

1

ABRAHAM LINCOLN AND THE SELF-MADE MYTH

Richard Hofstadter

I happen, temporarily, to occupy this White House. I am a living witness that anyone of your children may look to come here as my father's child has.
—ABRAHAM LINCOLN to the 166th Ohio Regiment

IIis ambition was a little engine that knew no rest.
—WILLIAM H. HERNDON

I

The Lincoln legend has come to have a hold on the American imagination that defies comparison with anything else in political mythology. Here is a drama in which a great man shoulders the torment and moral burdens of a blundering and sinful people, suffers for them, and redeems them with hallowed Christian virtues—"malice toward none and charity for all"—and is destroyed at the pitch of his success. The worldly-wise John Hay, who knew him about as well as he permitted himself to be known, called him "the greatest character since Christ," a comparison one cannot imagine being made of any other political figure of modern times.

If the Lincoln legend gathers strength from its similarity to the Christian theme of vicarious atonement and redemption, there is still another strain in American experience that it represents equally well. Although his métier was politics and not business, Lincoln was a preeminent example of that self-help which Americans have always so admired. He was not, of course, the first eminent American politician who could claim humble origins, nor the first to exploit them. But few have been able to point to such a sudden ascent from relative obscurity to high eminence; none has maintained so completely while scaling the heights the aspect of extreme simplicity; and none has combined with the attainment of success and power such an intense awareness of humanity and moral responsibility. It was precisely in his attainments as a common man that Lincoln felt himself to be remarkable, and in this light that he interpreted to the world the significance of his career. Keenly aware of his role as the exemplar of the self-made man, he played the part with an intense and poignant consistency that give his performance the quality of a high art. The first author of the Lincoln legend and the greatest of the Lincoln dramatists was Lincoln himself.

Lincoln's simplicity was very real. He called his wife "mother," received distinguished guests in shirtsleeves, and once during his presidency hailed a soldier out of the ranks with the cry: "Bub! Bub!" But he was also a complex man easily complex enough to know the value of his own simplicity. With his morbid compulsion for honesty he was too modest to pose coarsely and blatantly as a Henry Clay or James G. Blaine might pose. (When an 1860 campaign document announced that he was a reader of Plutarch, he sat down at once to validate the claim by reading the *Lives*.) But he did develop a political personality by intensifying qualities he actually possessed.

Even during his early days in politics, when his speeches were full of conventional platform bombast, Lincoln seldom failed to strike the humble manner that was peculiarly his. "I was born and have ever remained" he said in his first extended campaign speech, "in the most humble walks of life. I have no popular relations or friends to recommend me." Thereafter he always sounded the theme. "I presume you all know who I am—I am humble Abraham Lincoln....If elected I shall be thankful; if not it will be all the same." Opponents at times grew impatient with his self-derogation ("my poor, lean, lank face") and a Democratic journal once called him a Uriah Heep. But self-conscious as the device was, and coupled even as it was with a secret confidence that Hay called "intellectual arrogance" there was still no imposture in it. It corresponded to Lincoln's own image of himself, which placed him with the poor, the aged, and the forgotten. In a letter to Herndon that was certainly not meant to impress any constituency, Lincoln, near his thirty-ninth birthday, referred to "my old, withered, dry eyes."

There was always this pathos in his plainness, his lack of external grace. "He is," said one of Mrs. Lincoln's friends, "the ungodliest man you ever saw." His colleagues, however, recognized in this a possible political asset and transmuted it into one of the most successful of all political symbols—the hard-fisted rail-splitter. At a Republican meeting in 1860 John Hanks and another old pioneer appeared carrying fence rails labeled: "Two rails from a lot made by Abraham Lincoln and John Hanks in the Sangaman Bottom in the year 1830." And Lincoln, with his usual candor confessed that he had no idea whether these were the same rails, but he was sure he had actually split rails every bit as good. The time was to come when little Tad could say: "Everybody in this world knows Pa used to split rails."

Humility belongs with mercy among the cardinal Christian virtues. "Blessed are the meek, for they shall inherit the earth." But the demands of Christianity and the success myth are incompatible. The competitive society out of which the success myth and the self-made man have grown may accept the Christian virtues in principle but can hardly observe them in practice. The motivating force in the mythology of success is ambition, which is closely akin to the cardinal Christian sin of pride. In a world that works through ambition and self-help, while inculcating an ethic that looks upon their results with disdain, how can an earnest man, a public figure living in a time of crisis, ratify his aspirations and yet remain morally whole? If he is, like Lincoln, a man of private religious intensity, the stage is set for high tragedy.

II

The clue to much that is vital in Lincoln's thought and character lies in the fact that he was thoroughly and completely the politician, by preference and by training. It is difficult to think of any man of comparable stature whose life was so fully absorbed into his political being. Lincoln plunged into politics almost at the beginning of his adult life and was never occupied in any other career except for a brief period when an unfavorable turn in the political situation forced him back to his law practice. His life was one of caucuses and conventions, party circulars and speeches, requests, recommendations, stratagems, schemes, and ambitions. "It was in the world of politics that he lived," wrote Herndon after his death. "Politics were his life, newspapers his food, and his great ambition his motive power." Like his father, Lincoln was physically lazy even as a youth, but unlike him had an active forensic mind. When only fifteen he was often on stumps and fences making political speeches, from which his father had to haul him back to his chores. He was fond of listening to lawyers' arguments and occupying his mind with them

Herndon testifies that "He read specially for a special object and thought things useless unless they could be of utility, use, practice, etc."[1] When Lincoln read he preferred to read aloud. Once when Herndon asked him about it he answered: "I catch the idea by two senses, for when I read aloud I hear what is read and I see it...and I remember it better, if I do not understand it better." These are the reading habits of a man who is preparing for the platform.

For a youth with such mental habits—and one who had no business talents in the narrower sense—the greatest opportunities on the Illinois prairies were in the ministry, law, or politics. Lincoln, who had read Paine and Volney, was too unorthodox in theology for the ministry, and law and politics it proved to be. But politics was first: at twenty-three, only seven months after coming to the little Illinois community of New Salem, he was running for office. Previously he had worked only at odd jobs as ferry man, surveyor, postmaster, storekeeper, rail-splitter, farm hand, and the like; and now, without any other preparation, he was looking for election to the state legislature. He was not chosen, but two years later, in 1834, Sangamon County sent him to the lower house. Not until his first term had almost ended was he sufficiently qualified as a lawyer to be admitted to the state bar.

From this time to the end of his life—except for the years between 1849 and 1854, when his political prospects were discouraging—Lincoln was busy either as officeholder or office-seeker. In the summer of 1860, for a friend who wanted to prepare a campaign biography, he wrote in the third person a short sketch of his political life up to that time:

> 1832—defeated in an attempt to be elected to the legislature; 1834—elected to the legislature "by the highest vote cast for any candidate"; 1836, 1838, 1840—re-elected; 1838 and 1840—chosen by his party as its candidate for Speaker of the Illinois House of Representatives, but not elected; 1840 and 1844—placed on Harrison and Clay electoral tickets "and spent much time and labor in both those canvasses" 1846—elected to Congress; 1848—campaign workers for Zachary Taylor, speaking in Maryland and Massachusetts, and "canvassing quite fully his own district in Illinois, which was followed by a majority in the district of over 1500 for General Taylor"; 1852—placed on Winfield Scott's electoral ticket, "but owing to the hopelessness of the cause in Illinois he did less than in previous presidential canvasses"; 1854—". . . his profession had almost superseded the thought of politics in his mind, when the repeal of the Missouri Compromise aroused him as he had never been before"; 1856—"made over fifty speeches" in the campaign for Fremont; prominently mentioned in the Republican national convention for the vice-presidential nomination....

The rest of the story is familiar enough.

As a politician Lincoln was no maverick. On the bank question, on internal improvements, on the Mexican War (even at his own political expense), on the tariff, he was always a firm, orthodox Whig. He early became a party wheelhorse, a member of the Illinois State Whig Committee, and in the legislature a Whig floor leader. As Lord Charnwood puts it, "The somewhat unholy business of party management was at first attractive to him." It was during this period that he learned the deliberate and responsible opportunism that later was so characteristic of his statecraft.

In 1848, when he was still in Congress, Lincoln threw in his lot with the shrewd Whig leaders who preferred the ill-equipped but available Zachary Taylor to the party's elder statesman, Henry Clay, as presidential candidate. During the campaign he defended Taylor's equivocations by saying that, far from having no principles, Taylor stood for the highest of principles—"allowing the people to do as they please with their own business." Lincoln himself, because of an agreement to rotate the candidacy for his seat, did not run for re-election to Congress; had he done so, defeat would have been certain. When he tried to get an appointment to the General Land Office he was turned down; a less appealing offer of the Secretaryship of Oregon Territory he declined. For a while it seemed that his political career had come to an end. Thoroughly humbled by his depressing obscurity in Congress, he turned with reluctance to the law, overcome by a melancholy "so profound," says Beveridge, "that the depths of it cannot be sounded or estimated by normal minds. Certainly political disappointment had something to do with his despondency." His ambitions were directed toward public life; he had no legal aspirations, lucrative though his practice was. Years later, when the two were preparing their study of him, Herndon objected to Jesse Weik's desire to stress Lincoln's legal eminence: "How are you going to make a *great* lawyer out of Lincoln? His soul was afire with its own ambition and that was not law."

The repeal of the Missouri Compromise in 1854, which started the dissolution of both major parties and created a fluid political situation, once again aroused Lincoln's hopes. For some time he seems to have thought of the slavery extension issue as a means of revivifying the Whig Party, which he found it hard to abandon. For two years after the Republicans had formed local and state organizations in the Northwest he refused to join them, and even while supporting their candidate, Fremont, in 1856 he carefully avoided speaking of himself or his colleagues as Republicans. In the fall of 1854, hungering for the Senatorial nomination and fearing to offend numerous old-line Whigs in Illinois, he fled from Springfield on Herndon's advice to avoid attending a Republican state convention there.

One of his most terrible fits of melancholy overcame him when he failed to get the nomination the following year. "That man," says Herndon (whose adoration of Lincoln assures us we are listening to no hostile critic), "who thinks Lincoln calmly gathered his robes about him, waiting for the people to call him, has a very erroneous knowledge of Lincoln. He was always calculating and planning ahead. His ambition was a little engine that knew no rest." With all his quiet passion Lincoln had sought to rise in life, to make something of himself through his own honest efforts. It was this typically American impulse that dominated him through the long course of his career before he became interested in the slavery question. It was his understanding of this impulse that guided his political thought.

III

If historical epochs are judged by the opportunities they offer talented men to rise from the ranks to places of wealth, power, and prestige, the period during which Lincoln grew up was among the greatest in history, and among all places such opportunities were most available in the fresh territory north and west of the Ohio River—the Valley of Democracy.

Abraham Lincoln was nineteen years old when Andrew Jackson was elected President. Like most of the poor in his part of the country, Thomas Lincoln was a Jacksonian Democrat, and his son at first accepted his politics. But some time during his eighteenth or nineteenth year Abraham went through a political conversion, became a National Republican, and cast his first vote, in 1832, for Henry Clay.

The National Republican (later Whig) Party was the party of internal improvements, stable currency, and conservative banking; Lincoln lived in a country that needed all three. Doubtless there were also personal factors in his decision. If the Democrats spoke more emphatically about the equality of man, the Whigs, even in the West, had the most imposing and affluent men. That an ambitious youth should look to the more solid citizens of his community for political guidance was natural and expedient; the men Lincoln most respected in the Indiana town of his boyhood were National Republicans, great admirers of Henry Clay; and as Dennis Hanks mournfully recalled, Lincoln himself "always Loved Hen Clay's speeches." With one exception, John Hanks, who turned Republican in 1860, Abraham was the only member of the Lincoln or Hanks families who deserted the Democratic Party.

After a few years of stagnation Lincoln advanced with the utmost rapidity in his middle twenties. While many of the stories about the hardships of his youth celebrated in Lincoln legendry are true, it is noteworthy that success came to him suddenly and at a rather early age. At twenty-four he was utterly obscure. At twenty-eight he was the leader of his party in the Illinois House of Representatives, renowned as the winner of the fight to bring the state capital to Springfield, extremely popular in both Sangamon County and the capital itself, and partner of one of the ablest lawyers in the state. Of his first years in Springfield Herndon writes: "No man ever had an easier time of it in his early days than Lincoln. He had . . . influential and financial friends to help him; they almost fought each other for the privilege of assisting Lincoln . . . Lincoln was a pet . . . in this city." And, adds Herndon, "he deserved it." Success of this sort eases and fattens smaller men; for more restless souls it is a form of poison.

Like his "influential and financial friends," Lincoln belonged to the party of rank and privilege; it exacted a price from him. In time he was to marry into the family circle of Ninian Edwards, of whom it was once observed that he was "naturally and constitutionally an aristocrat and . . . hated democracy . . . as the devil is said to hate holy water." Lincoln's connection with such a tribe could only spur his loyalty to the democratic ways in which he had been brought up; he never did "belong," and Mary Todd's attitude toward him as a social creature was always disdainful.

In a letter written in 1858, discussing the growth of the Republican Party, he observed: "Much of the plain old Democracy is with us, while nearly all the old exclusive silk-stocking Whiggery is against us. I don't mean all the Old Whig party, but nearly all of the nice exclusive sort." Lincoln's keen sense of not belonging to the "nice exclusive sort" was a distinct political asset. Throughout his early career, no doubt, it enabled him to speak with sincerity for Jeffersonian principles while supporting Hamiltonian measures. For public and private reasons alike he was touchy about attempts to link him with the aristocrats because of his Whig affiliations, and once complained bitterly at being incongruously "put down here as the candidate of pride, wealth, and aristocratic family distinction."

And yet it was true that the young Lincoln fell short of being an outspoken democrat. In the social climate of Illinois he ranked as a moderate conservative. Running for re-election to the legislature in 1836, he submitted to a newspaper a statement of his views which included the following: "I go for all sharing the privileges of the government who assist in bearing its burdens. Consequently I go for admitting all whites to the right of suffrage who pay taxes or bear arms (by no means excluding females)." Now, the Illinois Constitution of 1818 had already granted the suffrage to all white male inhabitants of twenty-one or over without further qualification, so that Lincoln's proposal actually involved a step backward.[2]

Lincoln's democracy was not broad enough to transcend color lines, but on this score it had more latitude than the democracy professed by many of his neighbors and contemporaries. One of the extraordinary things about his strangely involved personality is the contrast between his circumspectness in practical politics wherever the Negro was concerned, and his penetration of the logic of the proslavery argument, which he answered with exceptional insight. His keen onslaughts against slavery, in fact, carry the conviction of a man of far greater moral force than the pre-presidential Lincoln ever revealed in action. After 1854, when he renewed his study of the slavery question, Lincoln was particularly acute in showing that the logic of the defenders of slavery was profoundly undemocratic, not only in reference to the Southern scene, but for human relations everywhere. The essence of his position was that the principle of exclusion has no inner check; that arbitrarily barring one minority from the exercise of its rights can be both a precedent and a moral sanction for barring another, and that it creates a frame of mind from which no one can expect justice or security. "I am not a Know-nothing," he wrote to Speed:

> How could I be? How can anyone who abhors the oppression of Negroes be in favor of degrading classes of white people? Our progress in degeneracy appears to me to be pretty rapid. As a nation we began by declaring that "all men are created equal." We now practically read it "all men are created equal except negroes." When the Know-nothings get control, it will read "all men are created equal, except negroes and foreigners and Catholics." When it comes to this, I shall prefer emigrating to some country where they make no pretence of loving liberty,—to Russia, for instance, where despotism can be taken pure, and without the base alloy of hypocrisy.

In Lincoln's eyes the Declaration of Independence thus becomes once again what it had been to Jefferson—not merely a formal theory of rights, but an instrument of democracy. It was to Jefferson that Lincoln looked as the source of his political inspiration, Jefferson whom he described as "the most distinguished politician of our history." "The principles of Jefferson are the definitions and axioms of free society," he declared in 1859. "The Jefferson party," he wrote privately at about the same time, "was formed upon its supposed superior devotion to the rights of men, holding the rights of property to be secondary only, and greatly inferior." The Democratic Party, he charged, had abandoned Jeffersonian tradition by taking the position that one man's liberty was absolutely nothing when it conflicted with another man's property. "Republicans," he added, in an utterly characteristic sentence which ought to be well remembered, "are for both the man and the dollar, but in case of conflict the man before the dollar." There is self portraiture in the remark: one sees the moral idealism of the man; it is there, unquestionably, but he hopes that the world will never force it to obtrude itself.

The Declaration of Independence was not only the primary article of Lincoln's creed; it provided his most formidable political ammunition. And yet in the end it was the Declaration that he could not make a consistent part of his living work. The Declaration was a revolutionary document, and this too Lincoln accepted. One of his early public statements declares:

> Any people anywhere being inclined and having the power have the right to rise up and shake off the existing government, and form a new one that suits them better. This is a most valuable, a most sacred right—a right which we hope and believe is to liberate the world.

Having said so much, he did not stop:

> Any portion of such people that can may revolutionize and make their own of so much territory as they inhabit. More than this, *a majority of any portion of such people may revolutionize, putting down a minority, intermingled with or near about them,* who may oppose this movement. Such a minority was precisely the case of the Tories of our own revolution. It is a quality of revolutions not to go by old lines or old laws; but to break up both, and make new ones.

The principle is reiterated with firmness in the First Inaugural Address.

So Lincoln, the revolutionary theorist. There was another Lincoln who had a lawyer-like feeling for the niceties of established rules and a nationalist's reverence for constitutional sanction. This Lincoln always publicly condemned the abolitionists who fought slavery by extra constitutional means—and condemned also the mobs who deprived them of their right of free speech and free press. This Lincoln, even before he was thirty, warned the young men of Springfield that disrespect for legal observances might destroy free institutions in America, and urged them to let reverence for the laws "become the political religion of the nation." This Lincoln suppressed secession and refused to acknowledge that the right of revolution he had so boldly accepted belonged to the South. The same Lincoln, as we shall see, refused almost to the last minute even to suppress rebellion by revolutionary means. The contradiction is not peculiar to Lincoln; Anglo-Saxon history is full of it.

As an economic thinker, Lincoln had a passion for the great average. Thoroughly middle-class in his ideas, he spoke for those millions of Americans who had begun their lives as hired workers—as farm hands, clerks, teachers, mechanics, flatboat men, and rail-splitters—and had passed into the ranks of landed farmers, prosperous grocers, lawyers, merchants, physicians, and politicians. Theirs were the traditional ideals of the Protestant ethic: hard work, frugality, temperance, and a touch of ability applied long and hard enough would lift a man into the propertied or professional class and give him independence and respect if not wealth and prestige. Failure to rise in the economic scale was generally viewed as a fault in the individual, not in society. It was the outward sign of an inward lack of grace—of idleness, indulgence, waste, or incapacity.

This conception of the competitive world was by no means so inaccurate in Lincoln's day as it has long since become; neither was it so conservative as time has made it. It was the legitimate inheritance of Jacksonian democracy. It was the belief not only of those who had arrived but also of those who were pushing their way to the top. If it was intensely and at times inhumanly individualistic, it also defied aristocracy and class distinction. Lincoln's life was a dramatization of it in the sphere of politics as, say, Carnegie's was in business. His own rather conventional version of the self-help ideology[3] is expressed with some charm in a letter written to his feckless stepbrother, John D. Johnston, in 1851:

> Your request for eighty dollars I do not think it best to comply with now. At the various times when I have helped you a little you have said to me, "We can get along very well now"; but in a very short time I find you in the same difficulty again. Now, this can only happen by some defect in your conduct. What that defect is, I think I know. You are not lazy, and still you are an idler. I doubt whether, since I saw you, you have done a good whole day's work in any one day. You do not very much dislike to work, and still you do not work much, merely because it does not seem to you that you could get much for it. This habit of uselessly wasting time is the whole difficulty.

Lincoln advised Johnston to leave his farm in charge of his family and go to work for wages.

> I now promise you, that for every dollar you will, between this and the first of May, get for your own labor...I will then give you one other dollar....Now if you will do this, you will soon be out of debt,

and, what is better, you will have a habit that will keep you from getting in debt again....You have always been kind to me, and I do not mean to be unkind to you. On the contrary, if you will but follow my advice, you will find it worth more than eighty times eighty dollars to you.

Given the chance for the frugal, the industrious, and the able—for the Abraham Lincolns if not the John D. Johnstons—to assert themselves, society would never be divided along fixed lines. There would be no eternal mud-sill class. "There is no permanent class of hired laborers among us," Lincoln declared in a public address. "Twenty-five years ago I was a hired laborer. The hired laborer of yesterday labors on his own account today, and will hire others to labor for him tomorrow. Advancement—improvement in condition—is the order of things in a society of equals." For Lincoln the vital test of a democracy was economic—its ability to provide opportunities for social ascent to those born in its lower ranks. This belief in opportunity for the self-made man is the key to his entire career; it explains his public appeal; it is the core of his criticism of slavery.

There is a strong pro-labor strain in all of Lincoln's utterances from the beginning to the end of his career. Perhaps the most sweeping of his words, and certainly the least equivocal, were penned in 1847. "Inasmuch as most good things are produced by labor," he began,

it follows that all such things of right belong to those whose labor has produced them. But it has so happened, in all ages of the world, that some have labored, and others have without labor enjoyed a large proportion of the fruits. This is wrong and should not continue. To secure to each laborer the whole product of his labor, or as nearly as possible, is a worthy object of any good government.

This reads like a passage from a socialist argument. But its context is significant; the statement was neither a preface to an attack upon private property nor an argument for redistributing the world's goods—it was part of a firm defense of the protective tariff!

In Lincoln's day, especially in the more primitive communities of his formative years, the laborer had not yet been fully separated from his tools. The rights of labor still were closely associated in the fashion of Locke and Jefferson with the right of the laborer to retain his own product; when men talked about the sacredness of labor, they were often talking in veiled terms about the right to own. These ideas, which belonged to the age of craftsmanship rather than industrialism, Lincoln carried into the modern industrial scene. The result is a quaint equivocation, worth observing carefully because it pictures the state of mind of a man living half in one economy and half in another and wishing to do justice to every interest. In 1860, when Lincoln was stumping about the country before the Republican convention, he turned up at New Haven, where shoemakers were on strike. The Democrats had charged Republican agitators with responsibility for the strike, and Lincoln met them head-on:

> ...I am glad to see that a system of labor prevails in New England under which laborers can strike when they want to, where they are not obliged to work under all circumstances, and are not tied down and obliged to labor whether you pay them or not! I like the system which lets a man quit when he wants to, and wish it might prevail everywhere. One of the reasons why I am opposed to slavery is just here. What is the true condition of the laborer? I take it that it is best for all to leave each man free to acquire property as fast as he can. Some will get wealthy. I don't believe in a law to prevent a man from getting rich; it would do more harm than good. So while we do not propose any war upon capital, we do wish to allow the humblest man an equal chance to get rich with everybody else. When one starts poor, as most do in the race of life, free society is such that he knows he can better his condition; he knows that there is no fixed condition of labor for his whole life.... That is the true system.

If there was a flaw in all this, it was one that Lincoln was never forced to meet. Had he lived to seventy, he would have seen the generation brought up on self-help come into its own, build oppressive business corporations, and begin to close off those treasured opportunities for the little man. Further, he would have seen his own party become the jackal of the vested interests, placing the dollar far, far ahead of the man. He himself presided over the social revolution that destroyed the simple equalitarian order of the 1840s, corrupted what remained of its values, and caricatured its ideals. Booth's bullet, indeed, saved him from something worse than embroilment with the radicals over Reconstruction. It confined his life to the happier age that Lincoln understood—which unwittingly he helped to destroy—the age that gave sanction to the honest compromises of his thought.

IV

A story about Abraham Lincoln's second trip to New Orleans when he was twenty-one holds an important place in the Lincoln legend. According to John Hanks, when Lincoln went with his companions to a slave market they saw a handsome mulatto girl being sold on the block, and "the iron entered his soul"; he swore that if he ever got a chance he would hit slavery "and hit it hard." The implication is clear: Lincoln was half abolitionist and the Emancipation Proclamation was fulfillment of that young promise. But the authenticity of the tale is suspect among Lincoln scholars. John Hanks recalled it thirty-five years afterward as a personal witness, whereas, according to Lincoln, Hanks had not gone beyond St. Louis on the journey. Beveridge observes that Lincoln himself apparently never spoke of the alleged incident publicly or privately,[4] and that for twenty years afterward he showed little concern over slavery. We know that he refused to denounce the Fugitive Slave Law, viciously unfair though it was, even to free Negroes charged as runaways. ("I confess I hate to see the poor creatures hunted down," he wrote to Speed, "...but I bite my lips and keep quiet.")

His later career as an opponent of slavery extension must be interpreted in the light of his earlier public indifference to the question. Always moderately hostile to the South's "peculiar institution," he quieted himself with the comfortable thought that it was destined very gradually to disappear. Only after the Kansas-Nebraska Act breathed political life into the slavery issue did he seize upon it as a subject for agitation; only then did he attack it openly. His attitude was based on justice tempered by expediency—or perhaps more accurately, expediency tempered by justice.

Lincoln was by birth a Southerner, a Kentuckian; both his parents were Virginians. His father had served on the slave patrol of Hardin County. The Lincoln family was one of thousands that in the early decades of the nineteenth century had moved from the Southern states, particularly Virginia, Kentucky, and Tennessee, into the Valley of Democracy, and peopled the southern parts of Ohio, Indiana, and Illinois.

During his boyhood days in Indiana and Illinois Lincoln lived in communities where slaves were rare or unknown, and the problem was not thrust upon him. The prevailing attitude toward Negroes in Illinois was intensely hostile. Severe laws against free Negroes and runaway slaves were in force when Lincoln went to the Springfield legislature, and there is no evidence of any popular movement to liberalize them. Lincoln's experiences with slavery on his journeys to New Orleans in 1828 and 1831 do not seem to have made an impression vivid enough to change his conduct. Always privately compassionate, in his public career and his legal practice he never made himself the advocate of unpopular reform movements.

While Lincoln was serving his second term in the Illinois legislature the slavery question was discussed throughout the country. Garrison had begun his agitation, and petitions to abolish slavery in the District of Columbia had begun to pour in upon Congress. State legislatures began to express themselves upon the matter. The Illinois legislature turned the subject over to a joint committee, of which Lincoln and his Sangamon County colleague, Dan Stone, were members. At twenty-eight Lincoln thus had occasion to review the whole slavery question on both sides. The committee reported proslavery resolutions, presently adopted, which praised the beneficent effects of white civilization upon African natives, cited the wretchedness of emancipated Negroes as proof of the folly of freedom, and denounced abolitionists.

Lincoln voted against these resolutions. Six weeks later—the delay resulted from a desire to alienate no one from the cause that then stood closest to his heart, the removal of the state capital from Vandalia to Springfield—he and Stone embodied their own opinions in a resolution that was entered in the Journal of the House and promptly forgotten. It read in part: "They [Lincoln and Stone] believe that the institution of slavery is founded on injustice and bad policy, but that the promulgation of abolition doctrines tends to increase rather than abate its evils." (Which means, the later Lincoln might have said, that slavery is wrong but the proposing to do away with it is also wrong because it makes slavery worse.) They went on to say that while the Constitution does not permit Congress to abolish slavery in the states, Congress can do so in the District of Columbia—but this power should not be exercised unless at "the request of the people of the District." This statement breathes the fire of an uncompromising insistence upon moderation. Let it be noted, however, that it did represent a point of view faintly to the left of prevailing opinion. Lincoln had gone on record as saying not merely that slavery was "bad policy" but even that it was unjust; but he had done so without jeopardizing his all-important project to transfer the state capital to Springfield.

In 1845, not long before he entered Congress, Lincoln again had occasion to express himself on slavery, this time in a carefully phrased private letter to a political supporter who happened to be an abolitionist.

> I hold it a paramount duty of us in the free States, due to the Union of the States, and perhaps to liberty itself (paradox though it may seem), to let the slavery of the other states alone; while, on the other hand, I hold it to be equally clear that we should never knowingly lend ourselves, directly or indirectly, to prevent that slavery from dying a natural death—to find new places for it to live in, when it can not longer exist in the old.

Throughout his political career he consistently held to this position.

After he had become a lame-duck Congressman, Lincoln introduced into Congress in January 1849 a resolution to instruct the Committee on the District of Columbia to report a bill abolishing slavery in the District. The bill provided that children born of slave mothers after January 1, 1850 should be freed and supported by their mothers' owners until of a certain age. District slaveholders who wanted to emancipate their slaves were to be compensated from the federal Treasury. Lincoln himself added a section requiring the municipal authorities of Washington and Georgetown to provide "active and efficient means" of arresting and restoring to their owners all fugitive slaves escaping into the District. (This was six years before he confessed that he hated "to see the poor creatures hunted down.") Years later, recalling this fugitive-slave provision, Wendell Phillips referred to Lincoln somewhat unfairly as "that slavehound from Illinois." The bill itself, although not passed, gave rise to a spirited debate on the morality of slavery, in which Lincoln took no part.

When Lincoln returned to active politics the slavery issue had come to occupy the central position on the American scene. Stephen Douglas and some of his colleagues in Congress had secured the passage of the Kansas-Nebraska Act, which, by opening some new territory, formally at least, to slavery, repealed the part of the thirty-four-year-old Missouri Compromise that barred slavery from territory north of 36° 30'. The measure provoked a howl of opposition in the North and split Douglas's party. The Republican Party, built on opposition to the extension of slavery, began to emerge in small communities in the Northwest. Lincoln's ambitions and interests were aroused, and he proceeded to rehabilitate his political fortunes.

His strategy was simple and forceful. He carefully avoided issues like the tariff, internal improvements, the Know-Nothing mania, or prohibitionism, each of which would alienate important groups of voters. He took pains in all his speeches to stress that he was not an abolitionist and at the same time to stand on the sole program of opposing the extension of slavery. On October 4, 1854, at the age of forty-five, Lincoln *for the first time in his life* denounced slavery in public. In his speech delivered in the Hall of Representatives at Springfield (and later repeated at Peoria) he declared that he hated the current zeal for the spread of slavery: "I hate it because of the monstrous injustice of slavery itself." He went on to say that he had no prejudice against the people of the South. He appreciated their argument that it would be difficult to get rid of the institution "in any satisfactory way." "I surely will not blame them for not doing what I should not know how to do myself. If all earthly power were given me, I should not know what to do as to the existing institution. My first impulse would be to free all the slaves and send them to Liberia, to their own native land." But immediate colonization, he added, is manifestly impossible. The slaves might be freed and kept "among us as underlings." Would this really better their condition?

> What next? Free them, and make them politically and socially our equals. *My own feelings will not admit of this*, and if mine would, we well know that those of the great mass of whites will not. Whether this feeling accords with justice and sound judgment is not the sole question, if indeed it is any part of it. A universal feeling, whether well or ill founded, cannot be safely disregarded.[5]

And yet nothing could justify an attempt to carry slavery into territories now free, Lincoln emphasized, for slavery is unquestionably wrong. "The great mass of mankind," he said at Peoria, "consider slavery a great moral wrong. [This feeling] lies at the very foundation of their sense of justice, and it cannot be trifled with....No statesman can safely disregard it." The last sentence was the key to Lincoln's growing radicalism. As a practical politician he was naturally very much concerned about those public sentiments which no statesman can safely disregard. It was impossible, he had learned, safely to disregard either the feeling that slavery is a moral wrong or the feeling—held by an even larger portion of the public—that Negroes must not be given political and social equality.

He had now struck the core of the Republican problem in the Northwest: how to find a formula to reconcile the two opposing points of view held by great numbers of white people in the North. Lincoln's success in 1860 was due in no small part to his ability to bridge the gap, a performance that entitles him to a place among the world's great political propagandists.

To comprehend Lincoln's strategy we must keep one salient fact in mind: the abolitionists and their humanitarian sympathizers in the nation at large and particularly in the Northwest, the seat of Lincoln's strength, although numerous enough to hold the balance of power, were far too few to make a successful political party. Most of the white people of the Northwest, moreover, were in fact not only not abolitionists, but actually—and here is the core of the matter—Negrophobes. They feared and detested the very thought of living side by side with large numbers of Negroes in their own states, to say nothing of competing with their labor. Hence the severe laws against free Negroes, for example in Lincoln's Illinois.[6] Amid all the agitation in Kansas over making the territory a free state, the conduct of the majority of Republicans there was colored far more by self-interest than by moral principle. In their so-called Topeka Constitution the Kansas Republicans *forbade free Negroes even to come into the state*, and gave only to whites and Indians the right to vote. It was not bondage that troubled them—it was the Negro, free or slave. Again and again the Republican press of the Northwest referred to the Republican Party as the "White Man's Party." The motto of the leading Republican paper of Missouri, Frank Blair's *Daily Missouri Democrat*, was "White Men for Missouri and Missouri for White Men." Nothing could be more devastating to the contention that the early Republican Party in the Northwest was built upon moral principle. At the party convention of 1860 a plank endorsing the Declaration of Independence was almost hissed down and was saved only by the threat of a bolt by the antislavery element.

If the Republicans were to succeed in the strategic Northwest, how were they to win the support of both Negrophobes and antislavery men? Merely to insist that slavery was an evil would sound like abolitionism and offend the Negrophobes. Yet pitching their opposition to slavery extension on too low a moral level might lose the valued support of the humanitarians. Lincoln, perhaps borrowing from the old free-soil ideology, had the right formula and exploited it. He first hinted at it in the Peoria speech:

> The whole nation is interested that the best use shall be made of these Territories. *We want them for homes of free white people. This they cannot be, to any considerable extent, if slavery shall be planted within them.* Slave States are places for poor white people to remove from, not to remove to. New free States are the places for poor people to go to, and better their condition. For this use the nation needs these Territories.

The full possibilities of this line first became clear in Lincoln's "lost" Bloomington speech, delivered at a Republican state convention in May 1856. There, according to the report of one of his colleagues at the Illinois bar, Lincoln warned that Douglas and his followers would frighten men away from the very idea of freedom with their incessant mouthing of the red-herring epithet: "Abolitionist!" "If that trick should succeed," he is reported to have said,[7] "if free negroes should be made *things*, how long, think you, before they will begin to make *things* out of poor white men?"

Here was the answer to the Republican problem. Negrophobes and abolitionists alike could understand this threat; if freedom should be broken down they might themselves have to compete with the labor of slaves in the then free states—or might even be reduced to bondage along with the blacks! Here was an argument that could strike a responsive chord in the nervous system of every Northern man, farmer or worker, abolitionist or racist: *if a stop was not put somewhere upon the spread of slavery, the institution would become nation-wide.*[8] Here, too, is the practical significance of the repeated statements Lincoln made in favor of labor at this time. Lincoln took the slavery question out of the realm of moral and legal dispute and, by dramatizing it in terms of free labor's self-interest, gave it a universal appeal. To please the abolitionists he kept saying that slavery was an evil thing; but for the material benefit of all Northern white men he opposed its further extension.

The importance of this argument becomes increasingly clear when it is realized that Lincoln used it in every one of his recorded speeches from 1854 until he became the President-elect. He once declared in Kansas that preventing slavery from becoming a nation-wide institution "is *the purpose* of this organization [the Republican Party]." The argument had a great allure too for the immigrants who were moving in such great numbers into the Northwest. Speaking at Alton, in the heart of a county where more than fifty percent of the population was foreign-born, Lincoln went out of his way to make it clear that he favored keeping the territories open not only for native Americans, "but as an outlet for *free white people* everywhere, the world over—in which Hans, and Baptiste, and Patrick, and all other men from all the world, may find new homes and better their condition in life."

During the debates with Douglas, Lincoln dwelt on the theme again and again, and added the charge that Douglas himself was involved in a Democratic "conspiracy...for the sole purpose of nationalizing slavery."[9] Douglas and the Supreme Court (which a year before had handed down the Dred Scott decision) would soon have the American people "working in the traces that tend to make this one universal slave nation." Chief Justice Taney had declared that Congress did not have the constitutional power to exclude slavery from the territories. The next step, said Lincoln, would be

another Supreme Court decision, declaring that the Constitution of the United States does not permit a *State* to exclude slavery from its limits...We shall lie down pleasantly, dreaming that the people of Missouri are on the verge of making their State free; and we shall awake to the reality instead, that the Supreme Court has made Illinois a slave State.

So also the theme of the "House Divided" speech:

> I do not expect the Union to be dissolved—I do not expect the House to fall—but I do expect it to cease to be divided. It will become all one thing or all the other. Either the opponents of slavery will arrest the further spread of it, and place it where the public mind shall rest in the belief that it is in the course of ultimate extinction or its advocates will push it forward, till it shall become alike lawful in all the States, old as well as new, North as well as South.
> Have we no tendency to the latter condition?[10]

The last sentence is invariably omitted when this passage is quoted, perhaps because from a literary standpoint it is anticlimactic. But in Lincoln's mind—and, one may guess, the minds of those who heard him—it was not anticlimactic, but essential. Lincoln was *not* emphasizing the necessity for abolition of slavery in the near future; he was emphasizing the immediate "danger" that slavery would become a nation-wide American institution if its geographical spread were not severely restricted at once.

Once this "House Divided" speech had been made, Lincoln had to spend a great deal of time explaining it, proving that he was not an abolitionist. These efforts, together with his strategy of appealing to abolitionists and Negrophobes at once, involved him in embarrassing contradictions. In northern Illinois he spoke in one vein before abolition-minded audiences, but farther south, where settlers of Southern extraction were dominant, he spoke in another. It is instructive to compare what he said about the Negro in Chicago with what he said in Charleston. Chicago, July 10, 1858:

> Let us discard all this quibbling about this man and the other man, this race and that race and the other race being inferior, and therefore they must be placed in an inferior position. Let us discard all these things, and unite as one people throughout this land, until we shall once more stand up declaring that all men are created equal.

Charleston, September 18, 1858:

> I will say, then, that I am not, nor ever have been, in favor of bringing about in any way the social and political equality of the white and black races [applause]: that I am not, nor ever have been, in favor of making voters or jurors of negroes, nor of qualifying them to hold office, nor to intermarry with white people....
> And inasmuch as they cannot so live, while they do remain together there must be the position of superior and inferior and I as much as any other man am in favor of having the superior position assigned to the white race.

It is not easy to decide whether the true Lincoln is the one who spoke in Chicago or the one who spoke in Charleston. Possibly the man devoutly believed each of the utterances at the time he delivered it; possibly his mind too was a house divided against itself. In any case it is easy to see in all this the behavior of a professional politician looking for votes.[11]

Douglas did what he could to use Lincoln's inconsistency against him. At Galesburg, with his opponent sitting on the platform behind him, he proclaimed: "I would despise myself if I thought that I was procuring your votes by concealing my opinions, and by avowing one set of principles in one part of the state, and a different set in another." Confronted by Douglas with these clashing utterances from his Chicago and Charleston speeches, Lincoln replied: "I have not supposed and do not now suppose, that there is any conflict whatever between them."

But this was politics—the premium was on strategy, not intellectual consistency—and the effectiveness of Lincoln's campaign is beyond dispute. In the ensuing elections the Republican candidates carried a majority of the voters and elected their state officers for the first time. Douglas returned to the Senate only because the Democrats, who had skillfully gerrymandered the election districts, still held their majority in the state legislature. Lincoln had contributed greatly to welding old-line Whigs and antislavery men into an effective party, and his reputation was growing by leaps and bounds. What he had done was to pick out an issue—the alleged plan to extend slavery, the alleged danger that it would spread throughout the nation—which would turn attention from the disintegrating forces in the Republican Party to the great integrating force. He was keenly aware that the party was built out of extremely heterogeneous elements, frankly speaking of it in his "House Divided" speech as composed of "strange, discordant, and even hostile elements." In addition to abolitionists and Negrophobes, it united high- and low-tariff men, hard and soft-money men, former Whigs and former Democrats embittered by old political fights, Maine-law prohibitionists and German tipplers, Know-Nothings and immigrants. Lincoln's was the masterful diplomacy to hold such a coalition together, carry it into power, and with it win a war.

Lincoln may have become involved in a gross inconsistency over slavery and the Negro, but this was incidental to his main concern. Never much troubled about the Negro, he had always been most deeply interested in the fate of free republicanism and its bearing upon the welfare of the common white man with whom he identified himself. On this count there was an underlying coherence in the logic of his career. His thesis that slavery might become national, although probably without factual foundation,[12] was a clever dialectical inversion of a challenge to the freedom of the common white man set forth by the most extreme Southern advocate of slavery. George Fitzhugh, a Virginia lawyer, had written and published a volume in 1854 entitled *Sociology for the South,* in which he carried to its logical conclusion the proslavery argument laid down by men like Calhoun. These men had said that Northern industrialism was brutal in its treatment of free labor, while Southern slavery was relatively kind to the Negro. Fitzhugh insisted that since slavery is the best condition for labor, all labor, and black or...white, should be owned by capital. "Slavery," Fitzhugh predicted, "will everywhere be abolished, or everywhere be reinstituted." Herndon had shown the volume to Lincoln, and Lincoln had read it with mounting anger and loathing. Although half-dozen Southern papers had toyed with his thesis, Fitzhugh was not taken too seriously in the South, but Lincoln seized upon his ultra-reactionary ideas as a symbol.[13]

Even as early as 1856 the Republicans had been exploiting the theme of the menace of slavery to free labor. The party put out a campaign pamphlet entitled: *The New Democratic Doctrine: Slavery not to be confined to the Negro race, but to be made the universal condition of the laboring classes of society. The supporters of this doctrine vote for Buchanan.* Lincoln carefully cut out the following editorial from a Southern paper and pasted it in his campaign scrapbook:

> Free society! We sicken of the name! What is it but a conglomeration of greasy mechanics, filthy operatives, small-fisted farmers, and moon-struck theorists? All the Northern and especially the New England states are devoid of society fitted for well bred gentlemen. The prevailing class one meets is that of mechanics struggling to be genteel, and small farmers who do their own drudgery; and yet are hardly fit for association with a southern gentleman's body servant. This is your free society which the northern hordes are endeavoring to extend to Kansas.

This was the direct antithesis of everything that Lincoln had been taught to believe—the equality of man, the dignity of labor, and the right to move upward in the social scale. It defied the beliefs of millions of free men in the North who, like Lincoln, were ambitious to move forward and believed that the most sacred thing free society could do was to give to the common man freedom and opportunity to make his own way. When Lincoln debated Douglas at Galesburg, Republican supporters carried a huge banner reading: "Small Fisted Farmers, Mud-sills of Society, Greasy Mechanics for A. Lincoln."

Flouting the aspirations of free labor cost the Southerners dear. The current of proslavery reaction had run its course, and it was somehow fitting that a man like Lincoln should use ideas like Fitzhugh's to destroy the Old South.

V

Before Lincoln took office the issues upon which he was elected had become obsolete. Seven states of the deep South had seceded. The great question was no longer slavery or freedom in the territories, but the nation itself. The Union, if it was to be maintained, as Lincoln, an ardent nationalist, thought it must, could be defended only by the sort of aggressive war that few Northerners wanted to wage. Psychologically on the defensive, the North had to be strategically on the offensive. One of Lincoln's most striking achievements was his tactical and ideological resolution of this difficulty.

By all rational calculation the Confederacy had much to lose and nothing to gain by war. Its strategic aim was merely to preserve itself as an independent state, an end that could be lost in war and achieved in peace. The North, on the other hand, once compromise and reconciliation had failed, had to wage a successful coercive war in order to restore the Union. Northern public opinion, which was in fierce agreement on the desirability of maintaining the Union, was reluctant to consider what saving the Union might cost. There was no more unanimity in the North on waging war to keep the Union than there had been in the South on seceding to destroy it. *Always there loomed the danger that an apparently unprovoked attack upon the Confederacy would alienate so many people in the Union and the world at large that it would hopelessly cripple the very cause for which the war would be fought.* Such an attack would certainly lose the support of the border states, still not withdrawn from the Union, which Lincoln was desperately eager to hold. He had deferred to this sentiment in his Inaugural Address, saying to the South: "The government will not assail you. You can have no conflict without being yourselves the aggressors."

And still there were the forts, the troublesome forts belonging to the government of the United States but located in Confederate territory. Particularly urgent was the problem of Fort Sumter, so placed in the mouth of Charleston harbor that it could hardly be reinforced without subjecting Union ships to the fire of Confederate batteries. Already Major Anderson's men there were running short of supplies and calling for help.

The situation had all the elements of a dilemma for both sides. But since Lincoln had to act first to save the fort from starvation, his was the initial problem. He had promised to maintain the Union, and protect, preserve, and defend the Constitution. It was now too late to restore the Union by compromise, because the Republican leaders, with his advice and consent, had rejected compromise in December.[14] To order Anderson to withdraw Fort Sumter's garrison at the demand of the Confederates was a tremendous concession, which Lincoln actually considered but rejected;

it would be an implicit acknowledgment of the legality of secession, and the Union would, by his own recognition, be at an end; the moral stock of the Confederacy would go soaring. And yet a military assault to bring relief to the fort would be a dangerous expedient. If it failed, it would ruin the already diminished prestige of his administration; success or failure, it would be looked upon by peace advocates and the border states as wanton aggression. However, there was one way out: the Confederates themselves might bring matters to a head by attacking Sumter before Anderson should be forced by shortages to evacuate.

It was precisely such an attack that Lincoln's strategy brought about. On March 29, 1861, the Secretaries of War and the Navy were ordered to co-operate in preparing a relief expedition to move by sea on April 6. Governor Pickens of South Carolina was notified that an attempt would be made to supply Fort Sumter "*with provisions only*," and not with arms, and was advised by Lincoln that "if such an attempt be not resisted, no effort to throw in men, arms, or ammunition will be made without further notice, or [*sic*] in case of an attack upon the fort."

To Northern opinion such a relief expedition would seem innocent enough—bringing food to hungry men. But to the Confederacy it posed a double threat: force would be used *if* the attempt to provision the fort were resisted; and should it not be resisted, an indefinite occupation by Union forces could be expected which would weaken the Confederate cause at home and sap its prestige abroad, where diplomatic recognition was so precious. Lincoln had now taken the burden of the dilemma from his own shoulders and forced it upon the Southerners. Now they must either attack the fort and accept the onus of striking the first blow, or face an indefinite and enervating occupation of Sumter by Anderson's soldiers. Could any supposedly sovereign government permit a foreign power to hold a fort dominating the trade of one of its few great harbors? As Professor James G. Randall has observed, the logic of secession demanded that the Confederates take the fort or that the Union abandon it.

Major Anderson refused a demand for prompt evacuation. Knowing that the Union relief fleet was approaching, the Confederates on the morning of April 12 began firing upon Sumter, and thus convicted themselves by an act of aggression. They had not only broken the Union, they had attacked it; and the reception of the deed at the North was everything that Lincoln could wish.

Lincoln's secretaries, Nicolay and Hay, observe in their monumental biography:

Abstractly it was enough that the Government was in the right. But to make the issue sure, he [Lincoln] determined that in addition the rebellion should be put in the wrong.... When he finally gave the order that the fleet should sail he was master of the situation...master if the rebels hesitated or repented, because they would thereby forfeit their prestige with the South; master if they persisted, for he would then command a united North.

Nicolay, in his *Outbreak of Rebellion,* asserted his belief that it was Lincoln's carefully matured purpose to force rebellion to put itself flagrantly and fatally in the wrong by attacking Fort Sumter. But there is even more intimate evidence of Lincoln's intention. On July 3 the newly appointed Senator from Illinois, Orville Browning (chosen to replace Douglas, who had just died), called upon Lincoln and held a conversation with him. Fortunately Browning kept a diary, and his entry for that evening reads:

> He [Lincoln] told me that the very first thing placed in his hands after his inauguration was a letter from Majr. Anderson announcing the impossibility of defending or relieving Sumter. That he called the cabinet together and consulted Genl Scott—that Scott concurred with Anderson, and the cabinet, with the exception of P M Genl Blair were for evacuating the Fort, and all the troubles and anxieties of his life had not equaled those which intervened between this time and the fall of Sumter. He himself conceived the idea, and proposed sending supplies, without an attempt to reinforce [,] giving notice of the fact to Gov Pickens of S.C. *The plan succeeded. They attacked Sumter—it fell, and thus, did more service than it otherwise could.*

If we may trust Browning, who was one of Lincoln's friends, it was the Confederate attack and not the military success of the expedition that mattered most. In a letter to Gustavus Vasa Fox, the extraordinary naval officer who had led the relief attempt, Lincoln concluded, "You and I both anticipated that the cause of the country would be advanced by making the attempt to provision Fort Sumter, even if it should fail; and it is no small conclusion now to feel that our anticipation is justified by the result."

This realistic bit of statecraft provides no reason for disparaging Lincoln, certainly not by those who hold that it was his legal and moral duty to defend the integrity of the Union by the most effective means at his command.[15] The Confederate attack made it possible to picture the war as a defensive one;[16] for some time it unified Northern sentiment. Who can say with certainty that the war could have been won on any other terms?

There was, for all this, a tremendous incongruity in Lincoln as a war leader. He did not want war; he wanted Union, and accepted war only when it seemed necessary to the Union. He had always been pre-eminently a man of peace. Probably the only time in his early political career when he seriously exposed himself by taking an unpopular stand on an important issue had been the occasion of his opposition to the Mexican War. His speech before Congress in 1848 ridiculing his own participation in the Black Hawk War is one of the classics of American frontier humor.

Evidently he did not expect a long fight. His first call for 75,000 volunteers required a three months' enlistment. (These figures must have come back to haunt him: in four years the war took some 618,000 lives on both sides.) But it soon enough became clear that the struggle would not be brief or easy. In a short time it loomed up as one of the major crises of modern history. To Lincoln fell the task of interpreting it to his people and the world.

There need be no doubt as to how Lincoln saw the conflict; he had innumerable occasions to state his view of it to Congress, to the country, even to foreign workingmen. It was, of course, a war to preserve the Union; but the Union itself was a means to an end. The Union meant free popular government, "government of the people, by the people, for the people."[17] But popular government is something deeper and more valuable than a mere system of political organization: it is a system of social life that gives the common man a chance. Here Lincoln returns again to his favorite theme—the stupendous value to mankind of the free-labor system. "This," he asserts gravely in his first extended message to Congress,

> is essentially a people's contest. On the side of the Union it is a struggle for maintaining in the world that form and substance of a government whose leading object is to elevate the condition of men—to lift artificial weights from all shoulders; to clear the paths of laudable pursuit for all; to afford all an unfettered start, and a fair chance in the race of life...this is the leading object of the government for whose existence we contend.

Such popular government has often been called an experiment, he went on, but two phases of the experiment have already been successfully concluded: the establishing and administering of it. There remains a final test—"its successful maintenance against a formidable internal attempt to overthrow it." The people must now demonstrate to the world that those who can fairly win an election can defeat a rebellion, and that the power of government which has been honestly lost by ballots cannot be won back by bullets. "Such will be a great lesson of peace: teaching men that what they cannot take by an election, neither can they take it by a war; teaching all the folly of being the beginners of a war."

Then there was his superb formulation of an everlasting problem of republican politics: "Must a government, of necessity, be too strong for the liberties of its own people, or too weak to maintain its own existence?"

Thus, skillfully, Lincoln inverted the main issue of the war to suit his purpose. What the North was waging, of course, was a war to save the Union by denying self-determination to the majority of Southern whites. But Lincoln, assisted by the blessed fact that the Confederates had struck the first blow, presented it as a war to defend not only Union but the sacred principles of popular rule and opportunity for the common man.

Here is a war aim couched in the language of Lincoln's old ideal, the language that had helped to make him President. Notice that while it is politically on the radical or "popular" side of the fight, it is historically conservative: it aims to preserve a long-established order that has well served the common man in the past. The Union is on the *defensive*, resisting "a war upon the rights of all working people." Sometimes Lincoln's language is frankly conservative. No men living, he insists, "are more worthy to be trusted than those who toil up from poverty. . . . Let them beware of *surrendering a political power which they already possess*, and which, if surrendered, will surely be used to close the door of advancement against such as they, and to fix *new* disabilities and burdens upon them, till all of liberty shall be lost." Again: "There is involved in this struggle the question whether your children and my children shall enjoy the privileges we have enjoyed."

Such being his conception of the meaning of the struggle, is it not understandable that Lincoln thinks in terms of restoring in its pristine simplicity that which has gone before? It is not understandable that he sets for his cause no such revolutionary goal as destroying the South's social fabric? Bring the South back, save the Union, restore orderly government, establish the principle that force cannot win out, and do it with the least cost in lives and travail—there is the Lincoln program. The tremendous forces of social revolution storm about his head, and in the end he bows to them. But not without doubt and hesitation. Not even without a struggle against his own destiny to become the symbol of freedom.

VI

From the beginning, then, everything was subordinate to the cause of Union. In his Inaugural Address, Lincoln repeated with pathetic vehemence his several earlier assurances that slavery would not be attacked in the states. He went farther. Congress had recently passed a constitutional amendment guaranteeing that the federal government would never interfere with slavery. Should the amendment be ratified by the states, it would nourish bondage for an epoch by fixing slavery fast in the constitutional structure of the nation. It would expressly make emancipation impossible except by voluntary action of the states severally. Although it was no part of his constitutional function, Lincoln did what he could to speed this amendment toward ratification by announcing that he considered it only an explicit statement of what was already implicit in the Constitution—"I have no objection to its being made express and irrevocable."

When war came, its goal was almost universally considered in the North to be as Lincoln declared it—to bring back the South with *slavery intact*. So general was this sentiment that when the aged John J. Crittenden of Kentucky introduced into Congress on the day after Bull Run a resolution declaring that the war was not being waged for conquest or subjugation nor to interfere with "the established institutions" of the seceded states, even Republicans of Jacobin leanings were afraid to vote against it. When Lincoln declared to Congress that he was determined not to allow the war to "degenerate into a violent and remorseless revolutionary struggle," he only voiced the initial opinion of a vast majority of Northerners. But before the war was eight months old, the House had significantly refused to re-enact the Crittenden resolution. Lincoln's mind would not change so readily.

As the conflict wore on, the difficulties of fighting a war against a slave power without fighting slavery became painfully evident. Fugitive slaves began to make their way into the Union lines. How were the generals to deal with them? In August 1861, the abolitionist General Fremont, sorely tried by guerrilla warfare in Missouri, declared martial law and proclaimed that all slaves of local owners resisting the United States where freemen. After failing to induce Fremont to revoke his proclamation voluntarily, Lincoln promptly countermanded it. Later he overruled an order of General David Hunter freeing slaves in Georgia, Florida, and South Carolina.

Antislavery men everywhere became impatient with this mode of conducting the war. They were fighting a power based on the labor of slaves, the greatest single wartime resource of the Confederacy. Not only did the administration refuse to issue an injunction to the slaves to free themselves and cease working for the secession cause, but it even withheld freedom from the blacks in those regions where its armies were penetrating the South. Fighting an attack upon the Constitution with the nicest constitutional methods had become preposterous.

Lincoln had genuine constitutional scruples, but his conservatism in everything pertaining to slavery was also dictated by political and strategic considerations. He was determined to hold the loyalty of the four border states, Maryland, Kentucky, Missouri, and Delaware, all of which were unwilling to participate in an antislavery crusade. The three larger states, as a glance at the map will show, were vital to Union strategy and to the safety of the capital itself. They were also contributing soldiers to the cause. Fremont's action, Lincoln reported, had had an extremely unfavorable effect on the Kentucky legislature, and in the field a whole company of volunteers upon hearing it had thrown down their arms and disbanded. Further, a great section of conservative Northern opinion was willing to fight for the Union but might refuse to support a war to free Negroes, and kept insisting that the war would become more bitter if the South saw that it was fighting avowed abolitionism. In everything he did, Lincoln had to reckon with the political potential of this sentiment, and he well understood its power, for it was a piece with the old anti-Negro feeling he had always known in Illinois politics.

To become President, Lincoln had had to talk more radically on occasion than he actually felt; to be an effective President he was compelled to act more conservatively than he wanted. The Radicals raged against him with increasing bitterness, and concluded, as one of their representatives reported after an interview, that he had "no antislavery instincts." As the war lengthened, Radical sentiment became stronger. Lincoln was in no position to thrust aside the demands of the very element in the country that supported the war most wholeheartedly. Men who had never thought of attacking the South's peculiar institution before secession were now ready to destroy in the most abrupt and ruthless way if by so doing they could hasten the end of the war. They argued that it was self-contradictory to fight the war without smashing slavery and with it the South's entire social structure. Calculating Republican leaders pointed out that to win the war without destroying the slave-owning class would only

> bring back the rebel States into full fellowship as members of the Union, with their full delegations in both Houses of Congress. They, with the pro-slavery conservatives of the Border States and the Democrats of the Northern states, will control Congress. Republicans and Republican principles will be in the minority under law, and this latter state would be worse than the former—worse than war itself.

There was, then, a logic to social revolution that Lincoln was vainly trying to override. He proposed the impossible, as Harry Williams has remarked: "to conduct the war for the preservation of the status quo which had produced the war."

Lincoln surveyed the scene with his extraordinary brooding detachment, and waited. (He had, reported Charles Francis Adams, Jr., "a mild, dreamy, meditative eye, which one would scarcely expect to see in a successful chief magistrate in these days of the republic.") He listened to the protests and denunciations of the Radicals and their field agents throughout the country, and politely heard abolition delegations to the White House. Like a delicate barometer, he recorded the trend of pressures, and as the Radical pressure increased he moved toward the left. To those who did not know him, it seemed that he did so reluctantly. The Radicals watched his progress with grim satisfaction—with the feeling, as Wendell Phillips expressed it, that if Lincoln was able to grow, "it is because we have watered him." But it is significant that such a haughty and impatient abolitionist as Senator Charles Sumner developed a deep respect and affection for Lincoln. According to one report, Lincoln said one day to Sumner: "We'll fetch 'em; just give us a little time...I should never have had votes enough to send me here, if the people had supposed I should try to use my veto power to upset slavery." To two famous Unitarian clergymen, William Ellery Channing and Moncure D. Conway, he observed that the masses of people were concerned only about military success and remained indifferent to the Negro. He added: "We shall need all the anti-slavery feeling in the country and more; you can go home and try to bring the people to your views; and you may say anything you like about me, if that will help. Don't spare me!"

It was all in keeping with his profound fatalism. He had always believed—and in conversations at Springfield had often told Herndon of his faith—that events are governed (the words are Herndon's) "by certain irrefragable and irresistible laws, and that no prayers of ours could arrest their operation in the least...that what was to be would be inevitable." It was the conviction of a man without haste and without malice, but it was not the philosophy of a reformer. Back in Illinois, Douglas, knowing and respecting Lincoln, had been asked if he was not a weak man. No, replied the Little Giant, but "he is preeminently a man of the atmosphere that surrounds him." Looking back upon events in 1864, Lincoln could say with a profound modesty: "I claim not to have controlled events but confess plainly that events have controlled me." As the Radicals gained in strength, he conducted a brilliant strategic retreat toward a policy of freedom.

To say that Lincoln's approach to the slavery question was governed by his penchant for philosophic resignation is not to say that he had no policy of his own. His program flowed from his conception that his role was to be a moderator of extremes in public sentiment. It called for compensated emancipation (at first in the loyal border states) assisted by federal funds, to be followed at length by deportation and colonization of the freed Negroes. To a member of the Senate he wrote in 1862 that the cost of freeing with compensation all slaves in the four border states and, the District of Columbia, at an average price of four hundred dollars per slave, would come to less than the cost of eighty-seven days of the war. Further, he believed that taking such action would shorten the war by more than eighty-seven days and "thus be an actual saving of expense." Despite the gross note of calculation at the end (one rescues 432,000 human beings from slavery and it turns out to be a saving of expense), the proposal was a reasonable and statesmanlike one, and it is incredible that the intransigence of all but one of the states involved should have consigned it to defeat.

The alternative idea of colonizing the Negroes abroad was and always had been pathetic. There had been in existence for a generation an active movement to colonize the slaves, but it had not sent out of the country more than the tiniest fraction of the annual increase of the slave population. By 1860 its fantastic character must have been evident to every American who was not determined to deceive himself. Nevertheless, when a deputation of colored men came to see Lincoln in the summer of 1862, he tried to persuade them to set up a colony in Central America, which, he said, stood on one of the world's highways and provided a country of "great natural resources and advantages." "If I could find twenty-five able-bodied men, with a mixture of women and children," he added, with marvelous naivete, "...I could make a successful commencement."

Plainly Lincoln was, as always, thinking primarily of the free white worker: the Negro was secondary. The submerged whites of the South and the wage workers of the North feared the prospect of competing with the labor of liberated blacks. The venerable idea of deporting emancipated Negroes, fantastic though it was, grew logically out of a caste psychology in a competitive labor market. Lincoln assured Congress that emancipation would not lower wage standards of white labor even if the freedmen were not deported. But if they were deported, "enhanced wages to white labor is mathematically certain....Reduce the supply of black labor by colonizing the black laborer out of the country, and by precisely so much you increase the demand for, and wages of, white labor."

In the summer of 1862 Congress passed a Confiscation Act providing that the slaves of all persons supporting the rebellion should be forever free. The Radicals had also proposed to make the measure retroactive and to provide for permanent forfeiture of the real estate of rebels. Lincoln was adamant about these features, and had no enthusiasm for the act in general, but finally signed a bill that had been modified according to his demands. Even with these concessions the Radicals had scored a triumph and forced Lincoln part way toward emancipation. He had prevented them from destroying the landed basis of the Southern aristocracy, but he had put his signature, however reluctantly, to a measure that freed the slaves of all persons found guilty of disloyalty; freed them on paper, at least, for the act was unenforceable during the war. It also guaranteed that escaped slaves would no longer be sent back to work for disloyal masters, and in this respect freed some slaves in reality.

When Lincoln at last determined, in July 1862, to move toward emancipation, it was only after all his other policies had failed. The Crittenden Resolution had been rejected, the border states had quashed his plan of compensated emancipation, his generals were still floundering, and he had already lost the support of great numbers of conservatives. The Proclamation became necessary to hold his remaining supporters and to forestall—so he believed—English recognition of the Confederacy. "I would save the Union," he wrote in answer to Horace Greeley's cry for emancipation. "...If I could save the Union without freeing any slave, I would do it; and if I could do it by freeing all the slaves, I would do it." In the end, freeing all the slaves seemed necessary.

It was evidently an unhappy frame of mind in which Lincoln resorted to the Emancipation Proclamation. "Things had gone from bad to worse," he told the artist F. B. Carpenter a year later, "until I felt that we had reached the end of our rope on the plan of operations we had been pursuing; that we had about played our last card, and must change our tactics, or lose the game. I now determined upon the adoption of the emancipation policy..." The passage has a wretched tone: things had gone from bad to worse, and as a result the slaves were to be declared free!

The Emancipation Proclamation of January I, 1863, had all the moral grandeur of a bill of lading. It contained no indictment of slavery, but simply based emancipation on "military necessity." It expressly omitted the loyal slave states from its terms. Finally, it did not in fact free any slaves. For it excluded by detailed enumeration from the sphere covered in the Proclamation all the counties in Virginia and parishes in Louisiana that were occupied by Union troops and into which the government actually had the power to bring freedom. It simply declared free all slaves in "the States and parts of States" where the people were in rebellion—that is to say, precisely where its effect could not reach.[18] Beyond its propaganda value the Proclamation added nothing to what Congress had already done in the Confiscation Act.

Seward remarked of the Proclamation: "We show our sympathy with slavery by emancipating the slaves where we cannot reach them and holding them in bondage where we can set them free." The London Spectator gibed: "The principle is not that a human being cannot justly own another, but that he cannot own him unless he is loyal to the United States."

But the Proclamation was what it was because the average sentiments of the American Unionist of 1862 were what they were. Had the political strategy of the moment called for a momentous human document of the stature of the Declaration of Independence, Lincoln could have risen to the occasion. Perhaps the largest reasonable indictment of him is simply that in such matters he was a follower and not a leader of public opinion. It may be that there was in Lincoln something of the old Kentucky poor white, whose regard for the slaves was more akin to his feeling for tortured animals than it was to his feeling, say, for the common white man of the North. But it is only the intensity and not the genuiness of his antislavery sentiments that can be doubted. His conservatism arose in part from a sound sense for the pace of historical change. He knew that formal freedom for the Negro, coming suddenly and without preparation, would not be real freedom, and in this respect he understood the slavery question better than most of the Radicals, just as they had understood better than he the revolutionary dynamics of the war.

For all its limitations, the Emancipation Proclamation probably made genuine emancipation inevitable. In all but five of the states freedom was accomplished in fact through the Thirteenth Amendment. Lincoln's own part in the passing of this amendment was critical. He used all his influence to get the measure the necessary two-thirds vote in the House of Representatives, and it was finally carried by a margin of three votes. Without his influence the amendment might have been long delayed, though it is hardly conceivable that it could have been held off indefinitely. Such claim as he may have to be remembered as an Emancipator perhaps rests more justly on his behind-the-scenes activity for the Thirteenth Amendment than on the Proclamation itself. It was the Proclamation, however, that had psychological value, and before the amendment was passed, Lincoln had already become the personal symbol of freedom. Believing that he was called only to conserve, he had turned liberator in spite of himself: *"I claim not to have controlled events but confess plainly that events have controlled me."*

VII

Lincoln was shaken by the presidency. Back in Springfield, politics had been a sort of exhilarating game; but in the White House, politics was power, and power was responsibility. Never before had Lincoln held executive office. In public life he had always been an insignificant legislator whose votes were cast in concert with others and whose decisions in themselves had neither finality nor importance. As President he might consult others, but innumerable grave decisions were in the end his own, and with them came a burden of responsibility terrifying in its dimensions.

Lincoln's rage for personal success, his external and worldly ambition, was quieted when he entered the White House, and he was at last left alone to reckon with himself. To be confronted with the fruits of his victory only to find that it meant choosing between life and death for others was immensely sobering. That Lincoln should have shouldered the moral burden of the war was characteristic of the high seriousness into which he had grown since 1854; and it may be true, as Professor Charles W. Ramsdell suggested, that he was stricken by an awareness of his own part in whipping up the crisis. This would go far to explain the desperation with which he issued pardons and the charity that he wanted to extend to the conquered South at the war's close. In one of his rare moments of self-revelation he is reported to have said: "Now I don't know what the soul is, but whatever it is, I know that it can humble itself." The great prose of the presidential years came from a soul that had been humbled. Lincoln's utter lack of personal malice during these years, his humane detachment, his tragic sense of life, have no parallel in political history.

"Lincoln," said Herndon, "is a man of heart—aye, as gentle as a woman is and as tender..." Lincoln was moved by the wounded and dying men, moved as no one in a place of power can afford to be. He had won high office by means sometimes rugged, but once there, he found that he could not quite carry it off. For him it was impossible to drift into the habitual callousness of the sort of officialdom that sees men only as pawns to be shifted here and there and "expended" at the will of others. It was a symbolic thing that his office was so constantly open, that he made himself more accessible than any other chief executive in our history. "Men moving only in an official circle," he told Carpenter, "are apt to become merely official—not to say arbitrary—in their ideas, and are apter and apter with each passing day to forget that they only hold power in a representative capacity." Is it possible to recall anyone else in modern history who could exercise so much power and yet feel so slightly the private corruption of Lincoln's personal eminence in the human calendar— that he was chastened and not intoxicated by power. It was almost apologetically that he remarked in response to a White House serenade after his re-election that "So long as I have been here, I have not willingly planted a thorn in any man's bosom."

There were many thorns planted in *his* bosom. The criticism was hard to bear (perhaps hardest of all that from the abolitionists, which he knew had truth in it). There was still in him a sensitivity that the years of knock-about politics had not killed, the remarkable depths of which are suddenly illumined by a casual sentence written during one of the crueler outbursts of the opposition press. Reassuring the apologetic actor James Hackett, who had unwittingly aroused a storm of hostile laughter by publishing a confidential letter, Lincoln added that he was quite used to it: "I have received a great deal of ridicule without much malice; and have received a great deal of kindness, not quite free from ridicule."

The presidency was not something that could be enjoyed. Remembering its barrenness for him, one can believe that the life of Lincoln's soul was almost entirely without consummation. Sandburg remarks that there were thirty one rooms in the White House and that Lincoln was not at home in any of them. This was the house for which he had sacrificed so much!

As the months passed, a deathly weariness settled over him. Once when Noah Brooks suggested that he rest, he replied: "I suppose it is good for the body. But the tired part of me is inside and out of reach." There had always been a part of him, inside and out of reach, that had looked upon his ambition with detachment and wondered if the game was worth the candle. Now he could see the truth of what he had long dimly known and perhaps hopefully suppressed—that for a man of sensitivity and compassion to exercise great powers in a time of crisis is a grim and agonizing thing. Instead of glory, he once said, he had found only "ashes and blood." This was, for him, the end product of that success myth by which he had lived and for which he had been so persuasive a spokesman. He had had his ambitions and fulfilled them, and met heartache in his triumph.

NOTES

1. For years Herndon kept on their office table the *Westminster Review*, the *Edinburgh Review*, other English periodicals, the works of Darwin, Spencer, and other English writers. He had little success in interesting Lincoln. "Occasionally he would snatch one up and peruse it for a little while, but he soon threw it down with the suggestions that it was entirely too heavy for an ordinary mind to digest."
2. The parenthetic inclusion of women was bold enough, however, assuming that Lincoln expected to be taken seriously. The words were written twelve years before the first Women's Rights Convention met at Seneca Falls, and even then, when Elizabeth Cady Stanton proposed to include suffrage among other demands, her colleague, the Quakeress Lucretia Mott, had chided: "Elizabeth, thee will make us ridiculous."
3. William C. Howells, father of the novelist, wrote in an Ohio newspaper shortly before Lincoln's inauguration as President that he and his wife represented "the western type of Americans." "The White House," he said, "has never been occupied by better representatives of the bourgoise [sic] or citizen class of people, than it will be after the 4th proximo. If the idea represented by these people can only be allowed to prevail in

this government, all will be well. Under such a rule, the practical individual man, who respects himself and regards the rights of others will grow to just proportions."

4. Herndon, however, attested that he heard Lincoln refer to having seen slaves on sale. Herndon's *Life of Lincoln* (Angle ed., 1930), p. 64. In a letter to Alexander H. Stephens, January 19, 1860, Lincoln wrote: "When a boy I went to New Orleans in a flat boat and there I saw slavery and slave markets as I have never seen them in Kentucky, and I heard worse of the Red River plantations."

5. Later, in the debate at Ottawa, Illinois, Lincoln repeated a larger passage containing this statement, and added: "this is the true complexion of all I have said in regard to the institution of slavery and the black race."

6. The Illinois constitutional convention of 1847 had adopted and submitted to a popular referendum a provision that instructed the legislature to pass laws prohibiting the immigration of colored persons. It was ratified by a vote of 50,261 to 21,297. If this vote can be taken as an index, the Negrophobes outnumbered their opponents by more than two to one. In 1853 the state was in effect legally closed to Negro immigration, free or slave. A Negro who entered in violation of the law was to be fined exorbitantly, and if unable to pay the fine could be sold into service. None of the of the Northwest allowed Negro suffrage.

7. The only existing version of this speech is not a verbatim report.

8. Stephen A. Douglas's appeal to this fear was as strong as Lincoln's: "Do you desire to turn this beautiful State into a free Negro colony in order that when Missouri abolishes slavery she can send one hundred thousand emancipated slaves into Illinois to become citizens and voters, on an equality with yourselves?" But Douglas had no comparable appeal to antislavery sentiment, and Lincoln was able to exploit the fact.

The conception that slavery was a menace to free labor throughout the nation was by no means new, nor peculiar to Lincoln. At the time of the Mexican War, Lowell had made Hosea Biglow say:

Wy, it's jest ez clear ez figgers, Clear ez one an' one make two, Chaps that make black slaves o' Diggers Want to make white slaves o' you.

Seward, in his "Irrepressible Conflict" speech, delivered four months after Lincoln's "House Divided" speech, declared: "The United States must and will, sooner or later, become either entirely a slaveholding nation or entirely a free-labor nation. Either the cotton and rice-fields of South Carolina and the sugar plantations of Louisiana will ultimately be tilled by free labor, and Charleston and New Orleans become marts for legitimate merchandise alone, or else the rye-fields and wheat-fields of Massachusetts and New York must again be surrendered by their farmers to slave culture and to the production of slaves, and Boston and New York become once more markets for trade in the bodies and souls of men." But largely because Lincoln was considered more conservative than Seward on the slavery question he was chosen for the party nomination in 1860.

9. Historians have dismissed these charges as untrue. Lincoln admitted that they were based on circumstantial evidence.

10. Lincoln is reported to have said to political friends of the "House Divided" utterance: "I would rather be defeated with this expression in my speech, and uphold it and discuss it before the people, than be victorious without it." (Herndon refused to believe it would harm him politically, assuring: "It will make you President.") It would probably be truer to say that Lincoln was making the great gamble of his career at this point than to say that he was sacrificing his political prospects for a principle. He had had his experience with pettifogging politics of the timid sort during his Congressional phase, and it had led only to disaster.

When Joseph Medill asked Lincoln in 1862 why he had delivered "that radical speech," Lincoln answered: "Well, after you fellows had got me into that mess and began tempting me with offers of the Presidency, I began to think and I made up my mind that the next President of the United States would need to have a stronger antislavery platform than mine. So I concluded to say something." Then Lincoln asked Medill to promise not to repeat his answer to others.

11. Lincoln was fond of asserting that the Declaration of Independence, when it said that all men are created equal, included the Negro. He believed the Negro was probably inferior to the white man, he kept repeating, but in his right to eat, without anyone's leave, the bread he earned by his own labor, the Negro was the equal of any white man. Still he was opposed to citizenship for the Negro. How any man could be expected to defend his right to enjoy the fruits of his labor without having the power to defend it through his vote, Lincoln did not say. In his Peoria speech he had himself said: "No man is good enough to govern another man, without that man's consent." In one of his magnificent private memoranda on slavery Lincoln argued that anyone who defends the moral right of slavery creates an ethic by which his own enslavement may be justified. ("Fragment on Slavery," 1854.) But the same reasoning also applies to anyone who would deny the Negro citizenship. It is impossible to avoid the conclusion that so far as the Negro was concerned, Lincoln could not escape the moral insensitivity that is characteristic of the average white American.

12. Historians are in general agreement with such contemporaries of Lincoln as Clay, Webster, Douglas, and Hammond that the natural limits of slavery expansion in the continental United States had already been reached. But even if slavery had spread into new territories, it hardly follows that it would have spread into the free states of the North.

    As to the territories, if natural causes were not sufficient to keep slavery from going there, Douglas's popular sovereignty probably would have done so. The free population of the North was expanding far more rapidly than the South's population, and it was much more mobile. Many Republicans accepted Douglas's assurances that slavery would be kept out of the territories by action of local settlers alone. After Douglas split with the more Southern faction of the Democratic Party headed by President Buchanan, there was even a movement among Republicans to coalesce with him and offer him the presidential nomination in 1860 on a popular-sovereignty platform! Why, it was reasoned, should opponents of the extension of slavery try to exclude it from the territories by an act of Congress that would be a gratuitous insult to the South, if the same end could be served by letting geography and popular sovereignty have their way? Part of Lincoln's achievement in the Lincoln-Douglas debates was to taunt Douglas into statements that made him absolutely unpalatable to free-soil Republicans. But the supreme irony can be found in the fact that early in 1861 the Republicans in Congress gave their votes to measures organizing the territories of Colorado, Nevada, and Dakota *without prohibiting slavery*. After beating Douglas in 1860, they organized the territories along the pattern of his policy, not Lincoln's.

13. Some of Lincoln's devices were a little sharp. A Springfield newspaper, the *Conservative*, opposed him and spoke in moderate language for acquiescence in extending slavery. Herndon, who knew the editor of the *Conservative*, once came upon an article in the Richmond *Enquirer* justifying slavery for both black and white laborers, a la Fitzhugh. Lincoln observed that it would be helpful if Illinois proslavery papers would take up such an extreme and vulnerable position. Herndon, with Lincoln's permission, induced the editor of the *Conservative* to reprint the *Enquirer's* article with approval. The editor fell for the scheme and his paper was "almost ruined" as a result.

14. Always a good party man, Lincoln feared the Republican Party would disintegrate if it sacrificed the one principle its variegated supporters held in common. Compromise, he wrote Thurlow Weed, December 17, 1860, "would lose us everything we gain by the election...would be the end of us."

15. Professor Kenneth Stampp concludes in his admirable review of the Sumter incident: "Although Lincoln accepted the possibility of war, which, in retrospect at least, was the inevitable consequence of his strategy of defense . . . the burden rested not on Lincoln alone, but on the universal standards of statesmanship and on the whole concept of "national interest'...The fact remains that southern leaders shared with Lincoln the responsibility for a resort to force. They too preferred war to submission."

16. "They well knew," said Lincoln of the Confederates in his July message to Congress, "that the garrison in the fort could by no possibility commit aggression upon them, They knew—they were expressly notified—that the giving of bread to the few brave and hungry men of the garrison was all which would on that occasion be attempted, unless themselves, by resisting so much, should provoke more."

17. In conversation with John Hay, Lincoln said: "For my own part, I consider the first necessity that is upon us, is of proving that popular government is not an absurdity."

18. There was also a cautious injunction to the "liberated" slaves "to abstain from all violence, unless in necessary self-defense," and another to "labor faithfully for reasonable wages." The latter has a sardonic ring.

2

ABRAHAM LINCOLN

Edmund Wilson

What precisely did Alexander Stephens mean when he said that for Lincoln the Union had risen to the sublimity of religious mysticism?

Whether or not it is true that Lincoln was troubled by the eloquence of the Methodist preacher mentioned by Francis Grierson, there is no evidence that, in early maturity, he ever saw the approaching crisis as an apocalyptic judgment or the possible war as a holy crusade. He was not a member of any church, and it is plain that in his earlier days, before he had become a great public figure, he was what was called a free-thinker. William Herndon, his law partner in Springfield, tells us that the young Lincoln had been associated, during his years at New Salem, with persons who had been strongly influenced by the skepticism of the eighteenth century, and that he had read Voltaire, Volney and Tom Paine. Later, in Springfield, when Herndon had brought to the office the books of Darwin, Spencer and Feuerbach, Lincoln had dipped into these. "He soon grew into the belief," says Herndon, "of a universal law, evolution, and from this he never deviated. Mr. Lincoln became a firm believer in evolution and [in] law. Of the truth of this there is no doubt and can be none. Mr. Lincoln believed in laws that imperiously ruled both matter and mind. With him there could be no miracles outside of law; he held that the universe was a grand mystery and a miracle. Nothing to him was lawless, everything being governed by law. There were no accidents in his philosophy. Every event had its cause. The past to him was the cause of the present and the present including the past will be the cause of the grand future and all are one, links in the endless chain, stretching from the infinite to the finite.

Everything to him was the result of the forces of Nature, playing on matter and mind from the beginning of time," which would continue to do so, "and will to the end of it...giving the world other, further and grander results." Herndon says that Lincoln did not believe "that Jesus was...the son of God any more than any man," or "that the Bible was the special divine relation of God as the Christian world contends," and he goes on to tell us that Lincoln, at some point in his middle twenties, before he had left New Salem, had even composed a long essay setting forth his views on religion, which he wanted to bring out as a pamphlet. But when he read it to the proprietor of the general store in which he was then working, his scandalized employer asked to look at it, then quickly thrust it into the stove. In 1842, when the thirty-three year old Lincoln delivers a remarkable address before the Springfield Temperance Society, it is quite evident that his hopes for the world are still confined to a human utopianism which does not yet embody the will of God. "Of our political revolution of '76 we are all justly proud," he says. "It has given us a degree of political freedom, far exceeding that of any other of the nations of the earth. In it the world has found a solution of the long mooted problem, as to the capability of man to govern himself. In it was the germ which was vegetated, and still is to grow and expand into the universal liberty of mankind." The march of this cause of political freedom, "cannot fail," he continues, "to be on and on, till every son of earth shall drink in rich fruition, the sorrow quenching draughts of perfect liberty. Happy day, when, all appetites controlled, all passions subdued, all matters subjected, *mind*, all conquering *mind*, shall live and move the monarch of the world. Glorious consummation! Hail fall of Fury! Reign of Reason, all hail!"

But when Lincoln was running for Congress in 1846, his Democratic opponent, a Methodist preacher, denounced him for infidelity. The candidate then made a point of writing and publishing in a local paper a statement of his religious views, the only one he ever made, which seems to have satisfied his public. When, however, we examine this closely, we discover that the supposed clarification is not really a confession of faith: it does not commit Lincoln to anything. Lincoln says that he has "never denied the truth of the Scriptures," but he does not say that he affirms this truth. "I have never spoken with intentional disrespect of religion in general, or of any denomination of Christians in particular"—which, of course, does not imply agreement. "It is true that in early life I was inclined to believe in what I understand is called the 'Doctrine of Necessity'—that is, that the human mind is impelled to action, or held in rest, by some power over which the mind itself has no control"; but he adds that he has only discussed this "with one, two, or three, but never publicly," and has "entirely left off for more than five years." "I have always understood this opinion to be held by several of the Christian denominations"—with which denominations, however, it is plain that he does not associate himself. He ends by remarking that he would not care to support any man for office "whom I know to be an open enemy of, and scoffer, at religion"—on the ground that no man "has the right to insult the feelings, and injure the morals, of the community in which he may live." There is nothing, so far, to conflict with Herndon's version of Lincoln's views. Herndon admits that Lincoln's "Doctrine of Necessity" had a conception of divinity behind it. "He firmly believed in an overruling Providence, Maker, God, and the great moral of Him written in the human soul. His—late in life—conventional use of the word God must not by any means be interpreted that he believed in a personal God. I know that it is said Mr. Lincoln changed his views. There is no evidence of this." This overruling Providence, this Deity, which we find in the degree to which Lincoln advances to political prominence, taking the place of such words as *Reason* and *mind* in such an utterance as the Temperance Society speech, wears sometimes the more secular aspect of the creative or the fatal operation of "history."

This conception of history as a power which somehow takes possession of men and works out its intentions through them is most familiar today as one of the characteristics of Marxism in which "history" has become the object of a semi-religious cult and has ended by supplying the basis for a fanaticism almost Mohamedan. But it was very widespread in the nineteenth century, and appeared in other contexts, at the time when the scientific study of the past had not yet detangled itself from the doctrine of divine Providence. When we find Lincoln speaking, as follows, in 1858 in the course of his debates with Stephen A. Douglas, we are made to feel the menace of "history" as a kind of superhuman force that vindicates and overrides and that manipulates mankind as its instruments: "Accustomed to trample on the rights of others, you have lost the genius of your own independence, and become the fit subjects of the first cunning tyrant who rises among you. And let me tell you that all these things are prepared for you with the logic or history, if the elections shall promise that the next Dred Scott decision and all future decisions will be quietly acquiesced in by the people." And again, in his message to Congress of December 1, 1862: "Fellow-citizens, *we* cannot escape history. We of this Congress and this administration will be remembered in spite of ourselves. No personal significance, or insignificance, can spare one or another of us. The fiery trial through which we pass, will light us down, in honor or dishonor, to the latest generation." But he needed something more in keeping than this doctrine of historical necessity with the Scriptural religious conceptions of his fellow Americans. His Methodist competitor for Congress had come close to injuring his reputation (just as Herndon's account in his *Life* of

Lincoln's early skepticism was to give rise to such an outcry on the part of the clergy that the book on its first appearance, as a result of their influence, was virtually banned; though several times reprinted, it has never been popular). But it was not really easy for Lincoln's public to suspect him of a critical attitude toward the Scriptures, for the Bible was the book he knew best: he had it at his fingertips and quoted it more often than anything else. And he must now have deliberately adopted the practice of stating his faith in the Union and his conviction of his own mission in terms that would not be repugnant to the descendants of the New England Puritans and to the evangelism characteristic of his time. In this he went much further than Herndon, with his confidence in Spencer and Darwin, was willing to recognize. Lincoln's speeches, on the eve of his inauguration, are full of appeals to the Deity. "A duty devolves upon me" he says, in his farewell address at Springfield, "which is, perhaps, greater than that which has devolved upon any other man since the days of Washington. He never would have succeeded except for the aid of Divine Providence upon which he at all times relied. I feel that I cannot succeed without the same Divine aid which sustained him, and on the same Almighty Being I place my reliance for support, and I hope you, my friends, will all pray that I may receive that Divine assistance without which I cannot succeed, but with which success is certain." He continues in this vein in his subsequent speeches; and we find him at last in his inaugural address describing the situation in the following terms: "If the Almighty Ruler of nations, with his eternal truth and justice, be on your side of the North or on yours of the South, that truth, and the justice, will surely prevail, by the judgment of this great tribunal, the American people"; and "Intelligence, patriotism, Christianity, and a firm reliance on Him who has never yet forsaken this favored land, are still competent to adjust, in the best way, all our present difficulty."

He is to revert several times in the years that follow to the attitude of God toward the war and as the struggle continues undecided, he becomes a good deal less sure that the moral issue is perfectly clear, the Almighty ruler of nations is committed to the side of the North. "The will of God prevails," we find him writing in a document to which Nicolay and Hay gave the title *Meditation on the Divine Will*, a note found after his death, which dates from the autumn of 1862, at a time when he was much discouraged by the failures George McClellan, his General-in-chief. "In great contests each party claims to act in accordance with the will of God. Both may be, and one must be, wrong. God cannot be for and against the same thing at the same time. In the present civil war it is quite possible that God's purpose is something different from the purpose of either party; and yet the human instrumentalities, working just as they do, are of the best adaption to effect his purpose. I am almost ready to say that this is probably true;

that God wills this contest, and wills that it shall not end yet. By his mere great power on the minds of the now contestants, he could have either saved or destroyed the Union without a human contest. Yet the contest began. And, having begun, he could give the final victory to either side any day. Yet the contest proceeds." Two years later in a letter to a Quaker lady, "we hoped," he writes, "for a happy termination of this terrible war long before this; but God knows best, and has ruled otherwise.... Surely he intends some great good to follow this mighty convulsion, which no mortal could make, and no mortal could stay." This line of anxious speculation is to culminate in the Second Inaugural Address. "Both," he writes there of the North and the South,

> read the same Bible, and pray to the same God; and each invokes His aid against the other. It may seem strange that any men should dare to ask a just God's assistance in wringing their bread from the sweat of other men's faces; but let us judge not that we be not judged. The prayers of both could not be answered; that of neither has been answered fully. The Almighty has his own purposes. "Woe unto the world because of offences! for it must needs be that offences come; but woe to that man by whom the offences cometh!" If we shall suppose that, American Slavery is one of those offences which, in the providence of God, must needs come, but which having continued through His appointed time, He now wills to remove, and He gives to both North and South this terrible war, as the woe due to those by whom the offence came, shall we discern therein any departure from those divine attributes which the believers in a Living God always ascribe to Him? Fondly do we hope—fervently do we pray—that this mighty scourge of war may speedily pass away. Yet, if God wills that it continue, until all the wealth piled by the bond-man's two hundred and fifty years of unrequited toil shall be sunk, and until every drop of blood drawn with the lash, shall be paid by another drawn with the sword, as was said three thousand years ago, so still it must be said "the judgments of the Lord are true and righteous altogether!"

We are far here from Herndon's office, closer to Harriet Beecher Stowe. If the need on Lincoln's part, as a public man, to express himself in phrases congenial to his public may have had some part in inducing him to heighten and personify the formulas of his eighteenth-century deism, if it is true that as the war went on and gave rise to more and more disaffection, it became more and more to his interest to invoke the traditional Lord of Hosts, it is nevertheless quite clear that he himself came to see the conflict in a light more and more religious, in more and more Scriptural terms, under a more and more apocalyptic aspect. The vision had imposed itself.

And now let us put aside this Scriptural phraseology and examine Lincoln's view of the war as a crisis in American history and his conception of himself as an American leader. Both of these emerge very early. Lincoln had always felt himself very close to the American Revolution. He had been seventeen when Jefferson died; his great hero was Henry Clay, who, in putting through the Missouri Compromise, had averted a break with the slave interests. He has from youth been acutely aware that the survival of the Union may still be threatened, and he has already had dreams of defending it. In a speech on *The Perpetuation of Our Political Institutions*, made before the Young Men's Lyceum of Springfield in 1838 when Lincoln was twenty-nine, he mounts up to the following impassioned climax. At the time of the American Revolution, he says of its heroes and leaders, "all that sought celebrity, and fame, and distinction, expected to find them in the success of that experiment.... They succeeded. The experiment is successful and thousands have won their deathless names in making it so.... This field of glory is harvested, and the crop is already appropriated. But new reapers will arise and *they*, too, will seek a field. It is to deny what the history of the world tells us is true to suppose that men of ambition and talents will not continue to spring up amongst us. And when they do, they will as naturally seek the gratification of their ruling passion as others have so done before them." You may assume that the young Lincoln is about to exhort his auditors to follow the example of their fathers, not to rest on the performance of the past but to go on to new labors of patriotism; but the speech takes an unexpected turn. "The question, then, is, can that gratification be found in supporting and maintaining an edifice that has been erected by others? Most certainly it cannot." He has been, it seems, preparing to deliver a warning: "Towering genius," he tells them, "disdains a beaten path. It seeks regions unexplored... It *denies* that it is glory enough to serve under any chief. It scorns to tread in the footsteps of *any* predecessor, however illustrious. It thirsts and burns for distinction; and, if possible, it will have it, whether at the expense of emancipating slaves or enslaving freemen. Is it unreasonable then to expect that some man possessed of the loftiest genius, coupled with ambition sufficient to push it to its utmost stretch, will at some time, spring up among us? And when such a one does, it will require the people to be united with each other, attached to the government and laws, and generally intelligent, to successfully frustrate his designs." Now, the effect of this is somewhat ambiguous: it is evident that Lincoln has projected himself into the role against which he is warning them. And a little less than two years later we find one of his political speeches winding up with the following peroration: "The *probability* that we may fall in the struggle *ought not* to deter us from the support of a cause we believe to be just: it *shall not* deter me. If ever I feel the soul within me elevate and expand to those dimensions not entirely unworthy of its mighty Architect, it is when I contemplate the cause of my country, deserted by all the world beside, and I standing up boldly alone and hurling defiance at her victorious oppressors."

The young Lincoln, then, was extremely ambitious: he saw himself in an heroic role. He is aware in the earlier of these two speeches that the political tug-of-war going on between the two sections of the country gives a chance for "some man possessed of the loftiest genius" to perform a spectacular feat. Such a man would "thirst and burn for distinction... whether at the expense of emancipating slaves or enslaving freemen." And, which was Lincoln to choose? He was not unsympathetic with the South. His father had come from Kentucky, and he told Herndon that his mother's father had been "a well bred Virginia planter." He has started his political career with the party of the propertied interests, the Whigs, and he never shows anything of the animus of the leader who has come up from poverty. He did not approve of slavery, but he did not such resent the slaves' masters and he was accustomed to say that if they of the North had found themselves in their opponents' situation they would undoubtedly behaved like the planters. He is at first philosophic about slavery. Lincoln was once taken by a Springfield friend, Joshua F. Speed, for a visit to the latter's family on their plantation near Louisville, Kentucky, and on his return he wrote to Speed's half sister (letter to Mary Speed, September 27, 1841) telling of their journey back:

By the way, a fine example was presented on board the boat for contemplating the effect of *condition* upon human happiness. A gentleman had purchased twelve negroes in different parts of Kentucky and was taking them to a farm in the South. They were chained six and six together. A small iron clevis was around the left wrist of each, and this fastened to the main chain by a shorter one at a convenient distance from the others; so that the negroes were strung together precisely like so many fish upon a trot-line. In this condition they were being separated forever from the scenes of their childhood, their friends, their fathers and mothers, and brothers and sisters, and many of them, from their wives and children, and going into perpetual slavery where the lash of the master is proverbially more ruthless and unrelenting than any other where; and yet amid all these distressing circumstances, as we would think them, they were the most cheerful and apparently happy creatures on board. One, whose offence for which he had been sold was an over-fondness for his wife, played the fiddle almost continually; and the others danced, sung, cracked jokes, and played various games with cards from day to day. How true it is that 'God tempers the wind to the shorn lamb,' or in other words, that He renders the worst of human conditions tolerable, while He permits the best, to be nothing better than tolerable.

Years later in a letter to the same friend (August 24, 1855), in which he discusses their political disagreements he gives this incident a somewhat different emphasis:

> You suggest that in political action now, you and I would differ. I suppose we would; not quite as much, however, as you may think. You know I dislike slavery; and you fully admit the abstract wrong of it. So far there is no cause of difference. But you say that sooner than yield your legal right to the slave—especially at the bidding of those who are not themselves interested, you would see the Union dissolved. *I* am not aware that *anyone* is bidding you to yield that right; very certainly *I* am not. I leave that matter entirely to yourself. I also acknowledge *your* rights and my obligations, under the constitution, in regard to your slaves. I confess I hate to see the poor creatures hunted down and caught and carried back to their stripes and unrewarded toils; but I bite my lip and keep quiet. In 1841 you and I had together a tedious low-water trip on a Steam Boat from Louisville to St. Louis. You may remember, as I well do, that from Louisville to the mouth of the Ohio there were, on board, ten or a dozen slaves, shackled together with irons. That sight was a continual torment to me; and I see something like it every time I touch the Ohio, or any other slave-border. It is hardly fair for you to assume that I have no interest in a thing which has, and continually exercises, the power of making me miserable. You ought rather to appreciate how much the great body of the Northern people do crucify their feelings, in order to maintain their loyalty to the constitution and the Union.

But in the critical year of 1858 the forty-nine-year-old Lincoln, now a public figure, who has served in Congress and is running against Stephen A. Douglas for the Senate takes definitely a new stand. The struggle over slavery in Kansas and Nebraska was intensifying political antagonisms. The new Republican party had already been organized—in 1854—by Democratic and Whig opponents of the Kansas-Nebraska Act, and northern Democrats who had not become Republicans were now being alienated by the efforts of the Democratic President James Buchanan, to forestall secession by appeasing the South. The debates, in their campaign for the Senate, between the Republican Lincoln and one of these anti-Buchanan Democrats drove Lincoln to make bold statements and to formulate a point of view which still exerts a very strong authority over the Northerner's conception of the Civil War. He had already in Springfield, on June 16, made his "House Divided" speech which reverberated all through the political world and which is echoing still in our minds: " 'A house divided against itself cannot stand.' I believe this government cannot endure permanently half *slave* and half *free*. I do not expect the Union to be *dissolved*—I do not expect the house to *fall*—but I *do* expect it will cease to be divided. It will become *all* one thing, or *all* the other." How much Lincoln had staked on this speech is attested by W. H. Herndon who tells Weik, in one of his letters, that Lincoln "was good while preparing it...he was at it off and on about one month." When he read it to Herndon, "I emphatically said to him: 'Lincoln, deliver and publish your speech just as you have written it.' " This speech figured constantly in the debates with Douglas, and after Lincoln was defeated by him, "hundreds of friends," says Herndon, "flocked into the office and said to Lincoln, 'I told you that speech would kill you'."

While the Lincoln-Douglas debates were going on, Senator W. H. Seward of New York State, taking his cue from Lincoln, delivered in Rochester on October 25 another anti-slavery speech which was also to have long reverberations:

Russia yet maintains slavery and is a despotism. Most of the other European states have abolished slavery and adopted the system of free labor. It was the antagonistic political tendencies the two systems which the first Napoleon was contemplating when he predicted that Europe would ultimately be either all Cossack or all republican. Never did human sagacity utter a more pregnant truth. The two systems are at once perceived to be incongruous. But they are more than incongruous— they are incompatible. They never have permanently existed together in one country, and they never can. It would be easy to demonstrate this impossibility, from the irreconcilable contrast between their great principles and characteristics....

Hitherto, the two systems have existed in different states, but side by side within the American Union. This has happened because the Union is a confederation of states. But in another aspect the United States constitute only one nation. Increase of population, which is filling the states out to their very borders, together with a new and extended network of railroads and other avenues, and an internal commerce which daily becomes more intimate, is rapidly bringing the states into a higher and more perfect social unity or consolidation. Thus, these antagonistic systems are continually coming into closer contact, and collision results.

Shall I tell you what this collision means? They who think it is accidental, unnecessary, the work of interested or fanatical agitators, and therefore ephemeral, mistake the case altogether. It is an irrepressible conflict between opposing and enduring forces, and it means that the United States must and will, sooner or later, become either entirely a slaveholding nation, or entirely a free-labor nation. Either the cotton and rice-fields of South Carolina and the sugar plantations of Louisiana will ultimately be tilled by free labor, and Charleston and New Orleans become marts for legitimate merchandise alone, or else the rye-fields and wheat-fields of Massachusetts and New York must again be surrendered by their farmers to slave culture and to the production of slaves, and Boston and New York become once more markets for trade in the bodies and souls of men.

This social-political issue was thus dramatized by the rising and militant Republicans as presenting sensational alternatives, a choice which would affect all history; but the issue held also to be shown as fundamentally a moral one. In the last of his debates with Douglas (October 15), Lincoln speaks with a frankness and a vehemence which, in the previous ones, he has hardly released: his answer to his opponent becomes a sermon. Slavery is a *wrong,* and not merely "social and political" but "moral."

> That is the real issue. That is the issue that will continue in this country when these poor tongues of Judge Douglas and myself shall be silent. It is the eternal struggle between these two principles—right and wrong— throughout the world. They are the two principles that have stood face to face from the beginning of time; and will ever continue to struggle. The one is the common right of humanity and the other the divine right of kings. It is the same principle in whatever shape it develops itself. It is the same spirit that says, "You work and toil and earn bread, and I'll eat it." [Loud applause.] No matter in what shape it comes, whether from the mouth of a king who seeks to bestride the people of his own nation and live by the fruit of their labor, or from one race of men as an apology for enslaving another race, it is the same tyrannical principle.

In his more famous Cooper Institute speech of February 27, 1860, on the eve of his campaign for the presidency, he reiterates this with even more eloquence:

> If slavery is right, all words, acts, laws, and constitutions against it, are themselves wrong and should be silenced, and swept away. If it is right, we cannot justly object to its nationality—its universality if it is wrong, they cannot justly insist upon its extension—its enlargement. All they ask, we could readily grant, if we thought slavery right; all we ask, they could as readily grant, if they thought it wrong. Their thinking it right, and our thinking it wrong, is the precise fact upon which depends the whole controversy. Thinking it right, as they do, they are not to blame for desiring its full recognition, as being right: but, thinking it wrong, as we do, can we yield to them? Can we cast our votes with their view, and against our own?...Neither let us be slandered from our duty by false accusations against us nor frightened from it by menaces of destruction to the Government nor of dungeons to ourselves. LET US HAVE FAITH THAT RIGHT MAKES MIGHT, AND IN THAT FAITH, LET US, TO THE END, DARE TO DO OUR DUTY AS WE UNDERSTAND IT.

Now, Lincoln—as he explains in his debates with Douglas—did not think that, aside from his right to be free, the Negro deserved to be set on a basis of equality with the white man. "I have no purpose," he says, "to introduce political and social equality between the white and black races. There is a physical difference between the two, which, in my judgment, will probably forever forbid their living together on the footing of perfect equality and inasmuch as it becomes a necessity that there must be a difference, I as well as Judge Douglas am in favor of the race to which I belong having the superior position. [Cheers. 'That's the doctrine.']" Nor had he approved of the Abolitionists. He believed that their furious agitation only made the situation worse; and even later, when the Republican party included a strong Abolitionist element, he took pains to dissociate himself from it. Yet his declarations that slavery was a *moral* issue, his talk about "right" and "wrong," made a connection between his policies and the spirit of the New England crusaders who were to turn the conflict of interests between the Northern and Southern states into a Holy War led by God. Though Lincoln was defeated in his contest with Douglas, his rivalry had prodded the latter into giving full expression to views sufficiently unfavorable to slavery to be quite inacceptable to the slave-owners and had thus deepened the split in the Democratic party which was to give the Republicans their chance; and Lincoln himself now stood out as a formidable public figure. He had indeed his heroic role, in which he was eventually to seem to tower—a role that was political through his leadership of his party; soldierly through his rank of commander-in-chief of the armies of the United States; spiritual—for persons like Grierson—as the prophet of the cause of righteousness. And he seems to have known that he was born for this.

Now, aside from this self-confident ambition, what kind of man was Lincoln? There has undoubtedly been written about him more romantic and sentimental rubbish than about any other American figure, with the possible exception of Edgar Allan Poe; and there are moments when one is tempted to feel that the cruelest thing that has happened to Lincoln since he was shot by Booth has been to fall into the hands of Carl Sandburg. Yet Carl Sandburg's biography of Lincoln, insufferable though it sometimes is, is by no means the worst of these tributes. It is useless if one tries to consult it for the source of some reported incident, but it does have its unselective value as an album of Lincoln clippings. It would, however, be more easily acceptable as a repository of Lincoln folk-lore if the compiler had not gone so far in contributing to this folk-lore himself. Here is Sandburg's intimate account of the behavior of Lincoln's mother, about whom almost nothing is known: "She could croon in the moist evening twilight to the shining face in the sweet bundle, 'Hush I lush thee, hush thee, thy father's a gentleman!' She could toss the bundle into the air against a far, hazy line of blue mountains, catch it in her two hands as it came down, let it snuggle to her breast and feed, while she asked, 'Here we come—where from?' And after they had both sunken in the depths of forgetful sleep the early dark and past midnight the tug of a mouth at her nipples in the gray dawn matched in its freshness the first warblings of birds and the morning stars leaving the earth to the sun and dew." And here is his description of Lincoln in the days when, according to Herndon, he was in love with Ann Rutledge, about whom we know hardly more than we do about Lincoln's mother: "After the first evening in which Lincoln had sat next to her and found that bashful words tumbling from his tongue's end really spelled themselves out into sensible talk, her face, as he went away, kept coming back. So often all else would fade out of his mind and there would be only this riddle of a pink-fair face, a mouth and eyes in a frame of light corn-silk hair. He could ask himself what it meant and search his heart for an answer and no answer would come. A trembling took his body and dark waves ran through him sometimes when he spoke so simple a thing as 'The corn is getting high, isn't it?'" The corn is getting high indeed! To one of the most vigorous passages of Lincoln's debates with Douglas, his biographer has added the following comment: "He [Lincoln] was a sad lost man chanting a rhythm of the sad and lost." [It should be noted that in a new edition of Sandburg's *Lincoln* a good deal of this matter has been removed.]

Carl Sandburg is not obnoxious when he is strumming his homely guitar and singing American ballads or in his chunks of Middle Western rhapsody that combine the density of a Chicago block with the dryness of a Kansas drought; but Lincoln took him out of his depth, and the result was a long sprawling book that eventually had Lincoln sprawling. The amorphous and coarse-meshed Sandburg is incapable of doing justice to the tautness and the hard distinction that we find when, disregarding legends, we attack Lincoln's writings in bulk. These writings do not give the impression of a folksy and jocular countryman swapping yarns at the village store or making his way to the White House by uncertain awkward steps or presiding like a father, with a tear in his eye, over the tragedy of the Civil War. Except in the debates with Douglas and some of his early productions, there is very little humor in these writings, and only the gravest sentiment. The dignity of the public utterances and the official correspondence of the Presidency is only infrequently varied by some curtly sarcastic note to a persistently complaining general or an importunate office-seeker. This is a Lincoln intent, self-controlled, strong in intellect, tenacious of purpose.

The raw realities of Lincoln's origins—the sordidness of his childhood environment, the boorishness of his first beginnings—are unflinchingly presented by Herndon, and the public has always found them repellent; but Herndon brings into the foreground Lincoln's genius and his will to succeed as the more romantic writers do not. From those who knew Lincoln best, we learn that he was naturally considerate, but essentially cold and aloof, not really caring much. Herndon tells us, about anyone but his wife and children. He seems always to have had the conviction of his own superiority. The legend of the log-cabin, the illiterate father, the rail-splitting, the flat-boat and all the rest has vulgarized Lincoln for the vulgar even in making him a backwoods saint. Aside from the possibility of his finding himself sustained by his belief that he came from good stock, he was able to derive self-confidence from knowing that, through physical strength, through sound character, through active brains and through personal charm, he had been able, with no other advantages, to establish himself as a person of importance in rude pioneer Illinois, where most people started from scratch and where one had to have sound qualifications in order to command respect. Though Henry Adams makes a point of telling us that Lincoln, at his Inaugural Ball, had difficulty in managing his gloves, we never feel that he is seriously ill at ease or that he finds himself with others at any sort of disadvantage. "Mr. Lincoln was a curious being," says Herndon in a letter to Weik. "He had an idea that he was equal to, if not superior to, all things; thought he was fit and skilled in all things, master of all things, and graceful in all things" adding however, that he "had not good judgments; he had no sense of the fitness, appropriateness, harmony of things." "With all [Lincoln's] awkwardness of manner," wrote Don Piatt, a journalist who had seen a good deal of him, "and utter disregard of social conventionalities that seemed to invite familiarity, there was something about Abraham Lincoln that enforced respect. No man presumed on the apparent invitation to be other than respectful. I was told at Springfield that this accompanied him through life. Among his rough associates, when young, he was a leader, looked up to and obeyed, because they felt of his muscle and its readiness in use. Among his associates at the bar it was attributed to his wit, which kept his duller associates at a distance. But the fact was that this power came from a sense of reserve force of intellectual ability that no one took account of save in its results." John Hay, who was Lincoln's secretary and observed him at close range all the time he was in the White House, insisted that it was "absurd to call him a modest man. No great man is ever modest. It was his intellectual arrogance and unconscious assumption of superiority that men like Chase and Sumner could never forgive." It was this, too, that made it possible, even in suppressing opponents, for him to exercise a magnanimity unusual for a politician, especially in a period of crisis—as when he continued to keep Salmon P. Chase in his cabinet at the time when the latter was working against him and allowing Chase's followers to attack him in leaflets which he refused to read.

Two other descriptions of Lincoln by persons who had closely observed him insist upon his intellectual qualities. "Mr. Lincoln's perceptions," said Herndon, in a speech after Lincoln's death, "were slow, cold, clear and exact. Everything came to him in its precise shape and colour. To some men the world of matter and of man comes ornamented with beauty, life and action, and hence more or less false and inexact. No lurking illusion or other error, false in itself, and clad for the moment in robes of splendour, ever passed undetected or unchallenged over the threshold of his mind—that point that divides vision from the realm and home of thought. Names to him were nothing, and titles naught—assumption always standing back abashed at his cold, intellectual glare. Neither his perceptions nor intellectual visions were perverted, distorted or diseased. He saw all things through a perfect mental lens. There was no diffraction or refraction there. He was not impulsive, fanciful, or imaginative, but calm and precise." Add to this the following passages from the letters of the Marquis de Chambrun, writing to his mother from America. "Mr. Lincoln," he says,

> stopped to admire an exceptionally tall and beautiful tree growing by the roadside and applied himself to defining its particular beauties: powerful trunk, vigorous and harmoniously proportioned branches, which reminded him of the great oaks and beeches under whose shade his youth had been passed. Each different type he compared, in technical detail, to the one before us. His dissertation certainly showed no poetic desire to idealize nature; but if not that of an artist, it denoted extraordinary observation, mastery of descriptive language and absolute precision of mind....No one who heard him express personal ideas, as though thinking aloud, upon some great topic or incidental question, could fail to admire his accuracy of judgment and rectitude of mind. I have heard him give opinions on statesmen and argue political problems with astounding precision. I have heard him describe a beautiful woman and discuss the particular aspects of her appearance, differentiating what is lovely from what might be open to criticism, with the sagacity of an artist. In discussing literature, his judgment showed a delicacy and sureness of taste which would do credit to a celebrated critic.

It must have been the Frenchman who turned Lincoln's attention to literature and beautiful women. But it is true that his sense of style was developed to a high degree. His own style was cunning in its cadences, exact in its choice of words, and yet also instinctive and natural; and it was inseparable from his personality in all of its manifestations. This style pervades Lincoln's speeches, his messages to Congress, his correspondence with his generals in the field as well as with his friends and family, his interviews with visitors to the White House and his casual conversation. Lincoln's editor, Mr. Roy P. Basler, in a study of Lincoln's style prefixed to a volume of selections from his writings, explains that the literary education of Lincoln was a good deal more thorough than used to be thought. "A careful examination," he says, of the books on elocution and grammar "which Lincoln studied both in and out of school will not impress anyone with Lincoln's poverty of opportunity for the study of grammar and rhetoric. It is safe to say that few children today learn as much through twelve years of formal schooling in these two subjects as one finds in the several text books which Lincoln is supposed to have studied." For it is true that the schoolbooks of the early nineteenth century taught not only the mechanics of writing—that is, of grammar and syntax—but also the art of rhetoric—that is, of what used to be called "harmonious numbers" and of dramatic and oratorical effectiveness. Here is a passage from a private letter dealing with personal matters which was written by Lincoln in his thirty-third year: "The second [cause of his correspondent's melancholy] is, the *absence of all business and conversation of friends,* which might divert your mind, and give it occasional rest from that *intensity* of thought, which will sometimes wear the sweetest idea threadbare and turn it to the bitterness of death," Here, in the final phrases, the balance of vowels and consonants, the assonance and alliteration, the progression from the long "e's" of "sweetest idea," over which one would want to linger, to the short and closed vowels of "bitterness of death," which chill the lyrical rhythm and bite it off at the end—all this shows a training of the literary ear that is not often taught in modern schools. The satirical *Letter from the Lost Townships* written in 1842, which nearly cost Lincoln a duel, handles colloquial language with a similar sense of style: it is quite a successful experiment in the vein of homely frontier humor that Mark Twain was to bring to perfection; and the poems that Lincoln wrote four years later, when he revisited his old home in Indiana, show even a certain skill in a medium in which he was less at home. He is describing a neighbor who had gone insane and whose daft doleful singing he now remembers:

> I've heard it oft, as if I dreamed,
>   Far-distant, sweet, and lone;
> The funeral dirge it ever seemed
>   Of reason dead and gone.

To drink its strains, I've stole away,
    All silently and still,
Ere yet the rising god of day
    Had streaked the Eastern hill.

Air held his breath; the trees all still
    Seemed sorr'wing angels round.
Their swelling tears in dew-drops fell
    Upon the list'ning ground.

In his *Eulogy on Zachary Taylor*, delivered in 1850 in striving for a loftier eloquence, he resorts, with less successful results, to a kind of constricted blank verse. Yet in prose, as in verse, he is working for the balance of eighteenth-century rhythms, and he learns to disembarrass these of eighteenth-century pomposity. He will discard the old-fashioned ornaments of forensic and congressional oratory, but he will always be able to summon an art of incantation with words, and he will know how to practice it magnificently—as in the farewell to Springfield, the Gettysburg speech and the Second Inaugural Address—when a special occasion demands it. Alone among American presidents, it is possible to imagine Lincoln, grown up in different milieu, becoming a distinguished writer of a not merely political kind. But actually the poetry of Lincoln has not all been put into his writings. It was acted out in his life. With nothing of the deliberate histrionics of the Roosevelts or of the evangelical mask of Wilson, he created himself as a poetic figure, and he thus imposed himself on the nation.

For the molding by Lincoln of American opinion was a matter of style and imagination as well as of moral authority, of cogent argument and obstinate will. When we put ourselves back into the period, we realize that it was not at all inevitable to think of it as Lincoln thought, and we come to see that Lincoln's conception of the course and meaning of the Civil War was indeed an interpretation that he partly took over from others but that he partly made others accept, and in the teeth of a good deal of resistance on the part of the North itself. If you are tempted to suspect that the Lincoln myth is a backward-reading invention of others, a closer acquaintance with the subject will convince you that something like the reverse is true. Though Lincoln is not responsible for the element of exaggeration, humorous or sentimental, with which he himself has been treated, we come to feel that the mysticism of a Grierson in his *Lincoln and The Valley of Shadows*, as well as the surprising nobility, at once classical and peculiarly American, of the Grant of the *Personal Memoirs*, are in some sense the creations of Lincoln, and that Lincoln has conveyed his own legend to posterity in an even more effective way than he did to the America of the sixties.

Should we, too, have accepted this vision if we had lived at the time of the Civil War? Can an American be sure he would have voted for Lincoln, that he would even have wanted him as a candidate, in the election of 1864? The war was then in its fourth year, and hundreds of thousands of men had been killed without, as it seemed to many, having brought a decision nearer. Lincoln had just called for a draft of half a million more, though the draft the summer before had set off in New York City a series of riots in which a thousand people had been killed or injured: Negroes had been shot and lynched, and Unionists' houses had been burned to the ground. The writ of habeas corpus had been suspended by Lincoln in spite of much public disapproval and an obstinate filibuster in Congress, and one of Lincoln's bitterest of critics, the Democratic Congressman Clement L. Vallandigham, who had demanded that the fighting be stopped and the quarrel submitted to foreign arbitration, had been sent to jail for the duration of the war (though his sentence was later commuted to banishment behind the Confederate lines). To the Albany Democratic Convention. which had passed a set of resolutions condemning the suppression of civil liberties, the President had addressed a retort which asserted his uncompromising policy and showed his argumentative style at its most compelling: "The man who stands by says nothing when the peril of his government is discussed, cannot be misunderstood. If not hindered, he is sure to help the enemy: much more if he talks ambiguously—talks for his country with *buts* and *ifs* and *awls*" (he should have said *ans*). Could this nasty situation have been averted? Should the war not have earlier been brought to an end? Could it not, in fact, have been prevented? Should Fort Sumter have been relieved? Would it not have been a good deal less disastrous if the South had been allowed to secede? All of these questions have been debated: and yet—except, of course, in the South—the ordinary American does not often ask them. He does not doubt now that Lincoln was right. Did he not, by reducing the Confederacy to an unconditional surrender, save the Union and liberate the slaves? Lincoln's conduct of the Civil War is usually now accepted as one of the most conclusive and most creditable exploits of our history. If the war left a lasting trauma, and resulted in, not an apocalypse, but, on the one hand, a rather gross period of industrial and commercial development and on the other, a severe disillusionment for the idealists who had been hoping for something better, these are matters about which we in the North have rarely thought and even less often spoken. We have, in general, accepted the epic that Lincoln directed and lived and wrote. Since it was brought to an end by his death the moment after the war was won, we are able to dissociate him entirely from the ignominies and errors of the Reconstruction and to believe he would have handled its problems better.

But let us see what Lincoln's epic leaves out. Of the strategy of the economic interests at work in the Civil War, which has been analyzed by Charles A. Beard in *The Rise of American Civilization*—a highly unconventional book when it was published in 1927—you will get no inkling from Lincoln, for the reason that he had none himself. The tariff for the benefit of Northern manufacturers—which prevented the South from buying goods from England more cheaply than they could from the North and had constituted one of their grievances—was raised higher during the years of the war than it ever had been before; the government presented enormous grants to the various railroad companies; and a prospect of high wages for labor encouraged by the absence of men in the army was averted, on behalf of the employers by the Immigration Act of 1864, which authorized the importing of labor under terms that could compel the immigrant to pay for the cost of his journey by pledging his wages for as long as twelve months. At the end of the Civil War, the industrialists were firmly in the saddle, but for what this implied for the future Lincoln had had no idea.

He refers on several occasions to the relations of capital and labor, and does not seem to be aware how completely the Republican party is already the champion of the former, for he always arrives at the conclusion that capital overrates its importance, since labor can get along without capital whereas capital cannot get along without labor, and is, in fact as he says, "the fruit of labor, and could never have existed if labor had not first existed." Though he examined the mechanical devices that were brought to him in the years of his Presidency and is reported to have understood them, he does not seem to have been much impressed by the development of machinery in America or even much interested in it. In a speech before the Wisconsin State Agricultural Society, in 1859, he takes a rather a dubious view of the prospects of the steam plow, and a lecture delivered in the same year on the subject of "Discoveries, Inventions, and Improvements" is a curious production for its period and was quite comprehensibly not a success, since most of the speech was devoted to extolling the value to humanity of language and the art of writing, the only discovery, invention or improvement that appears to have excited his enthusiasm. This was perfectly natural for Lincoln, since he evidently felt that the use of the Word was the only technique he needed; and for him, in his impoverished youth, it had been also a discovery and an improvement. Nor did he compensate for his indifference to industry by a sympathetic solicitude for agriculture. He does not seem to have looked back with pleasure on his labors in his boyhood on his father's farm, much publicized though these were, and when he writes to a friend who is working the land, it is usually in the vein of "I am so glad it is you and not I who are trying to run that farm." Though he tells his Wisconsin audience that, since the farmers in the United States constitute the largest occupational group, they are "most worthy of all to be cherished and cultivated," he hopes that he will not be expected to flatter them "as a class" or "to impart to you much specific information on agriculture," because, as he says, "you have no reason to believe, and do not believe, that I possess it."

Lincoln begins as a provincial lawyer and soon becomes a politician of more than provincial importance. His real vocation was for what we call statesmanship, and, as a statesman, he was entirely absorbed by the problems created by secession—though, under pressure of the necessity of winning the war, he was forced to become something of a military strategist. From the moment of his advent to the Presidency just after the withdrawal of seven states, he had of course little opportunity to occupy himself with anything else.

It is partly these limitations that give Lincoln's career its unity, its consistency, its self-contained character. He is not tempted to dissipate his energies; he has no serious conflicts of interest. Everything hangs together. He is conscious from the first of his public role, not only in relation to the history of his country but also in relation to the larger world, for which all the old values will he modified, the social relations altered, if it is possible to prove to it the practicability of the principles of our revolutionary documents. With conviction and persistence he performs this role, and he is always articulate in it. He has always had a sense of drama, as appears in the debates with Douglas, which seem actually to have proved effective when they were recently put on the stage, and now every word that he utters belongs to his part as President. In order to appreciate Lincoln's lines, you have, of course, to know the whole drama. A foreigner who did not know our history might be able to hear the music of the Second Inaugural and the Gettysburg Addresses yet at the same time not fully grasp the reasons for the powerful emotional effect that they have on Lincoln's fellow-Americans; and as for the letter to Mrs. Bixby, such a visitor might be quite at a loss to account for the elaborate trouble that has been taken to track Mrs. Bixby down and to authenticate that the letter is really by Lincoln and not by his secretary John Hay. These things must be felt in their contexts, where they speak to us with all the power of Lincoln's inspired conception of his role in the Civil War.

The dreams and premonitions of Lincoln are also a part of this drama, to which they contribute an element of imagery and tragic foreshadowing that one finds sometimes in the lives of poets—Dante's visions or Byron's last poem—but that one does not expect to encounter in the career of a political figure: Lincoln's recurrent dream of a ship on its steady way to some dark and indefinite shore, which seemed to prophesy that the war would be going well, since it had always been followed by a victory; his ominous hallucination, after the election of 1860, when, lying exhausted on a sofa, he saw in a mirror on the wall a double reflection of his face, with one image paler than the other, which his wife had taken as a sign that he would he elected to a second term but that he would not live to complete it. He repeated this story to John Hay and others the night of his second election, and a few days before his death he had spoken of a more recent dream, in which he had seen a crowd of people hurrying to the East Room of the White House and, when he followed them, found his own body laid out and heard voices saying, "Lincoln is dead." Herndon tells us that in the early days in Springfield, Lincoln would say to him. "Billy, I fear that I shall meet with some terrible end." But although he had been shot at in '62 when he was riding in the streets of Washington, he would not have a bodyguard; he explained that he wanted the people to know that "I come among them without fear." He would take walks in the middle of the night alone. It was only in the November of 1864 that four plain-clothesmen were posted at the White House. On his way back to Washington from his visit to Richmond just after the city's surrender, he read to his companions on the boat the scene from *Macbeth* that contains the lines:

> Duncan is in his grave;
> After life's fitful fever he sleeps well;
> Treason has done his worst: nor steel, nor poison,
> Malice domestic, foreign levy, nothing,
> Can touch him further.

The night before Lincoln was murdered, he dreamed again of the ship approaching its dark destination. He had foreseen and accepted his doom; he knew it was part of the drama. He had in some sense imagined this drama himself—had even prefigured Booth and the aspect he would wear for Booth when the latter would leap down from the Presidential box crying, *"Sic simper tyrannis!"* Had he not once told Herndon that Brutus was created to murder Caesar and Caesar to be murdered by Brutus? And in that speech made so long before to the Young Men's Lyceum in Springfield, he had issued his equivocal warning against the ambitious leader, describing this figure with a fire that seemed to derive as much from admiration as from apprehension—that leader who would certainly arise among them and "seek the gratification of [his] ruling passion," that "towering genius" who would "burn for distinction, and, if possible...have it, whether at the expense of emancipating slaves or enslaving freemen." It was as if he had not only foreseen the drama but had even seen all around it with a kind of poetic objectivity, aware of the various points of view that the world must take toward its protagonist. In the poem that Lincoln lived, Booth been prepared for, too, and the tragic conclusion was necessary to justify all the rest.

It is not to be doubted that Lincoln, in spite of his firm hand on policy, had found his leadership a harrowing experience. He had himself, one supposes, grown up in pain. The handicaps imposed by his origins on his character and aspirations must have constrained him from his earliest years, and his unhappy relations with women, the tantrums and aspirations of his rather vulgar wife and the death of two of his sons must have saddened and worried and humiliated him all through his personal life. The humorous stories and readings that his cabinet sometimes found so incongruous only served, as he once explained, as a relief from his fits of despondency, his constant anxiety about the war. Though not warm in his personal relationships, he was sensitive to the pain of others. He had remembered from fourteen years before that the sight of the slaves on the steamboat had been "a continual torment," and though he had pardoned, whenever it was possible, the soldiers who had been sentenced to death, he had been compelled by his office to authorize the executions of two hundred and sixty-seven men. He must have suffered far more than he ever expressed from the agonies and griefs of the war, and it was morally and dramatically inevitable that this prophet who had crushed opposition and sent thousands of men to their deaths should finally attest his good faith by laying down his own life with theirs.

3

NATURALLY ANTI-SLAVERY: LINCOLN, RACE, AND THE COMPLEXITY OF AMERICAN LIBERTY

James Oliver Horton

In this age, when some charge any revision of political position as a "flip flop" and consider thoughtless consistency a praiseworthy political attribute, we would do well to remember one of the most important political figures in American history, President Abraham Lincoln, a man who learned from personal experience and changed his mind. In a letter written in 1864, one year before his assassination, Lincoln expressed a view of himself as firmly opposed to the institution of slavery. "I am naturally anti-slavery," he wrote. "If slavery is not wrong, nothing is wrong." Then he added an intriguing autobiographical note, "I can not remember when I did not so think, and feel."[1]

Although Lincoln did not have much direct contact with slavery during his early life, he did observe the general inhumanity of the institution. He saw slaves at labor, being sold, and being punished. He was generally appalled but he was constrained by his acceptance of the legitimacy of law. Significantly, he believed that the United States Constitution protected slaveholders' human property, placing it beyond the reach of his personal morality. No matter how he felt about slavery, under the law, slaves were personal property and the source of great wealth throughout the South.

This was the personal dilemma that Lincoln, the lawyer and politician, faced all of his professional life. His antislavery sentiments were substantial from the early years of his life, but they were moderate, and moderation restrained his actions until the circumstances of his life and the life of the nation changed dramatically in 1861.[2]

With the presidential election in the fall of 1860, Lincoln became the sixteenth president of the United States, but before he actually took office in March of 1861, seven of the largest slaveholding states from the Deep South—South Carolina, Mississippi, Florida, Alabama, Georgia, Louisiana and Texas—seceded from the United States, seized much federal property, and declared themselves an independent nation. By that spring the bloodiest war in American history was underway. It was only under these circumstances, through his constitutional powers as a war-time president, that Lincoln could finally bring himself to put his antislavery convictions into action. In doing so he moved from his position as moderate antislavery advocate to full-fledged abolitionist.

Historian Aileen Kraditor laid out the distinction between antislavery and abolition in her classic study, *Means and Ends in American Abolitionism*. Those who considered themselves antislavery opposed the institution but generally moderated their criticisms of slaveholders and sought compromise that might contain the spread of slavery and encourage voluntary emancipation. Many, like Supreme Court Justice John Marshall or antislavery Whig political leader Henry Clay, favored the African or West Indian colonization of all blacks freed from bondage. For them, the removal of emancipated African Americans was the only practical solution to the problem of American slavery. Lincoln favored colonization also, but his was a moderate colonization stance supporting voluntary emigration only.[3]

Abolitionists, on the other hand, as Kraditor explained, were uncompromising in their attack on slavery. They demanded immediate emancipation without consideration of colonization or expatriation. They attacked slaveholders as immoral, inhumane, sinful exploiters of human beings who cared only for their own elevation and financial gain. In the years before the Civil War, they regarded Lincoln with great suspicion and saw his antislavery position as hypocritical. "He is Southern by birth, Southern in his associations, and southern, if I mistake not, in his sympathies," charged one Illinois newspaper editor. "His wife, you know, is a Todd," the editor continued, "of a proslavery family, and so are all his kin."[4]

America's radical abolitionists attacked Lincoln for most of his political life, but most agreed with his constitutional analysis. They too believed that the national constitution protected slavery. Boston abolitionist editor William Lloyd Garrison condemned it as a slaveholder's document. On the 4th of July in 1854, reacting to the passage of the new more harsh

Fugitive Slave Law four years earlier, he burned a copy of the Constitution, calling it, "a covenant with death and an agreement with Hell." He then asked the crowd for an "Amen," as he proclaimed, "so perish all compromises with tyranny." Garrison represented the most radical abolitionists. There were many levels of antislavery between his stand and that of antislavery Whigs who were far more conservative on the issue. Lincoln may have been in some sense antislavery, but he was not an abolitionist in the Garrisonian sense of the term.[5]

Historian Allen Guelzo has pointed out that there is no evidence that Lincoln strongly opposed slavery on humanitarian grounds before the late 1840s. Although he was born in the slave state of Kentucky, Lincoln's father Thomas moved the family to free Indiana while Abraham was still a child. The presence of slavery was apparently one reason for the family's move, although it may have been that Thomas was offended as much by the economic competition he faced from slave labor as by the inhumanity of the institution itself. In any case, young Abraham grew to maturity in a free state. Lincoln lore has it that as a young man, while on a flatboat trip to New Orleans, he was appalled by the sight of slaves at auction, "Negroes chained, maltreated, whipped and scourged." John Hanks, Lincoln's cousin, who claimed to have been with him on this trip, recalled the impact of this encounter: "Lincoln saw it, his heart bled, said nothing much, was silent from feeling, was sad, looked bad, felt bad, was thoughtful and abstracted." Hanks was confident, as he said, "that it was on this trip that [Lincoln] formed his opinions of slavery; it ran its iron in him then and there."[6]

There is some doubt, however, that Hanks actually completed the trip to New Orleans. Further, Guelzo argues that, while Lincoln lived there, the free state of Illinois allowed slaves to be transported through and to be confined temporarily within its borders. At the time that Lincoln moved to Springfield in April of 1837, six of the 115 African Americans in the town were slaves. Although while serving in the Illinois General Assembly, in March of 1837, he had condemned a resolution criticizing antislavery protest, there is no evidence that Lincoln ever raised a word of protest about slaves held in his city of residence.[7] A decade later, he provided his legal services to slaveholder Robert Matson, who was attempting to use the Illinois courts to retain ownership of his human property. Matson was being sued by one of his slaves, Jane Bryant, who claimed that she and her family had been held in Illinois beyond the state's limit on the temporary residence of a slave. Despite Lincoln's court appearance on Matson's behalf, Bryant won her case.[8]

These events cast serious doubt on the extent to which Lincoln was "naturally anti-slavery" in his early life. Nor is there evidence that his antislavery sentiment engendered feelings of racial equality. Garrison and other abolitionists who organized the American Antislavery Society in 1833 pledged themselves to work for an end of slavery and to create a society in which African Americans could "share an equality with the whites, of civil and religious privileges." During the same period, however, Lincoln expressed doubts that all slaves necessarily suffered under slavery.[9] In the summer of 1841, he reacted to the sight of slaves chained together on a boat on the Ohio River with the observation that those so bound did not seem to mind their plight. "Amid all these distressing circumstances, as we would think them," he told a friend, "they were the most cheerful and apparently happy creatures on board." Lincoln's conclusion was clear: "They are not like us." Later, however, when Lincoln recalled the same incident, he did so with much more empathy for the captive slaves. "That sight was a continual torment to me," he wrote to a friend in 1855. By then Lincoln was apparently affected by slavery in ways not apparent earlier. Although he had not taken a strong stand against the harsh Fugitive Slave Law of 1850, within a few years of its passage he wrote, "I confess I hate to see the poor creatures hunted down, and caught, and carried back to the stripes, and unrewarded toils." Obviously, Lincoln was changing and growing during these years, a trait he would display for the rest of his life.[10]

Although he had not become an abolitionist by the mid 1850s, Lincoln had certainly grown more antislavery in his public positions. He increasingly opposed slavery as a moral evil but, under ordinary circumstances, he saw no legal way to remove it from states that sanctioned it. Yet he felt strongly that the institution should not be allowed to spread into territories that might be added to the nation in the future. Lincoln made this clear in his assessment of the Kansas Nebraska Act supported by Stephen A. Douglas, the U.S. senator from Illinois, who would become his chief political rival in the decade before the Civil War.

The act repealed a measure passed in 1820 that had admitted Maine to the union as a free state, balancing the admission of Missouri as a slave state. Except in Missouri, slavery was excluded from all the Louisiana Purchase lands north of the 36°30 parallel, Missouri's southern boundary. This Missouri Compromise closed the territories of Kansas and Nebraska to slavery, a proposition that ignited heated regional debate in the early 1850s. In an effort to walk a line between antislavery and proslavery opinion, Douglas proposed that the status of slavery in the territories, and any states carved from them, be determined by the popular vote of area residents. He and his supporters in the Senate argued that this was the most democratic solution to the question of slavery's expansion. Lincoln, however, stood staunchly opposed. In a speech delivered in Peoria, Illinois, in the fall of 1854 he set out his opposition to the act, especially those parts of it that allowed for the spread of slavery beyond the slaveholding South. Speaking of the repeal of the Missouri Compromise, he argued that it was "Wrong in its direct effect, letting slavery in Kansas and Nebraska—and wrong it its prospective principle, allowing it to spread to every other part of the wide world, where men can be found inclined to take it."[11]

Lincoln opposed the expansion of slavery because of the great inhumanity of the institution, because of its generally debilitating effect on the society, and because as he said, "it deprives our republican example of its justice in the world." Thus he disliked slavery for a complex set of reasons, not the least of which was the stain it created on the nation's democratic experiment in the eyes of the world. It "causes the real friends of freedom to doubt our sincerity, and...forces so many really good men amongst ourselves into an open war with the very fundamental principles of civil Liberty—criticizing the Declaration of Independence, and insisting that there is no right principle of action but self-interest."[12]

Yet, even by the 1850s, Lincoln remained relatively moderate in his antislavery stance. True to his roots in the Whig Party, he stopped short of publicly condemning slaveholders. "I have no prejudice against the Southern people," Lincoln told his Peoria audience. "They are just what we would be in their situation." It was the existence of slavery in the South, he believed, that made southern slave supporters what they were. He argued that they would not now create the institution if it did not already exist. Then he admitted that had he the power, he could not bring himself to "free [the slaves] and make them politically and socially, our equals." Lincoln saw any program for immediate emancipation as an impractical solution to the problem of slavery, although he suggested Americans consider some measure of unspecified gradual emancipation.[13]

As the decade of the 1850s wore on and sectional tensions increased, Lincoln shifted his partisan alliances to suit his peculiar antislavery stance. In a eulogy for Henry Clay in 1852, he expressed great admiration for this Whig Party leader, the author of important compromises with slavery, including the Compromise of 1850. That measure included not only the abolition of the slave trade in the District of Columbia but also the Fugitive Slave Law of 1850. That law provided greater protection for the slaveholder property; and it guaranteed no legal rights to anyone accused of being a fugitive slave, a provision that increased the danger that free blacks might be kidnapped into slavery. Lincoln also praised Clay's commitment to the American Colonization Society which sought to encourage the end of slavery by removing all blacks from the United States and resettling them in the West African colony of Liberia, founded by the Society in the early 1820s. Despite the condemnation heaped on this idea by free African Americans and abolitionists, black and white alike, Lincoln heartily endorsed the plan. Using Clay's words, Lincoln argued: "There is a moral fitness in the idea of returning to Africa her children whose ancestors have been torn from her by the ruthless hand of fraud and violence. Transplanted in a foreign land, they will carry back to their native soil the rich fruits of religion, civilization, law and liberty. May it not be one of the great designs of the Ruler of the universe (whose ways are often inscrutable by short-sighted mortals) thus to transform an original crime, into a signal blessing to that most unfortunate portion of the globe?"[14]

Lincoln completely ignored African American arguments that, by having served in the ranks of Revolutionary soldiers who brought the nation into existence and among those who in the War of 1812 had defended that nation's independence, their ancestors had won the right of citizenship for succeeding generations. In the decade before the Civil War, Lincoln saw this plan for black American removal as a practical means to emancipation, allowing freedom for African Americans without subjecting white Americans to fears of interracial tensions with their former slaves.[15]

Although his support of colonization was based on an assumption that a multi-racial America was not practical, this was one form of anti-slavery that Lincoln could claim. It was an antislavery that contributed to his move from the fracturing Whig Party toward the newly forming Republican Party during the mid-1850s. He was not among the first to join the Republicans formed in 1854, but within two years Lincoln helped to organize the new party in Illinois. Although most Republicans were not truly abolitionist, many held antislavery principles. Like Lincoln, many who joined the new party had come from the antislavery wing of the Whig Party.

The political tensions of the early 1850s that had torn the Whigs asunder and given birth to the Republican Party continued to grow, making compromise on the slavery question all but impossible. They also moved Lincoln farther along the road of antislavery. He had made a reputation for himself as a congressman from Illinois by opposing America's entry into the war with Mexico. He worried about the impact that such a war might have on slavery. At the end of his congressional term in 1849, however, it was not clear that Lincoln was interested in continuing a political career. He returned to the profession of law and was admitted to practice before the U.S. Supreme Court. It was the struggle over Kansas that brought him back to politics and to the subsequent slavery-related struggles of the 1850s.[16]

In 1857, the U.S. Supreme Court under Chief Justice Roger B. Taney, a Maryland slaveholder and staunch supporter of slavery, handed down a stunning rebuff to Dred Scott, a Missouri slave who had sued for his freedom on the grounds that his master, a military officer, had quartered him in free territory for an extended period. The eighty-year-old Taney wrote the court's opinion and read it aloud to a shocked and silent courtroom. He argued that the national founders never intended African Americans to be citizens. Thus, neither Scott nor any other black person had standing before the Court and therefore could not bring suit. Further, the Court ruled that Congress did not have the power to prohibit the expansion of slavery into any American territory. The Republican Party, that had based much of its platform on a firm stand against the expansion of slavery, strongly objected.

Lincoln stood with his party, and his political positions seemed to appeal to a wide range of Republican views. His brand of antislavery steadfastly opposed slavery's expansion, but his respect for the Constitutional protection for the institution reassured moderates and conservatives that he was no radical abolitionist. When his party selected him to run in 1858 for the Illinois U.S. Senate seat, he was careful to distinguish his position on slavery from those of Stephen A. Douglas, his Democratic opponent. By the late 1850s, Lincoln was ready to strongly state his views on the immorality of slavery and the danger it posed to the nation. In his "House Divided" speech given in Springfield, Illinois, in the early summer of 1858, Lincoln told his audience, "I believe that this government cannot endure, permanently half slave and half free." He believed that the founders had assumed that over time slavery would fade from the nation. Yet, the events of the 1850s, especially what he termed "the Nebraska doctrine" and the Dred Scott decision, had opened all the territories to slavery and even made possible its reintroduction into many of the currently free states. Lincoln warned of dire consequences. "We shall lie down pleasantly dreaming that the people of Missouri are on the verge of making their state free; and we shall awake to the reality, instead, that the Supreme Court has made Illinois a slave state."[17]

Clearly, Lincoln was growing more concerned about the ability of the nation to survive the slavery debate. Neutrality on the issue had become impossible for one committed to the preservation of the Union. During the series of campaign debates with Douglas, Lincoln spoke in antislavery terms. "What has ever threatened our liberty and property save and except this institution of Slavery," he asked those who had gathered in Alton. He argued that one cannot cure a cancer by allowing it to spread over the entire body. Restricting its spread was what Lincoln called "the old fashioned way, the way in which the [founding] fathers themselves set us the example."[18]

Yet Lincoln also understood that in the volatile world of mid-nineteenth century politics too strong an antislavery stance was dangerous. To hold the support of his party and that of all but a small minority of Republican constituents, he must continually distinguish himself from Garrison and the true abolitionists. Realizing Lincoln's vulnerability on this point, Douglas attempted to paint him as a "radical" on the issue of race. Douglas strongly suggested that Lincoln favored not only an end to slavery, but also a reorganization of society that would bring about a political and social equality of the races. In his defense, Lincoln stated what was obvious to African Americans. To be antislavery was not necessarily to believe in racial equality. Employing his most effective wit, Lincoln accused Douglas of rearranging his words so as to "prove a horse chestnut to be a chestnut horse."[19]

Leaving no doubt that he favored a system of white supremacy, Lincoln claimed that black people were inferior people, not the equals of whites in many things, "certainly not in color, perhaps not in moral or intellectual endowments." Still he believed that they were entitled to some rights. He argued that "there is no reason in the world why the [N]egro is not entitled to all the natural rights enumerated in the Declaration of Independence, the right to life, liberty and the pursuit of happiness."[20]

As the debates continued that summer, again and again Lincoln was forced to defend himself against the charge of seeking a social and political system of racial equality. In Charleston, Illinois, he drew cheers when he unequivocally laid out his stand on the racial issue. "I will say then that I am not nor ever have been in favor of bringing about in any way the social and political equality of the white and black races." He then turned to the specifics of his beliefs saying, "I am not nor ever have been in favor of making voters or jurors of [N]egroes, nor of qualifying them to hold office, nor to intermarry with white people." Douglas had suggested that intermarriage was one of the intended consequences of Lincoln's position. To this charge Lincoln replied, "I do not understand that because I do not want a [N]egro woman as a slave I must necessarily want her as a wife."[21]

Even though he pushed to proclaim his dedication to white supremacy, Lincoln would not completely surrender his antislavery stand. He drew a line between racial equality and his commitment to humanity at its most basic level in the American context. In Ottawa, Illinois, he told a crowd that there were some areas in which racial difference did not justify white supremacy. "In the right to eat the bread, without leave of anybody else, which his own hand earns," Lincoln argued, "[the black man] is my equal and the equal of Judge Douglas and the equal of every living man." Here was the crux of his antislavery position.[22]

Although on the eve of the Civil War Lincoln was no abolitionist, he did see African Americans as human beings with basic human rights. Slavery troubled him largely because it deprived human beings of those natural rights enumerated in the Declaration of Independence. It was in large part his moderation on this central question of the era that made Lincoln attractive to Republicans who nominated him as their party's candidate for the presidency in 1860. During his campaign and even after his election, Lincoln struggled against those who, as he said, labeled him a fanatical "Black Republican" whose goal was to incite "insurrection, blood and thunder among the slaves." In defense of himself and his party, Lincoln charged that slaves did not need Republican prodding to rise in revolt. He cited as evidence the Nat Turner rebellion in 1831, more than two decades before the founding of the Republican Party. To those who argued that Republicans had encouraged and supported John Brown's 1859 raid on Harpers Ferry as the first step toward slave insurrection, Lincoln pointed out that Nat Turner's band, with no Republican support, had killed more than three times as many as had died at Harpers Ferry. After condemning Brown's efforts and assuring his critics that Brown was not a Republican, Lincoln argued that due to the lack of rapid communication between slaves no extensive slave rebellion was possible at that time. As he put it, "The indispensable concert of action cannot be attained."[23]

Southern slaveholders never believed that Lincoln or any other Republican could be trusted to respect their property rights in slaves. Despite Lincoln's personal and professional history and his protestations to the contrary, they continued to see him as an abolitionist. The debate on this issue and on how the South should respond to an election of a Republican president split the Democratic Party, as southern Democrats peeled away from the national organization to form their own party. Moreover, a fourth party split off from the southern faction, calling itself the Union Party and insuring hopelessly fractured opposition to the Republican candidate. As a result, Lincoln won the presidency with a majority of the electoral votes but less than 40 percent of the popular vote. He carried not a single southern or border state.

Southern claims that Lincoln was a front for abolitionist power carried a ring of irony for most abolitionists, especially in northern black communities that formed the backbone of abolitionism. African Americans generally supported the Republicans with great reluctance, viewing them as only the least offensive of the unsatisfactory alternatives available to them. During the summer before the 1860 election, black leaders who toured the North speaking to white abolitionists and free blacks bemoaned their limited political choices. H. Ford Douglass, a former Virginia slave who had become leader among Chicago blacks, addressed an abolitionist 4th of July picnic in Framingham, Massachusetts. He drew a great response when he labeled the political parties "barren and unfruitful," explaining that none "seeks to lift the [N]egro out of his fetters, and rescue this day from odium and disgrace." He singled out Lincoln, classing him with an outdated form of conservative antislavery. He challenged his audience to explain the difference "between the anti-slavery of Abraham Lincoln, and the anti-slavery of the old Whig party, or the antislavery of Henry Clay." He then answered his own challenge. "There is no difference between them." Finally, with a polemical flourish that stirred his listeners, he claimed the antislavery of Clay and Lincoln to be "just as odious to the antislavery cause and antislavery men as ever was John C. Calhoun," the notorious South Carolina defender of slavery.[24]

Thus, most black leaders greeted the Lincoln victory with ambivalence and skepticism. Their fears were not allayed by his inaugural address in which the new president pledged not to interfere with slavery in the states where it was sanctioned by law. This gesture, meant to reassure the slaveholding South, infuriated African Americans and illustrated for many the futility of looking to the federal government to fulfill the promises of the American commitment to freedom. With sadness and anger they noted that the first act of the new "antislavery president" was to declare his unwillingness to move against slavery. Lincoln's words seemed to confirm in the minds of many blacks and their white abolitionist allies that the new chief executive was, as one claimed, but "the fag end of a series of proslavery administrations."[25]

Frederick Douglass, the powerful abolitionist speaker, newspaper editor, and former slave, disagreed with this depiction of Lincoln and the Republican Party. He understood that a Lincoln presidency would be no abolitionist administration, but he hoped that a Republican victory "over the wickedly aggressive pro-slavery sentiment of the country" might help to move the nation toward an antislavery position. Events in the wake of Lincoln's presidential victory in the fall of 1860 were not encouraging, however. In early December, Douglass and other abolitionists were attending a meeting in Boston in memory of John Brown when the gathering was overrun by those determined not to allow the abolitionists to speak. Things quickly degenerated, as abolitionists on the platform came under intense attack. Douglass was among those assaulted by the mob and finally expelled from the hall by the police. That this violent confrontation with obvious racial overtones could occur in the nation's most abolitionist city suggested that Douglass may have underestimated the depth of racist anti-abolitionist feeling in the North.[26]

Obviously, Lincoln was right in his analysis of the national mood on the issues of slavery and race. It is most probable that the conciliatory tone of his inaugural address was meant not only for the southern states in secession and for those border states considering the possibility but for much of the rest of the nation as well. By the time he took office, Lincoln may have been committed to antislavery, but he also remained an astute politician. He understood that the country would not welcome a bold antislavery stand from its new chief executive. Thus, he bided his time.

Ironically, it was the South that created the conditions under which Lincoln could justify a move against slavery. By seceding from the Union, Southerners removed slavery from the protections provided under the U.S. Constitution, and by engaging in a war against the United States, they allowed the president, under his wartime constitutional powers, to authorize the confiscation of their slave property. Although abolitionists, black and white, bristled when Lincoln argued that his major purpose in pursuing the war was to save the Union, in fact he may have been structuring a politically viable position from which to ultimately play out an antislavery strategy. By defeating the southern effort at unconstitutional secession and restoring order in the South, Lincoln saw himself as engaged in the most sacred responsibility of the presidency. Thus, he could mollify the mass of anti-abolitionist critics to his political right by arguing that slavery was a side issue compared with the major goal of preserving the constitutional Union.

On a visit to New York City just before taking office, President-elect Lincoln encountered William E. Dodge, a wealthy industrialist who urged him to compromise with the South, then in the early stages of secession. To do otherwise, Dodge argued, was to risk the financial ruin of many northern cities, including New York City where without southern business the economy would grind to a halt and grass would grow in the street. Lincoln's answer displayed his characteristic humor but also his total commitment to the Constitution which he argued must be "respected, obeyed, enforced, and defended, let the grass grow where it may."[27] His actions, he said, were directed at traitors who placed their human property above the nation itself. "I could not feel that, to the best of my ability, I had even tried to preserve the constitution, if, to save slavery, or any minor matter, I should permit the wreck of the government, country, and Constitution all together."[28]

His reasoning was sound in several ways. So long as the South remained under the shelter of the U.S. Constitution, it had little to fear from abolitionists, no matter how determined they might be to end slavery. This institution was fully protected by law and the authority of the commander-in-chief under his constitutional responsibilities. When, in 1859, John Brown and his small army had attempted to move against slavery, they were confronted not simply by the local militia, but by the U.S. Marines led by Colonel Robert E. Lee with the assistance of Lieutenant "Jeb" Stuart. Many abolitionists hailed the news of southern secession, believing that it would ultimately ensure the destruction of slavery.

Speaking to an excited abolitionist crowd that had just heard the news of southern threats of secession, one black leader quoted Shakespeare in proposing a message to the South. "Stand not upon the order of your going," he bid the South, "but go at once... there is no union of ideas and interests in the country, and there can be no union between freedom and slavery." He was not the first. For more than a decade before the Civil War, Garrisonians had demanded "No Union with Slavery." Now the South seemed to be acting to facilitate the conditions under which abolitionists might mount an effective assault on what they called the Slave Power. One asked rhetorically, "Do you suppose that Old John Brown will be the last?"[29]

The southern secessionists saw withdrawal from the United States as an important step to ensure the protection of slavery against abolitionist attack. South Carolina seceded just before Christmas in 1860, to be followed in short order by six additional states. The Confederate States of America, with West Point graduate, former Secretary of War, and U.S. Senator from Mississippi Jefferson Davis as provisional president, was established in early February of 1861, just as Lincoln was preparing to take office. Lincoln's inaugural message, conciliatory as it was, did little to abate the southern momentum, and after the Confederate attack on Fort Sumter, four additional states from the Upper South left the United States to join the Confederacy. No American president had ever faced such a crisis, and Lincoln required all of his considerable political skills to hold the rest of the nation together, including the four slave states—Maryland, Delaware, Kentucky and Missouri—that did not secede. The presence of these slaveholding states complicated any antislavery approach Lincoln might take, especially in the early years of the war.

The war disrupted the routine of slavery not only in the slave states that had seceded but in those that had remained in the Union as well. Fearing that any widespread slave uprising might drive the loyal slave states toward the Confederacy, Lincoln cautioned Union commanders to prevent slave insurrections, even as they waged war on the enemy. Thus, military units operated in accordance with the Fugitive Slave Act of 1850, returning fugitive slaves who escaped to Union lines. In August of 1861 John C. Frémont, commander in charge of the Western Department of the Army, declared martial law in Missouri to control the intense Confederate guerilla action there. He then issued an order freeing the slaves of all disloyal Missouri slaveholders. Lincoln, fearing border state reaction, revoked Frémont's order and removed him from command.[30]

Yet, the pressure to move against slavery, at least in the rebellious states, was growing. Also in August, Congress sought to strike a blow at the enemy by passing the First Confiscation Act which authorized Union commanders to seize rebel property. It also declared freedom for all slaves who labored for the Confederate military. Still Lincoln did not encourage his commanders to free slaves of Confederate masters. The next spring, arguing that no commander could move without specific authority of the president, he overruled an emancipation order issued by General David Hunter, U.S. commander in eastern South Carolina and Georgia. Despite complaints from the ranks that his policy of returning fugitive slaves to their masters turned the U.S. military into a force of slave catchers, Lincoln held fast to his position. Frederick Douglass, angered by the president's refusal to move in an antislavery direction, declared Lincoln "the most dangerous advocate of slave-hunting and slave-catching in the land."[31]

Meanwhile, slaves in the border states and those in Confederate areas who could reach Union lines were escaping in significant numbers. Lincoln's proposals for gradual compensated emancipation for slaveholders in states loyal to the Union, which were designed to calm border state fears, met with resistance. Only in the District of Columbia, where the federal government had direct control, was the plan put into effect. On April 16, 1862, Lincoln signed an act abolishing slavery in the capital and compensating masters with approximately $300 for each freed slave. Still, during the summer of 1862, a rising crescendo of voices calling for Lincoln to authorize a general emancipation for slaves in the rebellious states would not allow his antislavery conscience to rest. Delegations of abolitionist and Quaker groups brought their message to the White House. In August, Douglass chastised Lincoln for not enforcing Congress's Second Confiscation Act, passed in mid-July, that declared freedom for the slaves of disloyal masters. This new congressional action, Confederate victories on the battlefield, and the increasing difficulty of recruiting soldiers brought additional pressure for presidential action. By that time, Lincoln had already drafted a preliminary emancipation order, and in late July he shared a draft of his Emancipation Proclamation with his Cabinet.[32]

Such a proclamation was fraught with danger. With so much of the fighting going against the Union, many might consider it an act of desperation, a judgment which might weaken its impact. There was also the question of the status of former slaves after emancipation. As an answer to the second issue, Lincoln fell back on that decades-old solution, colonization. In an effort to address black resistance to his plan, Lincoln made history. The president of the United States invited a delegation of African Americans to meet with him at the White House. On the afternoon of August 14, 1862, five black leaders—H. Ford Douglass, Henry Highland Garnet, William Wells Brown, A. P. Smith, and Edward M. Thomas— arrived to meet with the president. Thomas, assuming leadership of the delegation, asked the president to address the group, which he did. What followed was a sobering example of Lincoln's racial assumptions, a disappointment to the delegation and to African Americans who later became aware of his words, published in the next day's edition of the *New York Tribune* and in September's edition of Frederick Douglass's newspaper, *Douglass' Monthly*.

Calling slavery the "greatest wrong inflicted on any people," Lincoln made clear his determination to bring the institution to an end. Once ended, however, he told the delegation, black people would never be able to enjoy true freedom or equality in the United States among whites. "I do not propose to discuss this," he said, "but to present it as a fact with which we have to deal." Then he made his racial assumptions clear. "You and we are different. We have between us broader difference than exists between almost any other two races." Since he believed that these differences could never be altered, Lincoln suggested what he saw as the only practical solution. He argued that slavery had been an evil influence on whites as well as blacks and that the races could never live together except under the influence of that evil. He concluded that "it is better for us both, therefore, to be separated." He then presented his plan of voluntary African American emigration to Africa, the Caribbean, or South America. The black men listened to the president politely but found his words discouraging and offensive.[33]

In reaction, Frederick Douglass wrote a scathing editorial in *Douglass' Monthly*, calling Lincoln an "itinerant colonization lecturer" and "a genuine representative of American prejudice and Negro hatred."[34] A. P. Smith wrote to the president saying what almost all black people felt and asking the questions that most would have asked, if given the chance. "[M]ust I crush out my cherished hopes and aspirations, abandon my home, and become a pander to the mean and selfish spirit that oppresses me? Pray tell us, is our right to a home in this country less than your own, Mr. Lincoln?" he asked rhetorically. He went on to proclaim his patriotism, comparing it to Lincoln's, and declared his strong resistance to African American colonization. Clearly, African American opposition to colonization was overwhelming.[35]

Within a few months Lincoln announced his intention to issue an Emancipation Proclamation at the turn of the New Year. On the grand day, African Americans waited hopefully for the official world. When it came, blacks were relieved to find that it contained no contingency for colonization. Henry Highland Garnet, who had been part of the black delegation that Lincoln had addressed at the White House, led a gathering at Cooper Institute in New York City. He pronounced the president, "an advancing and progressive man...the man of our choice and hope."[36]

The Proclamation also altered Douglass's appraisal of Lincoln, for much had changed. For many African American and white abolitionists in the United States and Europe, the war now became a holy crusade against slavery. Black troops were serving the Union cause, their actions impressing even the most skeptical. Despite the disadvantages they faced in service to their nation, they had responded to the call that Lincoln had built into the Emancipation Proclamation.

Douglass met Lincoln for the first time in August of 1863. As a recruiter of African American troops, Douglass had come to Washington to talk to federal officials about the inequities in pay and treatment imposed on blacks. After meeting with members of Congress and Secretary of War Edwin M. Stanton, he visited the White House where he was received by the president. As Douglass set out the case of action needed to redress the disadvantages black soldiers confronted, he was struck by Lincoln's directness. He said that he "saw at a glance the justice of the popular estimate of his qualities expressed in the prefix Honest to the name Abraham Lincoln."[37] The men discussed the plight of black soldiers, and Lincoln defended himself from the charge of being slow and vacillating on the question of emancipation and human rights for African Americans.

Douglass was impressed. "Mr. Lincoln listened with patience and silence to all I had to say." On the question of equal pay for black soldiers, Lincoln set out the politics of the situation. African Americans were paid roughly half the amount allotted to whites, but the president argued that, "the employment of colored troops at all was a great gain to the colored people...that they ought to be willing to enter the service upon any con dition." He went on to say that the inferior pay provided to black soldiers "seemed a necessary concession to smooth the way to their employment at all as soldiers." Yet, in the end, Lincoln seemed to agree to work to redress the pay inequities. As Douglass recalled, the president told him, "...ultimately they would receive the same."[38]

Although Douglass did not receive all he had hoped, the former slave came away from this meeting feeling that the president of the United States had treated him as an equal and that he had encountered a sincere man. Lincoln's assessment of public opinion on the issue of African Americans in uniform was accurate. The general white public opposed equal pay for black troops because of what it symbolized. One New Yorker expressed the prevailing sentiment saying, "it is unjust in every way to the white soldier to put him on a level with the black."[39]

The struggle for equal pay would continue for more than two years, but finally, as the war neared its end in March of 1865, Congress authorized equal pay for all black soldiers, retroactive to their actual dates of enlistment. Progress had been slow, as Lincoln acknowledged, but pay equity had finally been achieved. Through it all, Douglass maintained a realistic understanding of Lincoln, the politician, and was nevertheless impressed with "the solid gravity of his character."[40]

As the war continued, Lincoln's views on racial issues changed. He came to appreciate the contributions that African Americans were making to the cause and became more outspoken on the subject. His Emancipation Proclamation provided an antislavery focus to U.S. military efforts that persuaded several European nations to withhold recognition and aid from the Confederacy. In the United States, it raised the hopes of those committed to freedom, but others, especially the loyal slave states, were uneasy about the concept of emancipation. It promised freedom to the slaves held by those still in rebellion; and although it did not apply to slaves in loyal states, slaveholders in the loyal states complained that many of their slaves embraced the spirit of the proclamation and walked off the plantation.

Despite the new moral focus that the Proclamation added to the struggle, the early years of the war were less than promising for the Union cause. Setbacks on the battlefield for Northern forces and the unprecedented loss of life contributed to a pessimism that plagued much of the United States. Although General Ulysses S. Grant won a victory over Confederate forces during the spring of 1862 at Shiloh, Tennessee, 13,000 of his 63,000 men were killed in the process. Later that year, U.S. forces suffered another 14,000 losses at the second Battle of Manassas and yet another 12,000 casualties at the Battle of Fredericksburg, also in Virginia. During the summer of 1863, the Union suffered over 20,000 casualties and then in the spring of 1864, General Grant's forces lost over 7,000 men in a little over an hour, as they attacked entrenched rebels at Cold Harbor, Virginia. All told, during one month of fighting in the late spring of 1864 the United States lost some 50,000 of its soldiers.[41]

In light of these shocking casualties, Lincoln felt strong pressure to sue for peace at almost any cost. Democrats had gained control of the legislature in his home state of Illinois in 1862 and called for negotiations to end the war. Only the efforts of Richard Yates, the state's Republican governor, had prevented it from withdrawing support for the war.[42] Fearing that such reactions might lead to demands for a reversal of emancipation as a peace offering to the Confederacy, Lincoln called Douglass to the White House for another consultation. This time explaining the situation and his fears that an immediate peace might leave tens of thousands of slaves in southern bondage, he asked for Douglass's help. "I want you to set about devising some means of making [the slaves] acquainted with [The Emancipation Proclamation], and for bringing them to our lines." Douglass was again impressed. Recalling this meeting, he said of Lincoln, "He spoke with great earnestness."[43]

The president had every reason for concern. As the presidential election of 1864 approached, his analysis of the political situation seemed disturbingly accurate. He faced a stiff challenge from the Democratic candidate, General George B. McClellan, the former commander of the Army of the Potomac whom Lincoln had relieved from military duty because of differences over the general's handling of the war in Virginia. If McClellan and the Democrats should take control of the White House, emancipation would be in grave danger. This was a significant concern since some Republicans were convinced that Lincoln could not win a second term. The situation was made more alarming when in mid-July of 1864, barely four months before the election, Confederate forces moved into Maryland, within five miles of Washington, D.C.

Although the party was not united in its decision, Lincoln secured the Republican nomination for the presidency. The Republicans also endorsed a constitutional amendment to abolish slavery. Lincoln was reelected with 55 percent of the popular vote, and in January of 1865, with his support, Congress passed the Thirteenth Amendment to the Constitution to bring an end to slavery. Finally, Lincoln was politically free to state his antislavery views and to connect them more directly to the war. In his Second Inaugural Address, he told his audience that the presence of slave property, one-eighth of the nation's population, had constituted a "peculiar and powerful interest" for slaveholders. He told his listeners what almost all understood clearly, that this interest was "somehow the cause of the war." He then suggested that slavery was an offense in the sight of God and that the Almighty may very well have punished the nation through the ordeal of war. Perhaps, he speculated, America's punishment would be continued "until all the wealth piled by the bond-man's two hundred and fifty years of unrequited toil shall be sunk, and until every drop of blood drawn with the lash shall be paid by another drawn with the sword."[44]

The war had changed Lincoln. He was impressed and even touched by the service of black troops. He was certain that they had played a major role in saving the Union and bringing an end to slavery. Meetings with Frederick Douglass had also gone a great distance toward changing Lincoln's racial views. Whereas before the war he had spoken of African Americans as inferiors, his respect for Douglass was obvious, made public by Lincoln's own words. He had invited Douglass to the White House reception after the inaugural address, an unprecedented gesture of respect. Then after Douglass had talked his way into the gathering, past officials who could hardly believe that a black man was to be the special guest of the president at such an affair, Lincoln shocked many in the room, by not only acknowledging Douglass's presence but also his friendship. As Douglass remembered it, he walked into the East Room "amid a scene of elegance such as...I had never before witnessed." Lincoln, in the midst of conversation, saw him and immediately acknowledged his presence. "Here comes my friend Douglass," he announced. Then, taking Douglass's hand he said, "I am glad to see you. I saw you in the crowd today, listening to my inaugural address; how did you like it?" Finally, as if to expel any doubt, Lincoln added, "There is no man in the country whose opinion I value more than yours." When Douglass complimented the speech, Lincoln thanked him, as White House guests looked on with considerable interest. This was a great distance from Lincoln's position during his debates with Stephen A. Douglas in the late 1850s, when he doubted the intelligence of African Americans and denied advocating their basic citizenship rights.[45]

Lincoln had indeed become publicly antislavery, having gone on record in support of the Thirteenth Amendment. He also seemed to drop his earlier plans for the colonization of African Americans outside of America. A decade before, in Peoria, Illinois, Lincoln had suggested colonization as a solution to the problem of slavery. While he admitted the impracticality of such a plan, he told his audience, "My first impulse would be to free all the slaves and send them to Liberia—to their native land."[46] However, after his Emancipation Proclamation of 1863 and the enlistment of black troops thereafter, he fell publicly silent on the issue. Historian Richard Carwardine sees Lincoln's failure to mention colonization as an important signal of his major philosophical shift. "One intimation for the new direction in policy," Carwardine suggests, "was the dog that did not bark." It indicated what Stephen B. Oates has called "an eloquent silence, indicating that he [Lincoln] had concluded that Dixie's whites and liberated Negroes must somehow learn to live together."[47] He may have been convinced by the argument put forward by a variety of black leaders that African Americans were as much American as white Americans and more so than recent white immigrants. He was surely swayed by the gallant military service of the tens of thousands of black troops fighting to save the nation. Regardless of where he stood at the start of the war, by his second term as president Lincoln had moved closer to the position staked out more than three decades earlier by black revolutionary David Walker who asserted, "America is more our country, than it is the whites—we have enriched it with our blood and tears."[48]

None other than William Lloyd Garrison acknowledged the antislavery progress Lincoln had made. The abolitionist leader met with Lincoln shortly before the 1864 election. The two men talked privately for an hour, discussing the Emancipation Proclamation and Lincoln's drive toward the total abolition of slavery. Lincoln told Garrison that he favored a constitutional amendment to abolish slavery to be added to the Republican platform. This should be done immediately and with strong party support, Lincoln argued, so that it would not be thought contingent upon Union victory on the battlefield or upon his fate at the ballot box. Garrison, always suspicious of American politics and politicians, was impressed by the president's commitment to the complete removal of slavery. He emerged from the meeting firmly believing that Lincoln would "do all that he can see it right and possible for him to do to uproot slavery and give fair-play to the emancipated."[49] In a speech to a cheering crowd of the abolitionist faithful, Garrison expressed gratitude "to the humble rail-splitter of Illinois—to the Presidential chain-breaker of millions—Abraham Lincoln."[50] Abolitionist doubts about Lincoln's antislavery views faded rapidly as the president became more publicly open on the subject. In a speech to an Indiana army regiment in mid-March, just a few days after his inauguration, Lincoln employed his well-known wit to make the point. "Whenever I hear anyone arguing for slavery," he told the troops, "I feel a strong impulse to see it tried on him personally."[51]

Although downplayed as a cause of the war in the winter and spring of 1861, by the spring of 1865 slavery was clearly at the war's center. Within three weeks of his message to the troops in Indiana, all had changed. On April 9, Lee surrendered his forces to Grant at Appomattox Court House. Two days later in Washington, Lincoln addressed the question of reconstructing the conquered states. Abolitionists were urging that now that African Americans were about to be free, they should have the vote. Lincoln seemed willing to seriously consider this proposition. He even showed signs of being open to that social equality among the races that he had denied during his debates with Stephen A. Douglas in the Senate race of 1858. Speaking specifically about the conditions for the readmission of Louisiana to the United States, Lincoln acknowledged approvingly that the new state constitution had opened public schools to blacks and had empowered the legislature to give them the right to vote. He then expressed support for conveying the franchise on selected groups of African Americans. "I would myself prefer that it were now conferred on the very intelligent, and on those who serve our cause as soldiers." He seemed excited by what he saw as a new spirit that freedom had brought to African Americans. "The colored man too," he said, "in seeing all united for him, is inspired with vigilance, and energy, and daring."[52] The president seemed to be moving toward advocating a complete overturning of the ruling in the Dred Scott decision.

Lincoln's transformation was apparent to many in his audience that evening, including an actor named John Wilkes Booth. Booth was a southern sympathizer who had yet to fully accept the Confederate surrender. He hated Lincoln for humbling the South and was infuriated by the president's endorsement of citizenship rights for African Americans. He was so enraged by Lincoln's words that he vowed to kill the president. On April 14, 1865, Booth made good on his threats, assassinating Lincoln as the president sat watching a play with his wife in a private box at Ford's Theatre in Washington.

By the end of his life, Lincoln had grown to be what he said himself to be—antislavery. But he was still growing and showed definite signs of becoming much more. He was moving beyond his earlier views of white supremacy. His relationship with Frederick Douglass and the experience of the war in which he called on the service of African Americans were among the most influential factors in his personal growth. Although he did not live to see the states ratify the Thirteenth Amendment that finally abolished slavery across the nation, his actions had helped make it possible. African Americans generally understood his growth, and most loved him for it. In New York they gathered at Cooper Institute to protest the decision of the city council to exclude blacks from Lincoln's funeral procession as it passed through the city. Douglass addressed the crowd, denouncing the council's action and praising their fallen hero. In support of the city's African Americans, the *New York Evening Post* observed, "Our late President was venerated by the whole colored population with a peculiar degree of feeling...and [they] looked upon him as the liberator of their race. We have accepted the services of colored citizens in the war and it is disgraceful ingratitude to shut them out of our civil demonstration." The newspaper also published a letter by black minister John Sella Martin, who argued that Lincoln had formed a special relationship with African Americans whom "he had lifted by the most solemn official acts to the dignity of citizens and defenders of the union." Lincoln, he argued, would have wanted African Americans to be "allowed the honor of following his remains to the grave." It finally took a telegram from Charles Dana, Assistant Secretary of War, to persuade the council to reverse itself. Finally some two thousand blacks took up positions at the rear of Lincoln's funeral procession in the city.[53]

Elsewhere, African Americans stood by the thousands along the tracks that bore the train carrying Lincoln's body back to Illinois. By and large, blacks were realistic about Lincoln. Most understood the conservative antislavery man he had been and were devoted to the memory of the abolitionist he had become. However slowly, and with whatever complications, Lincoln had presided over the end of slavery. It was Lincoln's personal growth that ultimately led to his premature death. John Wilkes Booth assassinated him for destroying the slaveholding South and for his support of citizenship rights for black people. It was also his personal growth that led African Americans across the country to remember Abraham Lincoln as the Great Emancipator.[54]

NOTES

James O. Horton is the Benjamin Banneker Professor Emeritus of American Civilization and History at The George Washington University. He presented this paper as the 2006 McMurtry Lecture at The Lincoln Museum, Fort Wayne, Indiana. The Lincoln Museum thanks the family of R. Gerald McMurtry for sponsoring the publication of this article.

1. "A Lincoln to Albert G. Hodges, April 4, 1864," Michael P. Johnson, ed., *Abraham Lincoln, Slavery, and the Civil War: Selected Writings and Speeches* (Boston: St. Martin's Bedford Books, 2000), 285.
2. Roy P. Basler, ed., *The Collected Works of Abraham Lincoln* (New Brunswick, NJ: Rutgers University Press, 1953), 2:320.
3. Aileen Kraditor, *Means and Ends in American Abolitionism: Garrison and His Critics on Strategy and Tactics, 1834–1850* (New York: Vintage Books, 1967).
4. David Herbert Donald, *Lincoln* (New York: Simon & Schuster, 1995), 181.
5. Henry Mayer, *All on Fire: William Lloyd Garrison and the Abolition of Slavery* (New York: St. Martin's Press, 1998), 445.
6. Douglas L. Wilson and Rodney O. Davis, eds. *Herndon's Informants: Letters, Interviews, and Statements about Abraham Lincoln* (Urbana: University of Illinois Press, 1997), 457. See also Allen C. Guelzo, *Abraham Lincoln: Redeemer President* (Grand Rapids, MI: Wm. B. Eerdmans Publishing, 1999), 128.
7. Abraham Lincoln, "Protest in Illinois Legislature on Slavery," *Collected Works of Abraham Lincoln*, 1:75.
8. Guelzo, *Abraham Lincoln*, 126–127.
9. "Article Three," *The Constitution of the American Anti-Slavery Society: with the Declaration of the National Anti-Slavery Convention at Philadelphia, December, 1833* (New York: American Anti-Slavery Society, 1838).
10. Guelzo, *Abraham Lincoln*, 127–128.
11. "Speech on the Kansas-Nebraska Act at Peoria, Illinois," Johnson, *Abraham Lincoln*, 45.
12. Ibid.
13. Paul Finkelman, *Defending Slavery: Proslavery Thought in the Old South* (Boston: Bedford/St Martin's Press, 2003); "Speed to One Hundred Fortieth Indiana Regiment" (March 17, 1865) Basler, *Collected Works*, 8:361; Johnson, *Abraham Lincoln*, 45–46.
14. Basler, *Collected Works*, 2:132.
15. For African American reactions to plans for African colonization see, James Oliver Horton and Lois E. Horton, *In Hope of Liberty: Free Black Culture and Community in the North, 1700–1865* (New York: Oxford University Press, 1997), 177–202.
16. The U.S. defeat of Mexico in 1848 extended the nation by more than 500,000 square miles through the Southwest and on to California and the Pacific Ocean, enabling the possible expansion of territory that might be open to slavery.
17. "A House Divided, Speech at Springfield, Illinois, June 16, 1858," Johnson, *Abraham Lincoln*, 63, 68.
18. Seventh Lincoln-Douglas Debate, October 13, 1858, Johnson, *Abraham Lincoln*, 79.
19. First Lincoln-Douglas Debate, August 21, 1858, Johnson, *Abraham Lincoln*, 72.
20. Ibid.
21. Fourth Lincoln-Douglas Debate, September 18, 1858, Johnson, *Abraham Lincoln*, 73.
22. First Lincoln-Douglas Debate, August 21, 1858, Johnson, *Abraham Lincoln*, 72.
23. "Address at Cooper Institute, February 27, 1860," Maureen Harrison and Steve Gilbert, eds., *Abraham Lincoln: Word for Word* (San Diego, CA: Excellent Books, 1994), 249–274, 266–267.

24. James M. McPherson, *The Negro's Civil War: How American Negroes Felt and Acted during the War for the Union* (New York: Vintage Books, 1965), 5–6.

25. Donald Yacovone, ed., *Freedom's Journey: African American Voices of the Civil War* (Chicago: Lawrence Hill Books, 2004), 299.

26. See William S. McFeely, *Frederick Douglass* (New York: W.W. Norton and Co., 1991), 208–211.

27. Ron Soodalter, *Hanging Captain Gordon: The Life and Trial of an American Slave Trader* (New York: Atria Books, 2006), 98.

28. Johnson, *Abraham Lincoln*, 285.

29. *Chicago Daily Times and Herald*, November 20, 1860.

30. W. M. Brewer, "Lincoln and The Border States," *Journal of Negro History*, vol. 34 no.1, (January, 1949), pp. 46–72.

31. David W. Blight, *Beyond the Battlefield: Race, Memory and the American Civil War* (Amherst, MA: University of Massachusetts Press, 2002), 80.

32. Harold Holzer, Edna Greene Medford and Frank J. Williams, eds., *The Emancipation Proclamation* (Baton Rouge, LA: Louisiana State University Press, 2006).

33. *New York Tribune*, August 15, 1862.

34. *Douglass' Monthly*, September, 1862, quoted in Blight, Beyond the Battlefield, 80.

35. Holzer, Medford and Williams, eds., *The Emancipation Proclamation*, 19.

36. Holzer, Medford and Williams, eds., *The Emancipation Proclamation*, 22.

37. McFeely, *Frederick Douglass*, 229.

38. Frederick Douglass, *Life and Times of Frederick Douglass* (London: Collier Books, [1892] 1969), 348.

39. James McPherson, *The Negro's Civil War: How American Negroes Felt and Acted during the War for the Union*, 199.

40. Douglass, *Life and Times of Frederick Douglass*, 348.

41. Harry S. Stout, *Upon the Altar of the Nation: A Moral History of the Civil War* (New York: Viking, 2006), 338–349; James M. McPherson, *Battle Cry of Freedom: The Civil War Era*, (New York: Oxford University Press, 1988).

42. Arthur Charles Cole, *Centennial History of Illinois: The Era of the Civil War, 1848–1870* (Springfield, IL: Illinois Centennial Commission, 1919).

43. Douglass, *Life and Times of Frederick Douglass*, 358.

44. "Second Inaugural Address, Washington, DC, March 4, 1865," Johnson, *Abraham Lincoln*, 320–321.

45. *Douglass, Life and Times of Frederick Douglass*, 366.

46. "Slavery and the Repeal of the Missouri Compromise," Peoria, Illinois, October 16, 1854," Harrison and Gilbert, eds., *Abraham Lincoln: Word for Word*, 105–144, 196.

47. Richard Carwardine, *Lincoln: A Life of Purpose and Power* (New York: Alfred A. Knopf, 2006), 220; Stephen B. Oates, *Abraham Lincoln: The Man Behind the Myths* (New York: Harper Collins Publishers, 1984), 113–114.

48. *David Walker's Appeal*, edited with an introduction by Charles M. Wiltse, 3rd edition (June, 1830; New York: Hill and Wang, 1965), 76.

49. Mayer, *All On Fire*, 568.

50. *Liberator*, February 10, 1865.

51. Basler, *Collected Works*, 8:361.

52. Johnson, *Abraham Lincoln*, 332.

53. Victor Searcher, *The Farewell to Lincoln*, (New York: Abingdon Press, 1965) 139; Philip S. Foner, *History of Black Americans: From the Compromise of 1850 to the End of the Civil War* (Westport, CN: Greenwood Press, 1983), 449–450.

54. Michael Kauffman, *American Brutus: John Wilkes Booth and the Lincoln Conspiracies* (New York: Random House, 2004).

II

THE PRIVATE LINCOLN

4

A STRANGE, FRIENDLESS, UNEDUCATED, PENNILESS BOY

David Herbert Donald

LINCOLN'S EARLY FRIENDSHIPS

Everybody liked the boy, but he had no special friends.[1] Years later, after Abraham Lincoln was assassinated, old residents of Kentucky and Indiana remembered what a good boy he had been. "He was a modest and Sensitive lad—never coming where he was not wanted," Elizabeth Crawford recalled; "he was gentle, tender and Kind."[2] Dozens said they had been his friends, but no one claimed to have been his intimate.

I

Not much can be said about Lincoln's playmates in Kentucky, where he spent his first seven years. Nearly all the stories about his boyhood are apocryphal. For instance, the Reverend James Duncan recalled how with three dogs he and young Abraham chased a groundhog into a cleft in the rocks along the side of a creek. After working in vain for nearly two hours to force the creature out, Lincoln ran off about a quarter of a mile to the blacksmith shop and returned with an iron hook attached to the end of a pole, which he used to pry the creature out. The problem with this memory is that Lincoln would have been only two years old at the time.[3]

The only fairly authentic anecdote concerning Lincoln's Kentucky playmates recounts an adventure when he was about seven. He and Austin Gollaher were playing in Knob Creek, which ran near the Lincolns' cabin, and decided to cross it to look for some young partridges Lincoln had seen the previous day. Neither boy could swim. Gollaher succeeded in "cooning" his way across on a small sycamore pole, but when Abraham followed, he fell off into deep water, and Gollaher had to rescue him. "He was almost dead," Gollaher remembered years later, "and I was badly scared. I rolled and pounded him in good earnest" until he began to breathe again.[4]

When Abraham was about six, he trudged off to school with his older sister, Sarah, more in order to keep her company on the two-mile walk than in any expectation that he would learn to read and write. But Gollaher, looking through the golden haze of memory, said Abraham was "an unusually bright boy at school, and made splendid progress in his studies." During the few months he and Sarah attended school, another Kentuckian remembered, "He alwa[y]s appear[e]d to be very quiet during play time" and gained something of a reputation for liking solitude and for keeping his clothes cleaner than the other boys his age.[5]

But when all these stories are put together, they add up to very little. As his cousin Dennis Hanks correctly judged, "Abe Exhibited no special traits in Ky."[6]

II

Southern Indiana was not a place that encouraged young Abraham Lincoln to make close friends. When Thomas Lincoln moved his family from Kentucky to Perry County (later subdivided to form Spencer County), Indiana, in 1816, they settled in a wild region. The public land to which Thomas staked his claim in the Little Pigeon Creek area was so remote that for part of the distance from the Ohio River, he had to hack a path through unbroken forest for his family to follow. Dangerous animals prowled in the woods. Many years later, when Abraham Lincoln revisited the region, he was moved to verse:

When first my father settled here,
   'Twas then the frontier line:
The panther's scream, filled night with fear
   And bears preyed on the swine.[7]

There was little opportunity in this rough frontier region for young Abraham Lincoln to make friends with other children of his own age. Though he was only eight years old, he was large for his age, and his labor was needed to help clear away the undergrowth and chop down enough trees so that his father could plant corn. As he remembered it, he "had an axe put into his hands at once; and from that till within his twenty-third year, he was almost constantly handling that most useful instrument—less, of course, in plowing and harvesting seasons."[8]

After about a year, the family seemed fairly well settled, especially when Thomas Sparrow and his wife, Elizabeth Hanks Sparrow, Nancy Hanks Lincoln's aunt and uncle, moved from Kentucky and built their own cabin near the Lincolns'. Dennis Hanks, Elizabeth Sparrow's eighteen-year-old illegitimate nephew, accompanied them, and he enlivened both households with his irrepressible good spirits and endless loquacity.

Then disaster struck. People in the Little Pigeon Creek community began to be afflicted with the mysterious ailment they called milk sickness that was later discovered to be caused by milk from their cows that ran wild in the forest and had been eating the luxuriant but poisonous white snake-root plant. Dizziness, nausea, and stomach pains were followed by prostration, coma, and, usually within seven days, death. Both Thomas and Elizabeth Sparrow died. Then Nancy Hanks Lincoln fell sick and died on October 5, 1818, leaving behind her husband, her daughter, aged eleven, and Abraham.

The death of his mother was a critical event in Abraham Lincoln's life. There is no way to measure the effect of such a loss on a nine-year-old. Lincoln himself left no direct record of his grief over his mother's death, but there is evidence to suggest his deep sense of loss. In the 1840s, when he revisited his old Indiana neighborhood, he was moved to mournful verse:

> I range the fields with pensive tread,
>   And pace the hollow rooms,
> And feel (companion of the dead)
>   I'm living in the tombs.[9]

Love g Poetry

During the Civil War, in an attempt to console the bereaved child of a friend killed in battle, he wrote: "In this sad world of ours, sorrow comes to all; and, to the young, it comes with bitterest agony, because it takes them unawares.... I have had experience enough to know what I say."[10]

Death is always traumatic for small children, and in Abraham's case the blow was the more severe because his mother's death, at the age of twenty-five or twenty-six, was both premature and unexpected. There was no long period of illness during which her husband and children could reconcile themselves to the inevitable. The loss was the more devastating because of its finality. Though a religious woman, Nancy Hanks Lincoln apparently had no belief in an afterlife (nor did her son ever develop one), and on her deathbed she gave her children no assurance that she would see them in heaven but "told them to be good and kind to their father—to

Not necessarily true

one another and to the world."[11] There was no possibility for a healing period of mourning. Nancy Lincoln, like her aunt and uncle, was placed in a coffin her husband hastily constructed of rough boards and, without ceremony, was buried on a knoll a quarter of a mile from the cabin. No stone or other marker was erected over her grave.

Children experience the death of a parent with confused emotions. There is, of course, the immense and overwhelming sense of loss, but there is also often concealed anger at having been abandoned. Always there is a sense of guilt—guilt over being a survivor when a mother or father has been taken—which can be accompanied by a wholly irrational feeling that, especially in the case of a mysterious disease like the milk sickness, somehow the child may have done something or neglected to do something that caused the parent's death.[12]

Psychoanalysts agree that when a parent dies, a child needs most "the comforting presence of his surviving parent or of a known and trusted substitute."[13] But the undemonstrative Thomas Lincoln, who had to struggle simply to keep food on the family table, was not a man who could extend such comfort to his orphaned children, and there were no neighbors who could serve as mother substitutes.

The sense of abandonment that the Lincoln children felt because of the death of their mother induced fear that their father too might leave them. Indeed, within a year of Nancy's death, Thomas Lincoln did go back to Kentucky, leaving his two small children unprotected except for their teenage cousin, Dennis Hanks. When Thomas Lincoln returned with a new wife, Sarah Bush Johnston Lincoln, she found Abraham and Sarah dirty, hungry, and clad in tatters. The children became devoted to this warm and outgoing woman, a widow with two daughters and a son Abraham's age, who quickly brought order to the Lincoln household, but she arrived before Abraham had time fully to accept the loss of his mother. His father had remarried before an itinerant preacher read a funeral service over Nancy Hanks Lincoln's grave.

In such circumstances, children often have difficulty in making close connections with others. It is as if once their most intimate link, to a parent, has been destroyed, they are fearful lest they invite another devastating hurt.

III

During this period of incomplete mourning, Abraham was saved from social isolation by the presence of Dennis Hanks, engaging, garrulous, and self-promoting. Dennis was later to claim he had great influence on young Abraham. "I taught Abe his first lesson in spelling—reading and writing," he boasted. "I taught Abe to write with a buzzards quillen which I killed with a rifle and having made a pen—put Abes hand in mind [mine] and moving his fingers by my hand to give him the idea of how to write."[14] (He claimed also to have sparked Lincoln's interest in the law: "I bought the Statute[s] of Indiana and from that he Lerned the principles of Law and allso My Self.") Most of these claims were fabricated or highly exaggerated, though certainly the two worked together on the farm and hunted rabbits together. But Dennis was nearly ten years older than his cousin, and he was more like a benevolent uncle than a close friend.

Abraham never developed a warm friendship for his step-brother, John D. Johnston, who was about his own age. The reasons are obscure. Though Sarah Bush Johnston Lincoln was even-handed in her treatment of both boys, her husband was not; as a relative remembered, he "always appeared to think much more of his stepson John D. Johnston than he did of his own Son Abraham."[15] Perhaps Thomas Lincoln felt more temperamentally kin to John D., who was rather dull and lazy, if good-tempered, than he did to Abraham; possibly he felt threatened by Abraham and was unwilling to share the male role of authority with his talented son. At any rate, a relative recalled, he "never showed by his actions that he thought much of his son Abraham when a Boy, he treated [him] rather unkind than otherwise." Inevitably the two boys became rivals rather than friends. Dennis Hanks said they were enemies.[16]

Outside of Abraham's family circle, there were few boys of his own age in the Little Pigeon Creek community. The Lincoln family had no nearby neighbors. Spencer County was almost uninhabited when the Lincolns arrived, with a total population of only about 200 in an area nearly the size of the state of Rhode Island. In 1820, about forty families lived within a five-mile radius of the Lincolns' cabin; this means there were fewer than two families per square mile. Louis A. Warren, who made a careful study of the early land records and the 1820 census, calculated that at the time Abraham was eleven years old, there were seven, or possibly eight, families that lived within a mile of the Lincolns, and these included only ten boys (besides Abraham and John D. Johnston) and nine girls between the ages of seven and seventeen. It is not possible to ascertain the ages of the individual children, but these figures suggest that within a mile radius, there were, at most, only one or two other boys of Abraham's age, none living so close that they could see each other and play with each other daily.[17]

The Little Pigeon Creek neighborhood was not even a village, and there was nothing like a community center, but Abraham did have a chance to meet other children when he, with his sister and the three

Johnston children, attended the school that Andrew Crawford opened in a cabin about a mile from the Lincoln house. It closed after one term of three months. The next year, he enrolled in James Swaney's school, about four miles from home, but the distance was so great that, because of his farm chores, he attended only sporadically. The following year, he went for about six months to a school Azel W. Dorsey opened in the same cabin where Crawford had taught. His formal schooling then ended and, all told, as he himself summarized, "the ag[g]regate of all his schooling did not amount to one year."[18]

The somewhat sporadic services of the Little Pigeon Creek Baptist Church, which his father, stepmother, and sister joined in 1823, offered other opportunities for meeting children of his own age. Though not a member, Abraham listened to the sermons and after the service would often rally the other boys and girls around him. Then, climbing on a tree stump, he would repeat—or sometimes parody—the minister's words.

He became a leader of the children in the area, in part because he matured earlier than most others. Lincoln experienced the onset of puberty in his twelfth—possibly in his eleventh—year, when he began to shoot up in height. He became "a man though a boy." When the other children his age got into squabbles or engaged in pranks, Lincoln would say, "Leave off your boyish ways and be more like men."[19] More mature than the other students, he was nearly always at the head of his class. One of them thought Lincoln "got ahead of his masters—[They] could do him no further good: he went to school no more."[20] His excellence in his school work could have caused jealousy, but it didn't because he was generous in helping other children. Kate Roby remembered that once Schoolmaster Crawford stumped the class by insisting that they spell "defied," threatening to keep the children in school day and night until they got it right. After unsuccessfully trying every variant she could think of, she chanced to spy tall Abraham Lincoln through the window, who smiled and pointed his finger to his eye. Taking the hint, she immediately changed the letter "y" into an "i," and Crawford had to let the class out.

The absence of playmates—important at any age—was of crucial importance at this stage of Lincoln's development. In late childhood and early adolescence, most boys find a close friend—a "chum," to use the term favored by psychoanalyst Harry Stack Sullivan—from whom they are inseparable and with whom they share confidences, secrets, desires, and ambitions. By giving a boy a perspective on himself different from that offered by his family members, a chum can help in the difficult process of self-recognition and can help him to develop an autonomous personality.[21] When there are very few children of the same age in a community, some boys never find such an intimate friend, and the failure can have serious consequences for the rest of their lives. Boys who do not have chums often have difficulty later in establishing close, warm friendships, and there is some evidence that such boys are more likely to suffer from depression in later years.[22] Lincoln never had a chum.

IV

In 1831, when Lincoln, at the age of twenty-two, left his family and settled in New Salem, Illinois, he was—as he later described himself—"a strange, friendless, uneducated, penniless boy."[23] What he meant by "strange" is so obscure that the editors of his *Collected Works* thought that he meant to say "stranger." But to have Lincoln call himself a "stranger" requires that his self-description be changed to "a stranger, [a] friendless, uneducated, penniless boy." Lincoln chose his words carefully and such emendations are unwarranted. Probably Lincoln meant precisely what he said: to residents of New Salem who saw him for the first time, he did indeed seem strange. He had already attained his full height of six feet and nearly four inches, which made him a head taller than almost anybody else in the New Salem community. Rail-thin, with elongated arms and huge feet, he flapped around like some enormous immature bird when he walked. His clothing added to the oddity of his appearance: a cheap chip hat, perched precariously on his mass of black hair that had the texture of a horse's tail; a flimsy jacket or coat, so short that it left his midriff unprotected; and jeans that lacked six or more inches of reaching his heavy work shoes. He was, one observer said, "as ruff a specimen of humanity as could be found."[24] New Salem had never seen his like before.

He arrived in New Salem by accident, and he knew nobody in the community. Working for Denton Offutt, he, John D. Johnston, and his cousin John Hanks, who lived off and on with the Lincolns, were guiding a flatboat loaded with barrels of wheat, corn, and bacon down the Sangamon River, and it became lodged on the milldam at New Salem. When the boat began taking on water, Lincoln worked frantically with the others to lighten the load in the stern. As the boat started to right itself, he went ashore, borrowed an auger, and bored a hole in the bow. After the water poured out of the hole, he plugged it. Then the whole boat was lifted and eased over the dam. Impressed by Lincoln's ingenuity, Offutt swore that, once the trip down the Mississippi was concluded, he would set up a store in New Salem, with Lincoln as its manager. In July, Lincoln returned, but Offutt had not yet come back, and there was no store.

In September, when Offutt did arrive with his stock of goods, Lincoln set to work as his clerk, assisted by William G. ("Slicky Bill") Greene. They both slept on a cot in the little store; it was so narrow, Greene remembered, that "when one turned over the other had to do likewise."[25] Henry McHenry later recorded that Lincoln made "a good, obliging clerk and an honest one: he increased Offut[t']s business much by his simplicity—open—Candid—obliging and honest."[26]

Soon Lincoln came to know all the hundred or so inhabitants of the village, and, because business at the store was seldom pressing, he joined in their amusements. He liked to run in foot races, and he promptly demonstrated that with his long legs, he could outjump any other man in the village. Offutt's store became the place where the men of the town met daily to exchange news and gossip and to regale each other with jokes and anecdotes. Lincoln seemed to have an inexhaustible supply of both, and men gathered around him when he began one of his tall tales, recounted with great gusto.

He found easy acceptance in this small, closely knit trading community, but initially it was not certain that he would be as well received by the farmers and laborers from the surrounding countryside, who came to New Salem to trade, have their corn ground at the grist mill, and have a few drinks at one of the "groceries" (as saloons were then called).

Wild and undisciplined, these young country men virtually terrorized the more sedate residents of New Salem. Worst of them all were the "Clary's Grove boys," who lived in a hamlet several miles southwest of New Salem. They were not innately vicious—that is, they did not rob, steal, or murder. If the spirit moved them, they would help an invalid or a widow when a pond needed to be dug or a ditch to be trenched. But they were, as James Short, one of the New Salem residents, called them, "roughs and bullies," who made it a practice to entice any stranger into a game of cards, when—fairly or unfairly—they would win all his money and often beat him up afterward.[27]

Indeed, fighting was a favorite pastime, as it was all along the frontier. Sometimes these brawls served simply as a vent for excess energy, like a gymnastic exercise; but frequently, they were dead serious and included choking, hair pulling, and eye gouging. Often there was little or no pretext to set off a fight, which could involve the whole gang. A fight became a kind of initiation rite for a newcomer, to establish his place in the pecking order.

Inevitably the Clary's Grove boys turned their attention to Offutt's new clerk. Offutt himself provoked them by boasting that Lincoln was not merely the smartest but the strongest man in the town. Caring nothing for Lincoln's mental accomplishments, the Clary's Grove boys vowed to test his ability to fight.

Jack Armstrong, their leader, challenged Lincoln. Stout and burly, Armstrong was a tricky veteran of scores of contests, and he was a formidable fighter. Lincoln demurred. He disliked the tactics of the Clary's Grove boys, who favored rough-and-ready wrestling, with no rules and no holds barred. "I never tussled and scuffled and will not," he said, "dont like this wooling and pulling." He enjoyed "scientific" wrestling, a style in which opponents, following agreed-on rules, begin by taking holds and attempting to throw each other. Urged on by Offutt and others who placed bets on the outcome, the two men agreed to wrestle, not to fight.[28]

The outcome of the contest became a matter of legend in New Salem. According to some accounts, Lincoln was victorious; according to others, Armstrong "legged" Lincoln—a tactic forbidden by wrestling rules—and illegally brought him down. Some remembered that Armstrong's followers, angered by the defeat of their champion, tried to gang up on Lincoln, who vowed that he would lick them all, but only by fighting them one at a time. Others recalled a controversy over whether Offutt lost his bet, since Armstrong did bring Lincoln down, though by an outlawed maneuver. Douglas Wilson's scrupulous account of this episode in *Honor's Voice* concludes that the evidence is so confused and contradictory that it will never be possible to determine precisely what happened.

But of the importance of the fight in shaping Lincoln's years in New Salem, there can be little doubt. With some exaggeration, John Todd Stuart, Lincoln's future law partner, said, *"This was the turning point in Lincoln's life."*[29] This test of Lincoln's strength and courage earned him the admiration of the Clary's Grove boys, and Jack Armstrong became, and remained, his lifelong follower.

V

Lincoln's place in the New Salem social hierarchy was ensured. Oddly enough, the rough country boys were not put off by his idiosyncratic refusal to smoke and drink or by his peculiar fondness for books and reading. Perhaps his deficiencies in these areas were made up for by his ability to spin yarns, often scabrous or scatological. More were doubtless impressed by his strength. He could hurl a maul or a cannon ball farther than any competitor. Rowan Herndon claimed Lincoln could lift a box of rocks weighing between 1,000 and 1,300 pounds.[30] According to one frequently reported anecdote, he squatted beside a barrel of whiskey, raised it by the chimes, and drank out of the bung hole.

The rough boys about town began to accept him not merely as an equal but in some sense as a leader who appealed to their better instincts For instance, he put a stop to Jack Armstrong's plan to cure one of the town's chronic drunkards by nailing him in a barrel and rolling it down the steep cliff into the Sangamon River. Another time, when the boys, well lubricated after an election celebration, bet a feeble-minded resident that he could not ride his pony through a bonfire they had built, Lincoln made them call the bet off and send the man home, slightly scorched but, in general, none the worse off.

The next year (1832), the young men of the New Salem area gave a clear demonstration of the place Lincoln held in their regard. That spring, the Sauk and Fox Indians violated the treaty they had signed with the U.S. government to remove across the Mississippi River and returned to Illinois to reclaim their tribal lands. Illinois Governor John Reynolds called out the militia to help the federal troops resist the invasion. Like other able-bodied white males, Lincoln was obliged to enlist, and he did so willingly because Offutt's store had, in Lincoln's words, "winked out" and he had no job. On April 21, he and the other recruits from the New Salem neighborhood were sworn into service, and, as was customary, they proceeded to elect their own officers. William Kirkpatrick, a wealthy sawmill owner, had announced his candidacy for captain and expected to be elected, but someone also nominated Lincoln. When the voting took place, each candidate stepped out in front on the village green, and his supporters fell in behind him. To Kirkpatrick's surprise, two-thirds of the recruits lined up behind Lincoln, and most of the others soon followed.

It was a success that delighted Lincoln, because he relished being esteemed by his peers. As Charles Strozier has said, it marked him as being first among equals, not just a friend of the soldiers but their leader. Years later, in 1859, after he had been elected four times to the state legislature and once to the U.S. House of Representatives and after he had twice been his party's candidate for the U.S. Senate, Lincoln said that his election as militia captain was "a success which gave me more pleasure than any I have had since."[31]

The story of Lincoln's brief service in the Black Hawk War—he served for one month as captain of his company, until it was disbanded, and then reenlisted for another few weeks as a private in another company—is not memorable, but what is significant is the high esteem, approaching veneration, in which his men held him. It was not due to any special military skill or knowledge. Lincoln knew nothing of military science. When he was drilling the company by making them march across a field, he discovered that they were about to run into a fence with a narrow gate. Unable to remember the proper command, he ordered the company to halt, disband for two minutes, and re-form on the other side of the fence. Nevertheless, the men continued to admire his physical strength and his skill as a wrestler. In a series of contests, he was never thrown, or "dusted," as the phrase went, and his men thought he could beat anyone. The supporters of Lorenzo Dow Thompson, of a St. Clair County regiment, also believed their champion was invincible. So a contest was arranged, and, as Lincoln remembered many years later, "the whole army was out to see it." To the surprise of Lincoln's backers, many of whom had bet on the outcome of the contest, Thompson threw him not once but twice. When some protested that Thompson's holds were illegal, Lincoln silenced them and told them that his opponent had played fair. "Why," he said later, "that man could throw a grizzly bear."[32]

Rather against their will, Lincoln's men were also impressed by his moral as well as his physical courage. When an old Indian, bearing a certificate of good conduct from American authorities, stumbled into their camp, some of the Illinois volunteers wanted to kill him, saying that he was a spy. Lincoln stepped between his men and the shivering Indian and said that anyone who wanted to hurt the visitor would have to lick him first. Grumbling, the men let the Indian slip away.

Nonetheless, Lincoln remained very popular among the men in his company, who were considered "the hardest set of men" in the army.[33] They knew, as Rowan Herndon observed, that "he Could out jump the Best of them he Could out Box the Best of them he Could Beat all of them on anecdote." "Lincoln was their idol," another soldier recalled, "and there was not a Man but what was obedi[e]nt to every word he spoke and would fight [to] his death for Lincoln."[34] In their recollections of this period in Lincoln's life, the theme is unvaried. "Lincoln was a man I always loved," observed John M. Rutledge. "I was with him in the Black Hawk war he was my Captain a better man I think never lived on the earth."[35] According to one soldier, he "was idolized by his men and generally by all the Regiment... to which he belonged."[36] "All the men in the Company—as well as the Regiment to which he and they belonged loved him well," claimed another, "almost worshipped him."[37]

Long after the Black Hawk War, the loyalty of these men to Lincoln remained unshaken. Although most of them were Democrats and he was a Whig, they regularly supported him for public office. When he traveled Sangamon County campaigning for the state legislature, some of them accompanied him, at times lending muscular as well as moral support when audiences were unruly. But it is notable that even after Lincoln's death, when the temptation to claim closeness to the martyred President was almost irresistible, very few of these men claimed that Lincoln was their friend, and none professed any degree of intimacy with him.

VI

In his description of his arrival in New Salem, Lincoln also referred to himself as a boy. He was, in fact, twenty-two years old, an age when most young men had settled on a career and a good many were married and had begun families.[38] But Lincoln gave a first impression of coltish youthfulness. "Uncle" Johnny Potter was working on a high rail fence when he first saw Lincoln, who asked whether he could have something to eat. Mrs. Potter gave him boiled eggs for breakfast. When he was finished, Lincoln came out and "straddled over that five-rail fence as if it wasn't in the way at all." Out in the road, he turned back and said, "There's only one egg left; I believe I'd better make a clean thing of it." He straddled the fence again, got the egg, and "went off—laughing like a boy, shuffling the hot egg from one hand to the other and then peeling and eating it."[39] Lincoln evidently thought of himself as still immature, with all the exciting possibilities and all the dangers of manhood still ahead of him.

Later, when he was only in his forties, he would be called "Old Abe," but during his New Salem years, people thought of him as a boy. His appearance of immaturity—his susceptibility to the wild moods of a belated adolescence, his inability to deal with practical matters like buying clothes and doing his laundry, his willingness to drift from one occupation to another, whether it was storekeeper, riverboat man, soldier, postmaster, or surveyor—brought out the maternal instincts of New Salem matrons, and he looked to them as mother substitutes.

Shy with young women, he found it easy to talk with them, because most were older than he and, being married, could not be considered objects of sexual interest. Mentor Graham's daughter recalled that he frequently asked her mother "for advice on different questions—such as Love—prudence of movements etc—girls—etc etc."[40]

After the great wrestling match, Hannah Armstrong, Jack Armstrong's wife, took a strong interest in Lincoln, who became a frequent visitor. "Abe would Come out to our house," she remembered, "drink milk and mush—Corn bre[a]d—butter." He would bring her children candy and rock the cradle of her baby while she laundered his clothes. To keep briars from ruining his trousers, she "foxed" them with two buckskins-that is, she sewed the skins on the front of the garments, to keep them from being shredded.[41] Their friendship was so close that her roughneck husband kept up a running joke that Lincoln was the father of her youngest son. It was a story, one contemporary remembered, that "plagued Lincoln terribly."[42]

Elizabeth Abell, the wife of Dr. Bennett Abell, was another New Salem matron who found this disheveled and disorganized young man immensely appealing. Mrs. Abell, whom William Butler described as "a cultivated woman—very superior to the common run of women" on the frontier,[43] also did Lincoln's laundry and "foxed" another pair of his pants. She thought him "the best natured man I ever got acquainted with" and described him as "sensitive"—but also as "backward."[44]

Those were not traits that especially endeared him to the young women in the New Salem community, and, indeed, he showed very little interest in them. Even in Indiana, he had the reputation of not liking girls much because they were "too frivalous."[45] In New Salem, according to James Short, "he didn't go to see the girls much. He didn't appear bashful, but it seemed as if he cared but little for them." Once when a Virginia family with "Three stilish Daughters" stayed at the Rutledge tavern, where Lincoln was also boarding, he absented himself from the table for two or three weeks, doubtless embarrassed by his homely appearance and perhaps by his deficient table manners.[46]

But there are two apparent exceptions to Lincoln's failure to find friends among the young women of New Salem. According to William H. Herndon, his law partner, Lincoln fell deeply in love with Ann Rutledge, daughter of one of the founders of New Salem. Though she was promised to another man, she reciprocated his affection and—as the story—goes they arrived at some kind of understanding, if not an actual engagement. Then, in the terrible summer of 1835, Ann died, and Lincoln was devastated.

It is hard to know what to make of this story, which was first hinted at in an 1862 article in the *Menard Axis*, an obscure, anti-Lincoln newspaper, but was not widely known until Herndon began interviewing New Salem old-timers after Lincoln's death. Herndon's extravagant rhetoric, including assertions that Lincoln was so distraught after Ann Rutledge's death that "his mind wandered from its throne" and that he never loved another woman, including his wife of twenty-three years, made some historians skeptical, yet others strongly supported Herndon's story. It was not until 1945, after Herndon's papers had been opened to the public, that the great Lincoln scholar, J. G. Randall, was able to make a close analysis of the evidence. His brilliant appendix to his *Lincoln the President*, called "Sifting the Ann Rutledge Evidence," concluded that Herndon's story was largely myth. Unsupported by credible evidence, it did "not belong in a recital of those Lincoln episodes which one presents as unquestioned reality."[47] As Professor Randall's research assistant, I fully endorsed that view in my first book, *Lincoln's Herndon*, and tried to explain why Herndon promulgated this myth.

In recent years, there has been a tendency to reverse this judgment against Herndon's story, and John Y. Simon and Douglas L. Wilson have published well-reasoned studies that argue for the essential credibility of the Ann Rutledge story (minus Herndon's speculations about Lincoln's mental instability and his alleged lack of affection for his wife) Their close reading of Herndon's numerous interviews relating to Ann Rutledge persuaded me that Professor Randall's analysis had perhaps been too rigorous in demanding firsthand testimony of two independent witnesses.

Using that criterion, a historian would have to discard almost everything reported about Lincoln's first thirty-one years. Consequently in my *Lincoln* (1995), I gave a mild endorsement to the basic Ann Rutledge story (without accepting Herndon's rhetorical embellishments).

In the years since, I have reconsidered my position. This rethinking was not, for the most part, the result of the discovery of new evidence. Both Professor Randall and his critics used the same documents—mostly interviews that Herndon conducted. But the 1998 publication of *Herndon's Informants*, ably edited and exhaustively annotated by Douglas L. Wilson and Rodney O. Davis, has made it possible more easily and systematically to examine all the testimony that Herndon collected on this subject. Looked at anew, it is impressive for its contradictions. Members of the Rutledge family were certain that there had been a firm engagement between Lincoln and their sister; Mrs. Abell, who may have been Lincoln's closest confidant in New Salem, professed to know nothing about a love affair, though she testified to Lincoln's genuine grief at Ann's death.

With one exception, all this confusing and contradictory evidence that Herndon collected was secondhand, recollected months and even years after Lincoln's assassination and, of course, thirty or more years after Ann Rutledge's death. No letter from Ann Rutledge is known to exist, and her name is never mentioned in the thousands of pages of Lincoln's published correspondence. Only Isaac Cogdal, a Menard County farmer and stonemason, claimed to have spoken personally with Lincoln about his alleged love affair. In an interview Herndon recorded in 1865 or 1866, Cogdal said he visited Lincoln in his office during the months after he was elected President in 1860, and the two friends began reminiscing about "old times and old acquaintances" in New Salem. Presently Cogdal felt emboldened to ask: "Abe is it true that you fell in love with and courted Ann Rutledge?" "It is true," replied Lincoln, "true indeed I did. I have loved the name of Rutledge to this day.... I loved the woman dearly and sacredly: she was a handsome girl—would have made a good loving wife...I did honestly-and truly love the girl and think often—often of her now."[48]

This statement has remained a linchpin in accounts endorsing the Ann Rutledge story, even though Professor Randall cautioned that it had "unLincolnian quality."[49] Recently it has come under more sustained attack from C. A. Tripp, who questions the timing and the accuracy of Cogdal's reported interview with Lincoln. In a careful computer-aided analysis of all of Lincoln's known writings and sayings, Dr. Tripp shows that Lincoln never used several key words Cogdal attributed to him, or adopted the pattern of phrasing Cogdal reported, and concludes that Cogdal's "entire testimony reeks of fraud."[50]

The whole subject is—as Lincoln said in a very different context—so "environed with difficulties"[51] that it is hard to reach a reasoned judgment. My present negative opinion rests in part on a reexamination of Herndon's evidence and of Dr. Tripp's analysis, but in larger part, it derives from the context of what we know about Lincoln's friends and associates. At no other point in Lincoln's early life did he express his deep affection—much less his love—for any woman. He was not prepared for intimacy.

Doubts about his romance with Ann Rutledge are reinforced by examination of the one other instance in which he was interested enough in a woman to propose marriage. Several New Salem matrons, concerned about his lonely and forlorn condition, vainly attempted to match him with a Miss Short and a Miss Berry, but Mrs. Abell was more successful in promoting his interest in her sister, Mary Owens. Handsome and well educated, this daughter of a wealthy Kentucky family made a great impression when she visited her sister in 1833 or 1834, and Lincoln is supposed to have told Mrs. Abell that "if ever that girl comes back to New Salem I am going to marry her." When she did return, a half-hearted courtship began, only to end in farce. Granting Lincoln's "goodness of heart," Mary Owens found him "deficient in those little links which make up the chain of woman's happiness." He found her greatly changed since her earlier visit and complained of her age, "her want of teeth, weatherbeaten appearance in general." To the relief of both parties, their romance—if it could be called that—ended, and Lincoln concluded "never again to think of marrying; and for this reason; I can never be satisfied with any one who would be blockhead enough to have me."[52]

It is clear that in his New Salem days Lincoln's attachments were to older, married, and hence unavailable, women. He needed a mother more than he needed a wife.

VII

Like older women, older men—or at least those who were more settled in occupation and family, more established in their businesses—also often volunteered to help this lonely; friendless young man. Denton Offutt became his first patron in Illinois. Though Offutt was, as one New Salem resident said, "a wild—rec[k]less careless man,—a kind of wandering horse tamer," he was perceptive enough to see great possibilities in Lincoln and put him, without any experience at all, in charge of his general store and then of his grist mill "By God," he predicted, "Lincoln will yet be President of these U.S."[53] Other men also trusted him. When Lincoln returned from the Black Hawk War without a job, Rowan Herndon sold him half-ownership of his general store, with no cash payment. "I believed he was thoroughly honest," Rowan Herndon explained, "and...I accepted his note in payment of the whole. He had no money, but I would have advanced him still more had he asked for it."[54]

When the store, which Lincoln owned jointly with William Berry, failed and he was left without a job, friends again intervened to help him. One secured for Lincoln the appointment as postmaster of New Salem, and another persuaded John Calhoun, the chief surveyor for northern Sangamon County, to name Lincoln his deputy, even though he knew nothing of surveying. While learning his new trade, Lincoln was invited to live for six months with Mentor Graham, the local schoolmaster.[55]

Successful in his new occupations, Lincoln again ran into trouble when his notes—mostly incurred through the purchase of the store and the contents of an adjacent one that the Clary's Grove boys drove out of business—fell due. His financial distress was the greater because Berry, his partner, had died, and he felt obligated to pay all the indebtedness of their firm. In the judgment against him, the court ordered the sale of all his assets, including his horse and his surveying compass, flagstaff, chain, and other surveying equipment, without which he could not make a living. Quietly, James Short, a New Salem neighbor, bought them up and returned them to Lincoln.

Not all the help Lincoln was offered was material or financial. In addition to giving him room and board, Mentor Graham shared with him his meager knowledge of arithmetic and geometry, which he needed to become a surveyor. Jack Kelso, a man of some education, with whom Lincoln boarded for a time, stimulated him to read Shakespeare and Burns. It seemed to one New Salem resident that they were "always together-always talking and arguing."[56] Kelso was less successful in interesting Lincoln in fishing, his other passion, but the two men would often sit for hours on the bank of the Sangamon River and "quote Shakespear."

Bowling Green, the local justice of the peace, was also fond of Lincoln, who boarded with him too for a time. Always interested in legal proceedings and thinking of the law as a possible profession, Lincoln faithfully attended the hearings at Green's court. Looking for amusement, the corpulent Green delighted in Lincoln's sense of humor and in some cases allowed him to make comments, which, as one resident recalled, produced "a spasmotic [sic] shaking of the fat sides of the old law functionary."[57] He came soon to recognize the young man's shrewd intelligence and clear, logical mind. "There Was good Material in Abe," he told friends, "and he only Wanted Education."[58] Abner Y. Ellis, who knew Lincoln well, reported that Bowling Green was "his allmost second Farther [sic]," and recalled that Lincoln "Used to say that he owed more to Mr. Green for his advancement than any other Man."[59]

Even more important was the interest that John Todd Stuart took in the young man. The two served in the Black Hawk War, and after the expiration of their one month of obligatory service, both reenlisted as privates. Stuart, a college-educated Virginian, already established as a lawyer in Springfield, saw great promise in this young frontiersman who was so fond of books and reading. Learning that Lincoln had considered studying law but was discouraged because he lacked formal education, Stuart urged him on and offered to lend him books from his own law library. He also promoted Lincoln's political career. As a staunch Whig, he recognized that his party had a very poor chance in strongly Democratic Menard County unless the Whigs ran someone like Lincoln, who had no telltale political record, though he strongly favored Whiggish policies like governmental support for internal improvements and-even more important-had a loyal personal following. Though Lincoln was defeated in his first race for the state legislature in 1832, he was victorious in the 1834 election, when, with Stuart's consent, he maneuvered to secure votes of both Whigs and Democrats.

Once elected, Lincoln realized that he had to pay some of his debts and buy clothes appropriate for a legislator. He approached Coleman Smoot, a well-to-do farmer and stock raiser of the Indian Creek neighborhood, saying, "You must loan me money to buy Suitable Clothing for I want to make a decent appearance in the Legislature."[60] Unhesitatingly, Smoot loaned him two hundred dollars, quite a large sum at that time, being more than half a month's salary of the governor of the state. He asked for no security, because he knew that Lincoln had nothing of value to secure the loan.

VIII

By the time Lincoln left New Salem for Springfield, he had literally hundreds of supporters and admirers who thought of him as their friend. Over and over again, in their letters and in their later recollections, they expressed their admiration and affection for Lincoln. "His friendship," wrote William Engle, "was undying, it was eternal . . .; it was truly friendship in marble and marble in Clay."[61] "I was Lincolns frend," wrote Henry Clark; "he was my frind."[62] "Lincoln was a man I always loved," echoed John M. Rutledge.[63]

Certainly many from Lincoln's Indiana and New Salem years regarded him as their close friend, but it is less clear how attached he felt toward them. In a number of cases in his later life, mostly when he was making recommendations for appointments, he spoke of a correspondent as "my intimate and personal friend." But there is only one such reference to any of his New Salem acquaintances: he said the son of Dr. Bennett Abell and Elizabeth Abell was "the child of very intimate friends of mine."[64]

By temperament and early training Lincoln grew up as a man of great reserve, unable to reach out in the broad, good fellowship that so many politicians cultivate as they strive to be everyone's closest friend. In his early life, he had never had anyone in whom he could confide, and that was not a barrier he could break down as an adult. Herndon, who worked daily in the same law office with Lincoln for sixteen years, concluded, "He was the most reticent and mostly secretive man that ever existed: he never opened his whole soul to any man: he never touched the history or quality of his own nature in the presence of his friends."[65]

Indeed, Lincoln was so self-contained that he rarely seemed to reciprocate the affection of those who admired and assisted him. Some thought him incapable of friendship. "L[incoln] did forget his friends," John Todd Stuart told Herndon. "There was no part of his nature which drew him to acts of gratitude to his friends."[66] Others tried to explain his lack of strong personal attachments. "He was the warm friend of few men," concluded Illinois Governor Richard Oglesby, "but he was the true friend of Mankind."[67] "He was by some considered cold hearted or at least indifferent towards his friends," agreed Joseph Gillespie, long a political associate. "This was the result of his extreme fairness. He would rather disoblige a friend than do an act of injustice to a political opponent."[68] Leonard Swett, who did much to promote Lincoln's nomination for President in 1860, agreed that "beneath a smooth surface of candor and an apparent declaration of all his thoughts and feelings," Lincoln was a very private man, without intimate friendships: "He handled and moved man remotely as we do pieces upon a chessboard."[69]

NOTES

1. All studies of Lincoln's early life rely heavily on the interviews and letters that his law partner, William H. Herndon, collected shortly after his assassination. These documents are in the Herndon-Weik Collection at the Library of Congress. Fortunately for scholars, Douglas L. Wilson and Rodney O. Davis have published an authoritative, carefully annotated edition of these writings in their invaluable *Herndon's Informants: Letters, Interviews, and Statements about Abraham Lincoln* (Urbana: University of Illinois Press, 1998).
2. *Herndon's Informants*, p. 126.
3. Louis A. Warren, *Lincoln's Parentage & Childhood* (New York: Century Co., 1926), pp. 145–46.
4. *Herndon's Informants*, p. 235; Ida M. Tarbell, *The Early Life of Abraham Lincoln* (New York: S. S. McClure, 1896), p. 44.
5. *Herndon's Informants*, p. 241.
6. Ibid., pp. 103–104.
7. Roy P. Basler and others, eds., *The Collected Works of Abraham Lincoln* (New Brunswick, N.J.: Rutgers University Press, 1953–55), 1:386 (hereinafter cited as CW).
8. Ibid., 4:62.
9. Ibid., 1:379.
10. Ibid., 6:16–17.

11. David Herbert Donald, *Lincoln* (New York: Simon & Schuster, 1995), p. 26.
12. Surprisingly Kenneth J. Winkle, in *The Young Eagle: The Rise of Abraham Lincoln* (Dallas: Taylor Trade Publishing, 2001), pp. 14–15, argues that "Lincoln's experience with parental loss appears thoroughly unremarkable."
13. John Bowlby, *Attachment and Loss*, Vol. 3; *Loss: Sadness and Depression* (New York: Basic Books, 1980), p. 320.
14. *Herndon's Informants*, p. 37.
15. Ibid., p. 134.
16. Ibid., p. 176.
17. Louis A. Warren, *Lincoln's Youth: Indiana Years, Seven to Twenty-one, 1816–1830* (New York: Appleton-Century Crofts, 1959), p. 98.
18. CW, 4:62. As I have shown in "Education Defective: Lincoln's Preparation for Greatness" (*Lincoln Reconsidered* [New York: Vintage Books, 2001], pp. 63–74), Lincoln exaggerated the deficiencies in his education.
19. *Herndon's Informants*, p. 124.
20. Ibid., p. 131.
21. This discussion relies heavily on the work of Harry Stack Sullivan, *The Interpersonal Theory of Psychiatry* (New York: Norton, 1953), especially chap. 16. For a concise explanation of Sullivan's theories, together with empirical data supporting them, see James Youniss, *Parents and Peers in Social Development* (Chicago: University of Chicago Press, 1980). See also Robert L. Selman and Lynn Hickey Schultz, *Making a Friend in Youth* (New York: Aldine de Gruyter, 1990). I have also been influenced by the writings of Erik H. Erikson, especially his discussion of Gandhi and his "evil friend," Sheik Mehtab, one of "his counterplayers to whom he gave more of himself than he could afford and from whom he wanted he knew not what." From his intimate but troubled relationship with this unsuitable young man of a different religion and a vastly different background Gandhi developed his classic definition of true friendship as "an identity of souls rarely to be found in the world. Only between like natures can friendship be altogether worthy and enduring." Erikson, *Gandhi's Truth: On the Origins of Militant Nonviolence* (New York: Norton, 1969), pp. 133–40.
22. Catherine L. Bagwell, Andrew F. Newcomb, and William M. Bukowski, "Preadolescent Friendship and Peer Rejection as Predictors of Adult Adjustment," *Child Development* (Chicago: University of Chicago Press, 1930-date) 69 (February 1998): 150–51.
23. CW, 1:320.
24. Douglas L. Wilson, *Honor's Voice: The Transformation of Abraham Lincoln* (New York: Knopf, 1998), p. 53.
25. *Herndon's Informants*, pp. 17–18.
26. Ibid., p. 14.
27. Ibid., p. 73.
28. In *Honor's Voice*, chap. 1, Douglas L. Wilson offers a fascinating account of fighting and wrestling on the frontier.
29. Ibid., p. 20.
30. *Herndon's Informants*, p. 7.
31. CW, 3:512.
32. Wilson, *Honor's Voice*, p. 30.
33. *Herndon's Informants*, p. 353.
34. Ibid.
35. Ibid., p. 394.
36. Ibid., p. 18.
37. Ibid., p. 15.
38. But it was not unusual for a young man in his twenties, unmarried and without steady employment, to be thought of as a "boy." "Up to 1840, men in Springfield married at age twenty-seven, on average." Winkle, *The Young Eagle*, p. 62. The average age in the rural districts was probably lower.

39. Walter B. Stevens, *A Reporter's Lincoln*, ed. Michael Burlingame (Lincoln: University of Nebraska Press, 1998), pp. 5–6.
40. Wilson, *Honor's Voice*, p. 110.
41. *Herndon's Informants*, p. 525.
42. Wilson, *Honor's Voice*, p. Ill.
43. *Herndon's Informants*, p. 738.
44. Wilson, *Honor's Voice*, p. 112.
45. Ibid., p. 109.
46. Ibid., p. 110.
47. G. Randall, *Lincoln the President: Springfield to Gettysburg* (New York: Dodd, Mead, 1945), 2:341.
48. *Herndon's Informants*, p. 440.
49. Randall, *Lincoln the President*, 2:334.
50. C. A. Tripp, "The Strange Case of Isaac Cogdal," *Journal of the Abraham Lincoln Association* 23 (Winter 2002): 69–77.
51. CW, 5:438.
52. Ibid., 1:118–19.
53. *Herndon's Informants*, p. 18.
54. William H. Herndon and Jesse W. Weik, *Herndon's Life of Lincoln*, ed. Paul M. Angle (Cleveland: The World Publishing Company, 1930), pp. 88–89. [Hereinafter cited as Herndon's *Lincoln*.]
55. *Herndon's Informants*, p. 10.
56. Ibid., p. 528.
57. Donald, *Lincoln*, p. 41.
58. *Herndon's Informants*, p. 173.
59. Ibid., p. 501.
60. Ibid., p. 254.
61. Ibid., p. 32.
62. Ibid., p. 528.
63. Ibid., p. 394.
64. CW, 4:310.
65. Herndon, "Ann Rutledge & Lincoln," unpublished monograph, c. 1887, Herndon-Weik Collection.
66. *Herndon's Informants*, p. 63.
67. Ibid., p. 153.
68. Ibid., p. 507.
69. Ibid., p. 168.

5

MARY AND ABRAHAM: A MARRIAGE

Jean H. Baker

[handwritten annotations: binding? restricting? ✓ The death of you? Generally negative message on ✓ marrying women]

"Marriage is a noose." "When a man takes a wife, he ceases to dread hell." "Marry in haste and repent in leisure." "A woman is necessarily an evil, and he that gets the most tolerable one is lucky"—and so on. There is an edgy, bridegroom-beware quality to the old proverbs that make marriage into a joking matter, with the joke on women. Today, yesterday's derisive sayings may seem as far removed from contemporary reality as some of the herbal remedies of an earlier age. But unlike calomel and the wild datura vine, these reproachful wisdoms from the past still carry authority and reflect our uncertain attitudes about the matrimonial state. We remember them because marriage is a universal, habitual human behavior—the ultimate in institutional survivals, however modified. We also remember them because marriage is so little studied, and this vacuum of historical information returns us to the folklore of the past.

Consequently, evaluations of the Lincoln marriage are largely subjective. Lacking context and for that reason varying tremendously, they float outside of historical analysis and remove a typical middle-class marriage from its moorings. Writes David Donald in the most authoritative biography ever written about Lincoln, "For all their quarrels, [the Lincolns] were devoted to each other. In the long years of their marriage Abraham Lincoln was never suspected of being unfaithful to his wife. She, in turn, was immensely proud of him and was his most loyal supporter and admirer."[1]

But listen to what Michael Burlingame has written in *The Inner World of Abraham Lincoln* in a 58-page assessment of the Lincoln marriage, 56 pages of which are a condemnation of Mary Lincoln: "In 1864 [the President] pardoned a soldier who had deserted to go home and marry his sweetheart, [saying] 'I want to punish that young man...probably in less than year he will wish I had withheld that pardon.'" According to Burlingame, who argues that Lincoln regretted his marriage as much as he expected the young soldier to rue his, the Lincolns' marriage was a "fountain of misery."[2] Burlingame is certain that Mary Lincoln is responsible for this fountain of misery, without any acknowledgment that proverbs, peers, and popular culture had taught Lincoln to joke about marriage, although never his own.

Mostly the depictions of the Lincoln marriage as a disaster focus on Mary Todd Lincoln's failings. Of course, it has always been women who are held responsible for the quality of a marriage, for many reasons not the least of which is that men write history and have especially controlled the Lincoln story. After her husband was assassinated, Mary Lincoln told the biographer Josiah Holland that during their courtship she had "trespassed" on her husband's "tenderness of character."[3] Such a sense of guilt is hardly an unusual feeling for any recent widow or widower to acknowledge. But listen to how Douglas Wilson interprets the commonplace reaction of a widow. He writes: "Had she been a man, [Lincoln] would have known how to respond [to this trespass on his tenderness]: he could have ridiculed her in public, planted a malicious piece about her in the newspaper, or knocked her and left her a-kicking."[4] (These are things that, on at least one occasion, Lincoln did to various adversaries.) Certainly the pinnacle of this judgmental style of interpretation by opposing quotations emerges in the title of Michael Burlingame's short book— *Honest Abe, Dishonest Mary.*

My response is that we have too many historians deciding that they don't like Mary Lincoln and with extraordinary vehemence extrapolating their personal judgments onto the marriage. Douglas Wilson and Michael Burlingame don't like Mary Lincoln; that does not mean that Abraham Lincoln did not, nor, more relevantly, does it mean that the compact that Mary Todd and Abraham Lincoln fashioned in the nearly 23 years of their marriage was not a satisfying one from which both partners gained emotional support, physical satisfaction, and intellectual intimacy.

To be sure, an unsuccessful Lincoln marriage is historically serviceable. For the president's daily association with a woman he supposedly loathed makes him ever more the martyr of American mythology. The president who dealt so generously with the afflicted in public affairs learned, in this understanding, to do so through his private life with a shrew: "Lincoln daily practiced tolerance of a cantankerous female who was neither his first nor his greatest love."[5] And those who assess the Lincoln marriage as unhappy have provided their hero with some alternatives.

First there is Ann Rutledge, a woman who is often portrayed as Lincoln's first and *only* love. I must protest. Granted that Lincoln may have loved Ann Rutledge and may even have been engaged to her (she apparently was less loyal and was betrothed in her brief life of 22 years to two other men before becoming engaged to Lincoln), still Ann Rutledge died in 1835.[6] Lincoln married seven years later. According to the most rabid enthusiasts of the Ann Rutledge legend, Lincoln adored her throughout his life. Perhaps the reason has something to do with the hauntingly beautiful poem by Edgar Lee Masters from his *Spoon River Anthology* that expresses the romantic longing of men caught in the reality of humdrum relationships with wives transformed in their imaginations, according to one proverb, "from good girls to bad wives": "I am Ann Rutledge who sleeps beneath these weeds/Beloved in life of Abraham Lincoln/Wedded to him not through union/but through separation."

But poetry is not historical evidence, and we do not have any creditable evidence of this enduring love from its principal, save an offhand comment in 1860 that he thought of her often. Hearsay evidence is not admissible, at least in most courts, and Lincoln's is no comment of an enduring passion. Instead it is more the testimony of his lifelong obsession with death. Now mine is not the evidence of scholars, but a half-century later I remember my first love with nostalgic affection. He happened to have been killed in an automobile accident while I was in college. Still I find it absurd for me and for anyone to hold that he was an only love and that I never got over him, even though I still think of him. There are, to paraphrase F. Scott Fitzgerald, second acts in American love lives.

Recently a new contender for Lincoln's affection has emerged in Douglas Wilson's *Honor's Voice: The Transformation of Abraham Lincoln*. Her name is Mathilda Edwards, and she was 17 years old and living at Elizabeth and Ninian Edwards's home when she supposedly became Lincoln's great love just before he, age 33, married Mary Todd. To establish this point, both Burlingame and Wilson make much of two sources from the Herndon collection. Lincoln's friends James Matheny and Joshua Speed, the latter said to be himself in love with Mathilda Edwards, reported that Lincoln fell in love with Miss Edwards.

But there is conflicting evidence that they do not consider. Elizabeth Edwards, who lived in this Springfield household on Second Street, twice told Herndon that there was nothing to the relationship between Mathilda and Abraham Lincoln. Interviewed in 1865 and again in 1887, Elizabeth Edwards, who is the most credible witness on the matter, denied that

Lincoln loved Mathilda. Quoting from an interview with Elizabeth Edwards, "I asked Miss Edwards...if Mr. Lincoln ever mentioned the subject of love to her. Miss Edwards said O my word, he never mentioned such a subject to me. He never even stooped to pay me a compliment." And then Elizabeth goes on to say, "Mr. Lincoln loved Mary." Asked again in 1887, Elizabeth Edwards reiterated, "It is said that Miss Edwards had something to do in breaking Mary's engagement with Lincoln—it is not true. Miss Edwards told me that Lincoln never condescended to pay her even a poor compliment: it was the flirtation with Douglas that did the business."[7]

What the promotion of other women to Lincoln's true loves accomplishes is to undermine Mary Lincoln and to place an anecdotal vise on the Lincoln marriage, which makes Lincoln's wife into someone he did not want to marry and who, in retaliation, made his life, according to William Herndon, into a hell. Remember neither Abraham nor Mary ever left even a shred of documentary evidence that either of them loved anyone else. In fact, after Lincoln's assassination, Mary Lincoln wrote a friend that Lincoln had always assured her that she was his *only* love.[8]

Conveniently for the anyone-but-Mary school, there is another teenager waiting in the wings who may represent the millennium's candidate for Lincoln's true love. Sarah Rickard was the sister-in-law of Lincoln's friend William Butler. After the president's death, Rickard reported to Herndon that Lincoln had proposed marriage to her, and she had refused him because he seemed almost like an older brother.[9] In any case, with the addition of Sarah to his list of girlfriends, Lincoln, a man universally viewed as uncomfortable with women, is transformed into a veritable Don Juan.

The reason for this controversy over the Lincoln marriage is our flawed understanding of the history of that institution. While we easily locate Lincoln the Republican partisan and officeholder within his political times, we do not put his marriage within the context of nineteenth-century courtship and marriage. There is an additional reason. Given the culture of their time, the Lincolns did not leave much documentary evidence about their relationship, and this silence, especially since many of their letters to each other burned in a fire, has encouraged an ensuing battle of quotations from outsiders over the state of their marriage. Unlike today, when young adults feel comfortable asking the president of the United States about his underwear, most middle-class Americans 150 years ago were reticent about their relationships with spouses. They closed their bedroom doors to the prying eyes of outsiders. Besides being off-limits, marriage is not a topic that most historians are interested in, especially those who write about Lincoln. Instead it is consigned to the woman's world.

In recent years, sociologists and historians have begun to study marriage as a legal arrangement, a social custom, a gender practice, and a sexual statement that changes over time. Critical in this regard for the Lincolns was the fact that the patriarchal marriage of the eighteenth century that placed men as the rulers of the household was giving way in mid-nineteenth century America to a more companionate ideal in which wives and husbands sought mutual love and affection as individuals creating a satisfying partnership. Some, though not all, Americans of this period held a romantic vision of marriage as the joining together of individuals with unique personalities who adored each other because that newfound entity of the nineteenth century—their essential self—had discovered a complementary soul.[10] In what follows I would like to place the Lincoln marriage in the context of the scholarship that we have on courtship, wedding, marriage, and parenting, using mostly the words and behaviors of the marriage's two principals and avoiding the memories of their contemporaries. Perhaps that way we can end the divergence of opinion—"the battle of the quotations"—that has led historians to create a contentious subfield of Lincoln studies.

COURTSHIP: "A MAN CHASES A WOMAN UNTIL SHE CATCHES HIM"

For most young women in midcentury America, the period of courting was a time of gaiety and fun. During this time females exerted an authority they lost when they married and by common law became one with their husbands—and he legally the one. Certainly this was the case with the Kentucky belle Mary Todd who, as her brother-in-law Ninian Edwards said, "could make a bishop forget his prayers."[11] She was having a good time at the parties in Springfield, Illinois, after she settled in her sister Elizabeth's home in the late 1830s.

By this time, the earlier considerations of cows and land and marriages controlled by parents had given way to considerable power exerted by young women themselves over whom they would marry. Marriage was no longer a property arrangement, nor an agreement between families. By way of comparison, in the 1730s Benjamin Franklin sought a dowry from a possible bride in order to pay for his printing press, and when the mother of his intended refused, he promptly ended the courtship.[12] But in the new republic of the United States, arranged marriages disappeared.

Indeed, European travelers pointed to the freedom of mate choice as one of the signal differences between Europe and the United States. But within an institution in which men enhanced their standing and satisfied their wants, American wives often lost their ambitions. Alexis

[handwritten margin note: Now, marriages are based on what the girl wants, not the parents]

de Tocqueville, the perceptive French observer of the United States, noticed as much in *Democracy in America:* "In America a woman loses her independence forever in the bonds of matrimony...a wife submits to stricter obligations...her husband's home is almost a cloister."[13] Mary Lincoln had observed as much about an institution she once called "the crime of matrimony." "Why is it," wrote Mary Todd to one of her friends, "that married folks always become so serious?"[14]

Even if they could choose their mate without parental interference, still young middle-class women had to marry because they were denied any respectable means of earning a living save as teachers and governesses, at the same time that any means of self-protection within marriage was denied them. But their courting power was solely that of a veto. As one young American woman Eliza Southgate noted, "We have the liberty of refusing those we don't like, but not of selecting those we do."[15] Mary Todd had done to that several suitors. Once married, women were without rights as citizens; but in a catch-22, if they stayed single, they were ridiculed as spinsters. Thus for young American women, marriage was a necessity; it was the way they earned their living. But they surely had reasons to hesitate.

In an era when divorce was not a recognized statutory procedure and required in most instances special legislative action or a petition to a special court, marriage to a bad husband—to an alcoholic (and this was a period of the highest per capita alcohol consumption in our history) or to a wife-beater was a life-threatening mistake. The annals of nineteenth-century misery were full of women who fled their husbands to avoid abuse and were ordered home by the courts.

Meanwhile, men had reasons to hesitate before marrying, for as breadwinners they were responsible for providing for their wives and children. For a man like the upwardly mobile and very conscientious Abraham Lincoln, such circumstances gave cause for concern. As Abraham Lincoln wrote in 1837, "Whatever woman may cast her lot with mine, should any ever do so, it is my intention to do all in my power to make her happy and contented."[16] And that required a sufficient income to establish a household with a young woman who was accustomed to a standard of living far above that of Lincoln's childhood. "Men," writes a student of courtship, "hesitated to commit themselves to marry—until they felt emotionally ready and could be sure of acquiring the necessary financial resources. Emotional preparedness for marriage was simply defined: If a young man fell in love with a woman, he wanted—some day—to marry her."[17]

And as every study of marriage in the nineteenth century makes clear, many engagements were disrupted as the principals stepped back from their courtship to contemplate the permanency of their future condition. As we know, this was the case with Mary Todd and Abraham Lincoln.

Sometime in 1840 they had reached an agreement that they might marry; and then, on what Lincoln called "the Fatal First" of January 1841, they broke off their engagement. A year and a half later they were courting again; and as all the world knows, they married in November of 1842.

Many historians have taken the disruption of their courtship as a sign that Lincoln did not love Mary Todd, and they assume without any preponderance of evidence that he was the one who ended their engagement. Then, according to this interpretation, he renewed his troth because he valued honor over breaking his word or because he worried, having been attached for debt in New Salem, that he might be charged with breach of promise. I find these explanations implausible. Isn't it more dishonorable, especially in an age when true love is becoming the conventional practice, to marry a woman you don't love? And as for a breach of promise suit, this judicial procedure was infrequently used in the 1840s when a new tradition of courtship based on mutual love had replaced a previous generation's interest in property arrangements. In a resounding statement of her own commitment to the new way of courtship and marriage, Mary Todd wrote a friend in 1840 "...my hand will never be given where my heart is not."[18]

Besides, where is Mary Lincoln in this masculinized equation during a period in her life when she had considerable power? Well, in this misogynist rendering she is humiliated, marries Abraham Lincoln for vengeance, and spends the rest of her life succeeding in making her husband miserable, according to William Herndon in an interpretation that has influenced contemporary positions. Here we have left the commonsense world that should accompany historians and have entered the dramas of Italian opera as well as the gender wars. There is no compelling documentary evidence on why their engagement was broken or who broke it, so the field is rife for speculation.

The clash of contradictory opinions ranges from Ninian Edwards's assertion that Mary Todd released Lincoln from his pledge, through Elizabeth Edwards's position that her sister's flirting with Stephen Douglas disrupted the relationship, to Abner Ellis, the Springfield postmaster's, opinion that Mary backed out of the engagement. "Her refusal to comply actually made Mr. L sick."[19] And among modern historians, interpretations move from Ruth Randall's arguments that the Edwards family opposed the marriage and so Lincoln gave it up, to my view that she was furious when he was late to a party.

Douglas Wilson, an historian of Lincoln's early private life, contends that the Lincoln courtship was superficial. He argues that when Lincoln got to know Mary better he found out that he did not like her, but as a man of honor felt compelled to marry her. But Wilson overlooks two things—one specific to Mary Todd and the other to courting in the early nineteenth century. He forgets that Mary Todd had first come to Springfield in 1837 (although he notes it in an exculpatory footnote) at almost exactly the same time that Lincoln had arrived from New Salem. She had then gone home, to return a year later. Hence their acquaintanceship was probably longer than he maintains. Furthermore, a courtship in which the lovers write those delightful "Lost Townships" letters published in the *Sangamon Journal* is hardly a superficial one in which the couple does not know each other.

These famous letters have been used in a variety of different ways to infer a number of things about Lincoln and the duel he almost fought with James Shields. Initially Lincoln had made fun of Shields, the Illinois state auditor, in a devastating satire published in the *Sangamon Journal*. Learning that Lincoln had written them, Shields challenged the chagrined author to a duel that was only forestalled by last-minute negotiations. But Mary Todd had also written one of these letters, and for her and her future husband they stand as an amusing public means for the reconciliation of a private relationship. "I know he's a fighting man...," wrote Mary Lincoln, "but isn't marrying better than fighting, although it tends to run into it." In Mary's final effort, written within weeks of her marriage, "Happy groom! Is sadness far distant from thee? The fair girls dream only of past times and glee."[20]

The second point is that we are imposing our twentieth-century standards of courtship if we think that Mary Todd did not know Abraham Lincoln very well. In the nineteenth century, the public courtships of earlier periods were no longer observed by the community. Instead courting, which usually began with friendship, had moved inside, where outsiders were closed out. The mid-nineteenth century was a transitional period in this process, as what had been a public affair became more private and sheltered, often in the twentieth century in the back seat of an automobile. The Lincoln courtship occurred at an historical moment when some courting was out of the house and very public, taking place during picnics, sleigh rides, and Springfield's dancing parties—all of which are mentioned by Mary Todd. But as often, a romance developed in walks down country lanes, on parlor sofas such as the horsehair one in the Edwards's home, and in the bower of trees surrounding the house.[21] That is why there were few sightings of Abraham and Mary in busybody Springfield before their marriage in the fall of 1842.

And many mid-nineteenth-century courtships were briefer than those of the twentieth century. "Before marriage," writes John Gillis, "young people made and unmade relationships with bewildering rapidity, keeping open their options for a much longer period than young people do today."[22] This was a generation that did not know the meaning of going steady. Surely the number and variety of both Mathilda Edwards's and Mary Todd's beaux suggest different, less uniform courting arrangements than exist in our times.

On the other hand Lincoln, according to Charles Strozier and David Donald, had trouble moving from the familiarity of all-male gatherings to intimacy with a woman. According to Strozier, both Speed and Lincoln "found solace in discussing their forebodings about sexuality—their intimate maleness substituted for the tantalizing and frightening closeness of women." In Donald's words, "(Lincoln) was worried about how to go about transforming the adored object of chaste passion into a bed partner."[23] One measure of Lincoln's uncertainty was his age when he married. He was 33 years old, which is seven years older than the typical groom of this period. Most men in Springfield married at 24, and even those who had come to the city as bachelors were routinely married by 31.[24]

Other historians cite Lincoln's letters to his friend Joshua Speed as evidence of his uncertainty about marrying. In this interpretation, only after Speed answered that he was more contented married than single did Lincoln become involved with Mary Todd again. Yet if we place the Lincoln courtship within its contemporary context, such inquiries emerge as routine occurrences.[25] What Abraham Lincoln and Mary Todd did in delaying their marriage was such a commonplace episode that we don't have to use it as a predictive factor for their future happiness together.

In fact, the timing of the transition to marriage was the most controversial aspect of marrying, and especially young men often wrote their friends to inquire as to their evaluation of marriage. Abraham Lincoln was no different than Daniel Webster and Henry Channing and thousands of other American men when he sought counsel from a male friend about his experience. The real point here is that both Joshua Speed and Abraham Lincoln were nervous about marriage. For self-made men, the creation of their own family circle might inhibit the independence and autonomy they had so carefully crafted for themselves in a male environment in new urban settings. It was the great dilemma of the nineteenth century facing middle-class males: was a manly life compatible with the domesticity imposed by this new cultural ideal of companionate marriage? And on the other hand, could they be true men of the republic who grounded their civic spirit in the creation of a family unless they married?[26]

THE WEDDING: "A WEDDING IS DESTINY AND HANGING LIKEWISE"

Much has been made of the suddenness of the Lincoln wedding. In the event's classic symbol, the cakes were still warm; the bridesmaids recruited the day of the wedding; and there were only 30 guests. The groom is reported to have said that he was going to hell—a sentiment that other grooms of the time frequently seconded as they anxiously contemplated an uncertain future state. Note here those pessimistic proverbs about marriage that have infiltrated our cultural heritage. "He that marries late marries ill." "Marry in haste and repent at leisure." They represent just the kind of dark popular wisdom that Lincoln would latch onto to comment about marriage as a public event, but they do not indicate his private feelings about his own marriage. In fact he would acknowledge his marriage as a matter of "profound wonder." Rather than being interpreted as the awe that a 33-year-old man felt at the matrimonial state, even this comment has been interpreted to display his ambivalence about his marriage to Mary Todd.[27]

For the detractors of Mary Lincoln, the swiftness of the marriage sustains the proverb that a quick marriage is a bad one. In fact, after the very public disruption of their courtship, Mary Todd had told her sister that "it was best to keep the courtship from all eyes and ears."[28] Again our lack of historical understanding about weddings has contaminated the Lincoln story. Weddings of the nineteenth century were shorter and simpler affairs than they are today. Indeed, getting married on what would seem to us the spur of the moment was quite common.

For example, among the Adlai Stevenson family of nearby Bloomington during this period, several brides and grooms undertook similarly hasty (in our eyes, but not theirs) marriages.[29] In 1855, Lucy Stone and Henry Blackwell were married before breakfast, and on their way to New York by eight o'clock in the morning. The point is that there was no standardized wedding ritual, and while there were plenty of so-called prescription manuals that prescribed etiquette on a variety of other issues, few dealt with weddings. Nor were marriages obligatory family events as they are in contemporary America. Brides did not wear fancy satin gowns of lacy white; the concept of an organized catered reception was two generations away; any need for months of planning amid wedding consultants was unnecessary.

If we can move the Lincolns away from their uniqueness and use them to sustain generalizations about the history of weddings, their wedding took place at a transitional point in the history of middle-class American marriages. In the wonderful anecdote of the occasion, Judge William Brown, who was accustomed to more rustic civil ceremonies, cried out after the groom had promised to endow the bride with all his goods and chattels, lands, and tenements: "The statute fixes that, Lord Jesus Christ, God Almighty, Lincoln." Still Lincoln had contemplated his wedding long enough and loved his bride sufficiently to place an engraved gold ring on her finger with the inscription "LOVE IS ETERNAL."[30]

THE MARRIAGE: "A TRUE WIFE IS HER HUSBAND'S BETTER HALF"

Like their courtship and wedding, the Lincoln marriage is encrusted with conflicting quotations about its level of satisfaction. Certainly it is worth remembering that one observer's bad marriage may be another's heaven. Both Professors Burlingame and Wilson ask the question, how could Lincoln have married such a dreadful woman? But we could ask as well, what did Mary Todd see in Abraham Lincoln, the hardly handsome or gentrified product of the prairies of Kentucky, Indiana, and Illinois who still wore pants that were too short and who once burst into a party saying the "girls smelt good." In any case the marriage, a crucial one for these two who had cut themselves off from their surviving parents and birthplaces, endured amid compromises on both sides. Mary Lincoln acknowledged the completeness of the relationship and its companionship, once writing a friend that her husband had been "always lover-husband-father-all to me."[31]

And as for the close-mouthed Lincoln, it was his behavior, not his words, that testified to the strength of the relationship, whether it was his often-expressed desire to have Mary Lincoln home ("I really wish to see you," he telegraphed in 1863), his nursing of his wife after the death of their son Eddie in 1850 and the birth of Tad in 1853, and his appearance at the Springfield railroad station three nights in a row during a snowstorm in January 1861 to meet his wife who was returning from New York. Certainly the president shared some of the turmoil of his presidential life with her, meticulously advising her when she should come home if she took Tad out of Washington during the bad weather season. "Don't come on the night train; it is too cold," he warned in December 1864 with the solicitude that marked his relations with her. "I would be glad to see you and Tad," he telegraphed, as he acknowledged her deep interest in army matters and often sent news from the Virginia front. He encouraged her to join him in the last days of the war when he went several times to Virginia, and he was holding hands with her during the performance of *Our American Cousin* when he was assassinated. Even his failure to be at home—a chronic condition for nineteenth-century professional men— must be viewed in the context of nineteenth-century marriages where complaints by wives about their husband's absences were common.[32]

Leaving the impressionistic judgments aside, I would like to take three arenas of the Lincolns' life that brought the couple close together and then discuss several that drew them apart.

SOURCES OF CONGENIALITY: "BE ONE WITH ME IN ALL THINGS"

Most observers of the Lincoln marriage have been impressed with their sexuality. Sex was one of the bonds that made this marriage between two very different human beings a success. Again some male historians have argued without any evidence that the Lincolns' sex life ended after Tad's difficult birth in 1853 because Mary Lincoln did not have any more children. Alternatively it is supposed to have ended in 1856 when the Lincolns enlarged their house at Jackson and Eighth and no longer shared a bedroom, a conclusion that removes the couple from the growing affluence of midcentury middle-class Americans who sought bigger houses with more bedrooms. By the 1850s, many middle-class couples slept in separate bedrooms. For example, Letitia and Adlai Stevenson of Bloomington did so, and managed to add to their family. Despite malevolent speculation, there are almost no gynecological conditions resulting from childbirth that prevent sexual intercourse save a prolapsed uterus, which, given Mary Lincoln's lifestyle, she clearly did not suffer from. Again, the removal of the Lincoln marriage from its life and times has distorted our view on these matters.

Listen to the letters that Abraham and Mary Lincoln wrote to each other in 1847–1848 when Mary Lincoln had gone to Lexington to visit her family and Abraham Lincoln, an Illinois congressman, was living in a boarding house in Washington during winter. Lincoln had encouraged her departure; she was cooped up in two small rooms with two children under five, but as he acknowledges, "In this troublesome world we are never quite satisfied. When you were here, I thought you hindered me some in attending to business." Now he wants her back. "Come along as soon as possible," he writes in June 1848, signing himself "affectionately" and "most affectionately." "I shall be impatient till I see you....Come as soon as you can."[33] It is not the lament of a man who hates his wife. Nor are his telegrams to Mary Lincoln in the White House when she has left for the summer and he hopes that she will come back soon.

Earlier Mary had written a long letter to him that had a strain of sexuality in it: "How much, I wish instead of writing, we were together this evening. I feel very sad away from you....With love I must bid you good night." Then she scratched through with love, knowing that this night at least she would not physically love her husband.[34] Several times Mary Lincoln is quoted by neighbors as wishing that Mr. Lincoln were home more often so that she could love him more. And while women are ever accused of dressing for other women, Mary Lincoln's low-cut dresses and flirtatious style certainly drew attention to her, but they also pleased her husband.

On more than one occasion, her husband praised her stylishness in the presence of bystanders. He noticed when she adopted low necklines. "Whew," the president was quoted as saying, "our cat has a long tail tonight." Always moved by her looks in the way of long-married couples who pass imperfections lightly by (and Mary Lincoln did not age well), he praised his wife's appearance. Once Lincoln remarked at a White House reception, "my wife is as handsome as when she was a girl, and I a poor nobody then, fell in love with her and what is more, have never fallen out."[35]

Indeed, Mary had become pregnant almost immediately after their wedding, and while this was not unusual for American brides in an era without many effective means of artificial contraception, what is interesting about the Lincoln marriage is that the couple controlled their fertility. Robert Todd was born in August 1843, followed by Eddie in early 1846. There were no more children until after Eddie's death in 1850, and then immediately so. Willie was born in December 1850, followed, because he needed a playmate, by the fourth and last Lincoln son, Thomas "Tad" in April 1853. Compare this to Mary Lincoln's family of origin. Her father Robert Smith Todd had seven children by his first wife and after she died after childbirth, another eight by his second wife.

But by the 1850s, especially in towns and cities, couples like the Lincolns were responding to the fact that children were not potential units of labor available for work on the family farm as Lincoln had been for his father, but rather were projects that required considerable venture capital. That is one reason why the American fertility rate dropped from seven in 1800 to a fraction over six in 1820 and to a little over four in 1850. The reason was birth control, by which I mean any kind of action taken to prevent having children whether it be coitus interruptus, long-term breast feeding, or the devices such as condoms and "womb veils" that arrived in the Springfield post office in mysterious brown paper wrappers.[36]

Planning a family requires an intimacy about sexual relations that for aspiring couples meant shared companionate power over reproduction, as sex, according to a recent student, "became a powerful pervasive subject in the 19th century with birth control a part of it."[37] In an age when sexuality was being separated from reproduction and partners discussed the timing of their children, there was mutuality and openness about a critical aspect of the intersecting lives of wives and husbands.

At home there was also little tension in the Lincolns' life as parents, and parenting, sex, and money matters are the habitual arenas in which couples of both the nineteenth and twentieth centuries disagree. As we know from them and from their neighbors, both Mary and Abraham were permissive parents. Once on a train to Lexington, a fellow traveler was appalled at the behavior of what Lincoln affectionately called "the Little codgers."[38] Eddie and Robert were racing through the train, disturbing the other passengers. Lincoln's law partner William Herndon has left disgruntled accounts of the boys' visits to the law office he shared with Lincoln, where they dropped orange peels and pulled out legal files— with never a reprimand from their ever-approving father. In the White House, the children's antics, which included once waving a confederate flag and aiming a toy cannon at the cabinet, continued unchecked by any parental intervention. According to Mary Lincoln, her husband took pleasure that his children were "free-happy and unrestrained by parental tyranny.... 'Love is the chain whereby to lock a child to its parents.'" Or as the First Lady said, "We never controlled our children much."[39]

Fully engaged with the children—in a way that more traditional parents were not—Mary and Abraham gave birthday parties in their honor at a time when such celebrations were unusual. Mary dressed up and played a part in Robert's reenactment of Ivanhoe, giving advice to the brave knights to be more merciful than brawny. Neighbors remembered parties at the Lincolns' where the boys were trotted downstairs to recite poetry, usually Shakespeare and Burns. And when her half-sister Emilie Helm was soon to be a mother, she offered her own self-portrait as a "happy, loving, laughing Mama."[40]

Besides sex and their children, Mary Todd and Abraham Lincoln shared the politics of what Mary Lincoln liked to call the affairs of "our Lincoln party." Indeed the relationship between Mary and Abraham Lincoln is laced together with examples of their mutual interest in partisan politics. The daughter of a father who participated in Kentucky politics as a Whig state senator, Mary Lincoln was one of those nineteenth-century women who were interested in "the great game of politics." There were others, and we are in the process of finding out about the tangential, but nevertheless important, ways in which American women participated in parades, went to rallies, and even gave speeches in the 1840s and 1850s.[41] Mary Lincoln was such a woman; and even in the White House, the couple discussed the composition of his cabinet, as well as matters relating to the war and politics.

This was a couple who transformed a mutual interest in public events into a love affair. They had always shared an admiration for Henry Clay, Mary's neighbor in Lexington, and Whig politics. During the days of their courting, they had discussed election returns, and Mary Todd had commented in a letter to a friend about Lincoln's presence in the offices of the Whig newspaper during the 1840 election when, according to James Conkling, "some fifteen or twenty ladies were collected to listen to the Tippecanoe Singing Club." During their courtship, Lincoln gave Mary a list of the state legislative returns, and she tied it with a pink ribbon.[42]

After their marriage, Mary Lincoln maintained her interest in the male sphere of politics. It was partly her interest in public issues that brought her to Mrs. Spriggs's tiny Washington boarding house when Lincoln was a congressman in 1847. Few wives from the Midwest, much less mothers with small children, uprooted their households to be with their husbands in Washington, and Mary Lincoln was one of the few. And when Lincoln wanted to become the commissioner of the Land Office, it was his wife who undertook a letter-writing campaign. This shared interest in politics was one of the significant ways in which she related to her husband.

Lincoln's political career stalled in the 1850s, and it was Mary Lincoln who constantly encouraged him in his two unsuccessful senatorial campaigns. An ascension from Vandalia, the first capital of Illinois, to the White House would have left little room for a wife's advice. Instead, Lincoln's jagged course across the partisan landscape of nineteenth-century American party politics left plenty of opportunity for shared discussions of political strategies. At home, Lincoln received not only the applause that a typical wife might bestow; he received heartening reinforcement as well as intelligent discussion of ambitions that were mutual. "Mary insists that I am going to be Senator and President of the United States too," Lincoln told a reporter and then shook with laughter at the absurdity of it. Henry Whitney, a lawyer who traveled the circuit with Lincoln, recounted a similar incident.[43]

But this interest in politics made Mary Lincoln unpopular with some of Lincoln's friends, certainly with his secretaries in the White House, and ultimately with many historians. Women's lives in this period were to be led in private, not public. Women were not to hold discussions about politics and know the difference among Whigs, Know-Nothings, and Democrats. Women were not supposed to meddle in patronage matters. And certainly Mary Lincoln excelled in the latter. She sought positions for her relatives, and when she failed to get her way, she intercepted cabinet officers and pressed officials at her receptions. Often she pleaded in the name of the presidential "we."

To the extent that politics involves matters of power and authority, as first lady Mary Lincoln was consistently political. When she began her crusade to fix up the White House, which she, and others, thought resembled a shabby old hotel, she did so because she believed that it would be a physical statement of the power of the Union during the Civil War. She knew that the impressions of foreign ambassadors, especially those from Great Britain and France, were critical to the future of the republic. But the White House was her home, and in the separated spheres of the nineteenth century she was enacting what historians of women have classified as "domestic feminism." She was decorating a home for her family, and doing so at a time in which women were beginning to enter the public domain as consumers.

AVENUES OF SEPARATION: "ALAS FOR THOSE WHO LOVE AND CANNOT BLEND"

Of course, like others', this was not a marriage without conflict, although the stories of marital anguish—always for Lincoln rather than his wife— are overblown. The episodes of Mary Lincoln's pot-throwing and knife- wielding promoted, incredibly, into possible matricide are exaggerated and exceptional. But their avenues of separation involved differences in temperament and taste. He was frugal; she was sometimes a spendthrift. He was plebeian; she was to the manor born. On her bad days she was vol- atile and lost her temper; on his he was depressed and distracted. Often he was remote, and he was frequently absent from home. Certainly the president was embarrassed by his wife's spending during the Civil War, both on her clothes and on the White House—the flub-a-dubs that he complained about.

In one spectacular public instance, he was mortified by her behavior on the parade grounds near Malvern Hill in March 1865. She had arrived late to the parade grounds, and when she saw him riding alongside the handsome Mrs. General Ord, Mary Lincoln berated him before the high command of the Union Army. But like summer storms, these fits of temper and jealously subsided and the couple reconciled in a few days.[44]

Clearly there were outsiders who saw their marriage as a difficult relationship; clearly Mary Lincoln had a temper that she displayed to the world, instead of, one might conjecture, internalizing her complaints against her husband in silent anger or indifference. Clearly her husband was frequently inattentive to her, "deficient," as one woman once said of him, "in those little links which make up the great chain of woman's happiness...."[45]

CONCLUSION: "A UNION OF OPPOSITES"

In these differences Abraham Lincoln and Mary Todd Lincoln complemented each other—not in the ancient way of marriage as a little commonwealth with the husband and father as ruler and the wife and mother as subject. Rather, their relationship was part of the companionate ideal of a new close- ness of husband and wife—the "tender passion" of a nineteenth-century marital style based on difference—the union of opposites of a generation that sought congeniality of interests even as it established the paradox of separate spheres. Or as Mary Lincoln perceptively commented about her marriage, "for I well know how deeply grieved the P feels over any coolness of mine...fortunately for both my Husband and myself...our lives [together] have been eminently peaceful."[46]

Partly this mutuality grew because both spouses crossed over the boundaries that divided husbands and wives into separate spheres and that often established marriages grounded in parallel lives of different work, habitats, traits, and emotions. Given Mary Lincoln's interest in politics, her life overlapped with Abraham Lincoln's in an unusual shared endeavor, while he, with his egalitarian approach to their mutual authority in the home and with the children, entered the traditional woman's world. "Mr. Lincoln," according to his nephew, was always "a home man."[47] Today we expect marriages to be based on symmetrical roles with both partners sharing work, play, leisure activities, housekeeping, and child-raising. The Lincoln marriage puts us on the road to that kind of relationship and, from this perspective, is very modern.

The best way to remember the Lincoln marriage is to consider individual marriages arranged along a spectrum from total alienation to warm, empathetic relationships of intimacy. Somewhere along this line the Lincoln marriage falls. Placed in the context of other middle-class marriages of this period that separated husbands and wives into different spheres, the Lincoln marriage seems a close one. That is not to say that there were not squabbles and the frequent rain showers of Mary Lincoln's temper, which were matched by the lack of spousal congeniality occasioned by Lincoln's melancholy and episodes of neurasthenia. It is to say that its bad moments have been vastly exaggerated.

Remember this marriage was bound together by three strong bonds—sex, parenting, and politics—and keep in mind that story, corroborated by several observers, that when Lincoln learned he had won the Republican nomination and later the presidency, he hurried home, saying as he turned the corner, "Mary, Mary *we* are elected." It is as good a testament to the profound respect and affinity the Lincolns had for each other as any I can think of.[48]

NOTES

1. David Herbert Donald, *Lincoln* (New York: Simon & Schuster, 1995), 108.
2. Michael Burlingame, *The Inner World of Abraham Lincoln* (Urbana: University of Illinois Press, 1994), 260.
3. As quoted in Justin G. Turner and Linda Levitt Turner, *Mary Todd Lincoln: Her Life and Letters* (New York: Alfred A. Knopf, 1972), 293.
4. Douglas L. Wilson, *Honor's Voice: The Transformation of Abraham Lincoln* (New York: Alfred A. Knopf, 1998), 232.
5. Jean H. Baker, *Mary Todd Lincoln: A Biography* (New York: W. W. Norton & Co., 1987), xiii.

6. Douglas Wilson and Rodney Davis, eds., *Herndon's Informants: Letters, Interviews and Statements about Abraham Lincoln* (Urbana: University of Illinois Press, 1998), 604. Lincoln was clearly not as smitten by Rutledge as was his predecessor James Buchanan who, when his fiancée died, never married.

7. Ibid., 444, 623.

8. Turner and Turner, *Mary Todd Lincoln*, 296.

9. Wilson and Davis, eds., *Herndon's Informants*, 664.

10. Karen Lystra, *Searching the Heart: Women, Men and Romantic Love in 19th Century America* (New York: Oxford University Press, 1989), 28, 31, 57, 60, 102, 157–159, 180–183; Peter Gay, *The Tender Passion* (New York: Oxford University Press, 1986), 51–60.

11. Katherine Helm, *Mary, Wife of Lincoln* (New York: Harper and Brothers, 1928), 81.

12. Benjamin Franklin, *The Autobiography of Benjamin Franklin* (New York: St. Martin's Press, 1993), 78–79.

13. Alexis de Tocqueville, *Democracy in America* (New York: Harper Perennial, 1988), 592.

14. Turner and Turner, *Mary Todd Lincoln*, 21.

15. Quoted in E. Antonio Rotundo, *American Manhood: Transformations in Masculinity from the Revolution to the Modern Era* (New York: Basic Books, 1993), 112.

16. Roy P. Basler, ed., Marion Dolores Pratt, and Lloyd A. Dunlap, asst. eds., *The Collected Works of Abraham Lincoln*, 9 vols., 2 suppl. vols. (New Brunswick, New Jersey: Rutgers University Press, 1953–55, 1990), 1:78.

17. Ellen Rothman, *Hands and Hearts: A History of Courtship in America* (New York: Basic Books, 1984), 57.

18. Turner and Turner, *Mary Todd Lincoln*, 18; on breach of promise as an outmoded judicial procedure, Michael Grossberg, *Governing the Hearth: Law and Family in 19th Century America* (Chapel Hill: University of North Carolina Press, 1985), 35–38.

19. Quoted in Baker, *Mary Todd Lincoln*, 90; Wilson and Davis, eds., *Herndon's Informants*, 238, 623.

20. *Sangamon Journal*, September 9, 1842:16. The letters are also printed on August 5, and 24, 1842; Roy P. Basler, "The Authorship of the Rebecca Letters," *Abraham Lincoln Quarterly* 2 (June 1942): 80–90.

21. Andrew Cherlin, *Public and Private Families* (New York: McGraw Hill, 1999), 240–247; on Mary Todd and Abraham Lincoln courting inside, Wilson and Davis, eds., *Herndon's Informants*, 443.

22. John Gillis, *A World of Their Own Making: Myth, Ritual, and the Quest for Family Values* (Cambridge, Mass.: Harvard University Press, 1996), 135; also Stephanie Coontz, *The Social Origins of Private Life: The Social History of American Families, 1600–1900* (New York: Verso, 1988), 116; Rothman, *Hands and Hearts*, 60–63; John Modell, "Dating Becomes the Way of American Youth," *Essays on the Family and Historical Change*, ed. David Levine, et al. (Lubbock: Texas A & M University Press, 1983), 91–95.

23. Donald, *Lincoln*, 86; Charles Strozier, *Lincoln's Quest for Union: Public and Private Meanings* (New York: Basic Books, 1982), 43.

24. Kenneth Winkle, "Abraham Lincoln: Self-Made Man," forthcoming in the *Journal of the Abraham Lincoln Association*.

25. Rothman, *Hands and Hearts*, 60–63.

26. Rotundo, *American Manhood*, 115–136; Robert Griswold, *Family and Divorce in California, 1850–1890 Victorian Illusions and Every Day Realities* (Albany: State University of New York Press, 1982); Daniel Wise, *The Young Man's Counselor* (New York: Carlton and Porter, 1850), especially the chapters on energy and industry; Ronald Byars, "The Making of the Self-Made Man: The Development of Masculine Roles and Images in Ante-Bellum America" (Ph.D. diss., Michigan State University, 1979).

27. Basler, et al., eds., *Collected Works of Lincoln*, 1:305.

28. Wilson and Davis, eds., *Herndon's Informants*, 444, 665.

29. Jean H. Baker, *The Stevensons: Biography of an American Family* (New York: W. W. Norton & Co., 1993), 87–95, 103.

30. Helm, *Mary, Wife of Lincoln*, 93–94; Ruth Randall, *Mary Lincoln: Biography of a Marriage* (Boston: Little, Brown, 1953), 74.
31. Turner and Turner, *Mary Todd Lincoln*, 534.
32. Basler, et al., eds., *Collected Works of Lincoln*, 6:283, 371–372, 421, 434; 8:174; Randall, *Mary Lincoln*, 382.
33. Basler, et al., eds., *Collected Works of Lincoln*, 1:465, 477, 496. Evidently some of the Lincolns' private letters to each other were burned in a fire in Chicago after his assassination.
34. Turner and Turner, *Mary Todd Lincoln*, 34–36.
35. Elizabeth Keckley, *Behind the Scenes* (New York: Oxford University Press, 1988), 101–102; Turner and Turner, *Mary Todd Lincoln*, 113–114.
36. Linda Gordon, *Woman's Body, Woman's Right: A Social History of Birth Control* (New York: Viking, 1976), 49–62; Janet Brodie, *Contraception and Abortion in 19th Century America* (Ithaca, N.Y.: Cornell University Press, 1994), 205–224.
37. Brodie, *Contraception and Abortion*, 226; Ansley Coale and Melvin Zelnick, *New Estimates of Fertility and Population in the United States* (Princeton: Princeton University Press, 1963); Robert Wells, "Demographic Change and the Life Cycle of American Families," in Theodore Rabb and Robert Rotberg, eds., *The Family in History* (New York: Harper, 1971), 85–94.
38. Baker, *Mary Todd Lincoln*, 119–125; Wilson and Davis, eds., *Herndon's Informants*, 444.
39. Basler, et al., cds., *Collected Works of Lincoln*, 4;82; 1:391; Rufus Rockwell Wilson, ed., *Intimate Memories of Lincoln* (Elmira, N. Y: Primavera Press, 1945), 135.
40. Turner and Turner, *Mary Todd Lincoln*, 50.
41. Glenna Matthews, *The Rise of Public Woman: Woman's Power and Woman's Place in the United States* (New York: Oxford University Press, 1992); Elizabeth Varon, *We Mean to Be Counted: White Women and Politics in Antebellum Virginia* (Chapel Hill: University of North Carolina Press, 1998), 116–119.
42. James Conkling to Mcree, 21 September 1840, Conkling Papers; Basler, et al., eds., *Collected Works of Lincoln*, 1:299.
43. Henry Whitney, Life on the Circuit, 93.
44. Adam Badeau, *Grant In Peace: A Personal Memoir from Appomattox to Mt. McGregor* (Hartford: S. S. Scranton & Company, 1887), 356–362.
45. Wilson and Davis, eds., *Herndon's Informants, 256.*
46. Turner and Turner, *Mary Todd Lincoln*, 200.
47. Wilson and Davis, eds., *Herndon's Informants*, 485, Helm, *Mary, Wife of Lincoln*, 113.
48. William H. Ward, ed., *Abraham Lincoln: Reminiscences of Soldiers, Statesmen Old Citizens* (New York: Thomas Crowell, 1895), 32.

III

LINCOLN THE POLITICIAN

6

THE MASTER POLITICIAN

Richard N. Current

Among Americans the words *politics* and *politician* long have been terms of reproach. Politics generally means "dirty" politics, whether the adjective is used or not. Politicians, then, are dirty politicians unless they happen to be statesmen, and in that case they are not politicians at all.

A well-known American once defined politicians as "a set of men who have interests aside from the interests of the people, and who, to say the most of them, are, taken as a class, at least one long step removed from honest men." The author of this definition was Abraham Lincoln, and at the time he made it he was a twenty-eight-year-old member of the Illinois Legislature. He added: "I say this with the greater freedom because, being a politician myself, none can regard it as personal."

After his death Lincoln was hailed almost universally as a statesman, one of the greatest—if not the greatest—the country or the world had ever seen. To many of his admirers it seemed unthinkable that he had been at any time a practitioner of politics. He, after all, was "Honest Abe." He must have been above that sort of thing.

But some of his acquaintances and friends had thought of him as a master of the politician's art. In time historians looked carefully into his political interests and techniques, noting for example the day-to-day attention that, as President, he gave to dividing the spoils of government jobs and patronage. The defenders of Lincoln do not infer, however, that he was a mere grubby spoilsman. "In being a competent politician," they conclude, "he became a statesman."

No longer are many people likely to be shocked by the picture of Lincoln busy at a politician's chores. It is taken for granted that politics for him was a consuming interest. But his expertness remains a subject of some dispute.

What were his strengths and weaknesses? How successful was he, really, as a politician?

II

If Lincoln as President proved himself a political wizard, this could not have been due to native shrewdness or sagacity alone. As a genius, if indeed he was one, he must have been made, not born. This is borne out by the record of his apprentice years in national politics.

"His ambition," Herndon thought, "was a little engine that knew no rest." Besides his ambition he had experience in the State Legislature but almost nothing else to justify him when, as a young man in his thirties, he looked longingly toward a seat in the House of Representatives. He had no platform, no program. "You know that my only argument is that 'turn about is fair play,'" he stated frankly to a follower. He and two other hopefuls, adopting in this case the opposition party's principle of rotation in office, had agreed to take turns as the Whig candidate in their district. His turn had come, and he was determined to have it.

During his single term in Congress (1847–1849) the lone Whig from Illinois left no monument of constructive legislation, large or small. He put together, but did not press, a plan for the gradual, compensated emancipation of slaves in the District of Columbia, the plan to take effect only with the approval of the voters in the District. On the whole he gave little attention to legislative matters as such. His big concern was Presidential politics, and his congressional speechmaking was mostly campaign oratory. He devoted a great deal of time to unmaking one President, a Democrat, and making another, a Whig.

He found an issue and a candidate in the Mexican War. The war, just getting under way when he ran for Congress, appeared to be extremely popular in Illinois. Whigs and Democrats alike waved the flag and volunteered for service at the front. What Candidate Lincoln said on the subject is not recorded, but the *Sangamo Journal* of Springfield, a newspaper that was thought to express his views, took a consistently patriotic, pro-war stand. More than a year later, when the congressman-elect arrived in Washington, he saw that the Whig leaders of the nation were bent on condemning the war and denouncing the President, James K. Polk, as the author of it. If Lincoln ever had approved the war, he no longer did so. Soon he was out-Whigging most of his fellow Whigs.

Within a few weeks after he had taken his seat, he introduced his "spot" resolutions, in which he challenged Polk's statement that Mexico had started the war by invading the United States and shedding American blood upon American soil. The point of these resolutions the new congressman drove home when he got to the floor for his maiden speech. If the President could not or would not answer the inquiries satisfactorily, his silence would prove that he was deeply conscious of being in the wrong. It would prove that "he feels the blood of this war, like the blood of Abel, is crying to Heaven against him." It would prove that for some ulterior motive he had plunged the nation into a war, into a needless, hopeless conflict, the end of which was nowhere in sight.

The war President, busy with strategy and with plans for peace, did not bother to reply. He did not rise to Lincoln's baiting, nor, apparently, did he even notice it. Indeed, in all the pages of his voluminous diary, Polk never so much as mentioned Lincoln's name. And less than two weeks after the latter's speech on the endless war, a treaty of peace with Mexico was signed.

Lincoln was but following the party line—voting to condemn Polk and the war while voting supplies for it—yet his course in Congress made him unpopular with his constituents in Illinois. Whigs as well as Democrats muttered about him. They or their friends or relatives had fought in the war and had come home as heroes, dead or alive. They did not relish being told that they or their fallen comrades had made all the effort and the sacrifice in an unworthy cause, a war unnecessarily and unconstitutionally begun.

Herndon wrote to warn his friend and partner that his principles were wrong and his politics unwise. Lincoln insisted his principles, at least, were right. "I will stake my life, that if you had been in my place, you would have voted just as I did," he assured Herndon. "You are compelled to speak; and your only alternative is to tell the *truth* or tell a lie." Politics, Lincoln was saying, must take second place to honor, truth, and right.

And yet, in other letters he wrote, Lincoln made it plain that the Whig attitude toward Polk and the war had a very direct bearing on the Whig prospects in the Presidential election 1848. The Whigs were ready to use the war both ways—to their own advantage and to the disadvantage of the Democrats—by condemning the war President while running a war hero as a Whig candidate. Lincoln was an early and eager worker for the nomination of the victorious general, Zachary Taylor. The thing to do, as Lincoln saw it, was to approve Taylor and his part in the war without approving Polk and *his* part in it. "You should simply go for Genl. Taylor," Lincoln advised a fellow Whig; "because by this, you can take some

Democrats, and lose no Whigs; but if you go also for Mr. Polk on the origin and mode of prosecuting the war, you will still take some Democrats, but you will lose more Whigs, so that in the sum of the operation you will be loser." These look like the words of a calculating politician, not those of an inflexible supporter of right principle.

At the nominating convention in 1848, Lincoln labored manfully to turn his fellow Illinois delegates from Henry Clay's to Taylor's support. Taylor was nominated, without a platform, and he accepted without a statement of what he stood for. Clay and Daniel Webster, disappointed contenders themselves, naturally were not enthusiastic about the choice. Taylor was "a military man, and a military man merely," with "no training in civil affairs," Webster said. Such a nomination was "not fit to be made." The Democrats accused the Whigs of deserting their principles and riding on the coattails of a military hero.

Lincoln, campaigning for Taylor in and out of Congress, did not deny the coattail charge. He merely reminded the Democrats that, for many years, they had been using the coattail of another famous warrior, Andrew Jackson. "Like a horde of hungry ticks you have stuck to the tail of the Hermitage lion to the end of his life," Lincoln said memorably if inelegantly, "and you are still sticking to it, and drawing a loathsome sustenance from it, after he is dead." As for principles, Lincoln maintained that Taylor's views were no more obscure than those of the Democratic candidate. Taylor's views were not vague at all, he said. Had the general not made it clear already that on the public questions of the day he would respond to "the will of the people" as expressed in acts of Congress? Indeed, Taylor held to the best of principles—"the principle of allowing the people to do as they please with their own business."

While making the most of Taylor's military glory, Lincoln cleverly ridiculed the record of the Democratic candidate, Lewis Cass, who had served competently in the War of 1812. It was on this occasion that Lincoln referred to his having been a "military hero," himself, in the Black Hawk War. "Speaking of Gen. Cass' career reminds me of my own," Lincoln joked in Congress. "If Gen. Cass went in advance of me in picking whortleberries, I guess I surpassed him in charges upon the wild onions. If he saw any live, fighting Indians, it was more than I did; but I had a good many bloody struggles with the mosquitoes...."

Whortleberries, onions, and mosquitoes, coattails, hungry ticks, and a dead lion. No platform, no committed candidate, nothing but the will of the people, whatever it might turn out to be. Such was politics, such was statesmanship, as practiced by Congressman Lincoln in 1848. So far as the Presidential election was concerned, these tactics seemed to work. Taylor won.

But Lincoln lost. The Whig line, however effective it may have been in some parts of the country, destroyed the Whig majority in his own Congressional district. His distribution of his share of government jobs did little good, though he gave close attention to it. Barred by his taking-turns agreement, he did not seek reelection to Congress. The Whig whose turn it was, running perforce on Lincoln's record, was overwhelmingly defeated.

What was worse, Lincoln failed to get from the Taylor administration the government job (Commissioner of the General Land Office) which he desperately wanted and considered as no more than his just due. Prominent Whigs, including Webster and Clay, used their influence to aid a rival applicant. "It will now mortify me deeply if Gen. Taylor's administration shall trample all my wishes in the dust merely to gratify these men," Lincoln confided to a friend. All his wishes were trampled in the dust, and he was deeply mortified.

At the age of forty—frustrated, despondent, seemingly at the end of his public career—he certainly appeared to be no natural-born genius in politics. Perhaps he had been, so far, lucky. He had yet to grow in political skill as in other respects, and fortune was yet to favor him.

III

The events of the 1850s gave Lincoln his opportunity to get out of the woods and set foot again upon the path of politics. To help in his advancement, he now exploited to the utmost the magic in the names of two late, great politicians (or statesmen) of the Whig party, Webster and Clay.

Clay introduced in Congress the proposals that culminated in the Compromise of 1850, which supposedly put to rest the disturbing issues between North and South, including the question of slavery in the territories. Webster eloquently supported the Compromise with his argument that Congress need not act to keep slavery out of the West since God already had done so by creating geographical conditions unsuited to it there. Then Clay and Webster died, in 1852.

Two years later Lincoln's friend and rival Stephen A. Douglas maneuvered through Congress a bill for reopening the Louisiana Purchase to slavery and, allowing the settlers of Kansas and Nebraska to decide for themselves whether to permit slaveholding in those territories.

Now, the Compromise of 1850, though unpopular in New England, where the abolitionists cursed Webster, was generally approved in Illinois and the old Northwest. Its most conspicuous sponsors, Webster and Clay, were famed in the prairie country as Union-savers. But, throughout the North, the Kansas-Nebraska Act provoked wild demonstrations of outrage which Douglas had failed to foresee. The Republican party rose out of the protest, and the Whig party, already disintegrating, was speeded on the way to extinction. In Illinois, as in other states, thousands of hesitating Whigs were left without a party home.

Douglas, with presidential as well as senatorial ambitions, faced the task of winning to the Democratic party as many of the homeless Whigs as he could. Lincoln, with ambitions of his own, set himself to heading off his most dangerous rival and steering the undecided Whigs into the Republican camp. Douglas tried to convince them that, in the Kansas-Nebraska business, he had but carried on in the spirit of their dead heroes, Webster and Clay. Lincoln undertook to contradict him. Douglas the Democrat and Lincoln the Republican both sought votes by appealing to the memory of the departed Whig leaders, and each claimed to be their true and only disciple.

The argument had begun at least as early as the presidential campaign of 1852, when there was still a Whig party and Webster was still alive. At that time Lincoln accused Douglas of falsely crediting the Democrats with the Compromise of 1850 and brazenly stealing Clay's and Webster's ideas.

In 1854, after arousing opposition with his Kansas-Nebraska Act, Douglas emphasized the bipartisan nature of the Compromise of 1850, saying it had been the work both of Whigs like Clay and Webster and of Democrats like Lewis Cass. Then Lincoln protested: "The Judge [Douglas] invokes against me, the memory of Clay and Webster." He proceeded to ask: "For what is it, that their life-long enemy, shall now make profit, by assuming to defend them against their life-long friend?" And he answered his own query: "The truth is that some support from Whigs is now a necessity with the Judge, and for thus it is, that the names of Clay and Webster are now invoked."

Again, in 1856, when he was stumping for John C. Frémont, the first Republican presidential candidate, Lincoln countered Douglas by aligning himself on the side of the old Whigs. A Democratic newspaper reporter, dropping in on one of Lincoln's campaign talks, "heard him pronouncing, with thundering emphasis, a beautiful passage from Webster's compromise speech, and that too, *without the quotations.*"

This same contest for identification with Clay and Webster ran through the Lincoln-Douglas campaign of 1858. "It would be amusing, if it were not disgusting, to see how quick these compromise-breakers administer on the political effects of the political effects of their dead adversaries, trumping up claims never before heard of, and dividing the assets among themselves," Lincoln exclaimed in a speech at Springfield before the formal debates began. Then in the first joint debate at Ottawa, Douglas came back at his opponent by asserting that not he but Lincoln was the compromise-breaker. "Lincoln went to work to dissolve the Old Line Whig party," Douglas resumed in the second debate at Freeport. "Clay was dead, and although the sod was not yet green on his grave, this man undertook to bring into disrepute those great compromise measures of 1850, with which Clay and Webster were identified." In appearances by himself at Tremont and Carlinville Lincoln denied Douglas's charges and repeated that he stood exactly where Clay and Webster had taken their stand. In the third joint debate at Jonesboro, Douglas returned to the attack and, in the fourth at Charleston, he elaborated by saying that "no sooner was the rose planted on the tomb of the Godlike Webster" than Lincoln and others tried to abolitionize the good old Whig party.

Neither Webster nor Clay had been, in fact, the sole authors of the Compromise of 1850. That was essentially a bipartisan achievement. Douglas himself, more than any other one man or two men, engineered the final passage of the compromise bills, and they were carried by the overwhelming vote of Democrats as well as Whigs. The roles of Clay and Webster were afterward so much exaggerated as to become almost mythological. The man who was mainly responsible for the Compromise was also largely responsible for the misconceptions regarding it. Manipulating the great Whig reputations in such a way as to attract former Whigs to the Democratic party, Douglas so minimized his own role in the events of 1850 that he distorted history and dimmed his own fame.

That is ironical enough, but the story has still more irony in it.

Lincoln, as well as Douglas, had been using the names of the two bygone politicians, reputed to be giants, in order to win votes. Not that Lincoln personally was lost in reverence for the departed great. He never quite forgave Clay and Webster for their part in frustrating his hopes for a government job. Possibly he still had his old disappointment in mind when, as President, he agreed in a Cabinet conversation that they had been "hard and selfish leaders." Nevertheless, in the rivalry with Douglas it had seemed important to Lincoln that he show a parallel between his policy and theirs.

In later generations, after his martyrdom, the name of Lincoln acquired a political magic incomparably more potent than ever had been the name of Clay or Webster or anyone else among the sainted dead. For decades after the Civil War the Republicans used the incantation of Lincoln's name to extremely good effect. At first they held a monopoly on the political remains of Honest Abe. Eventually the Democrats undertook to get their share of these assets, and they began to claim the soul of Lincoln as rightfully theirs. The Socialists, the Communists, the Prohibitionists, and others put in their exclusive claims. Today, politicians of all parties feel called upon, no matter what they advocate, to show they stand foursquare with The Rail Splitter from Illinois. All who seek the favor of the American electorate take pains to "get right" with him.

A hundred years ago the habits of politicians were essentially the same. Lincoln, for one, devoted a good deal of effort to getting right with Clay and Webster.

IV

There is no need to question the sincerity of Lincoln in opposing Douglas and the Douglas program. As like as not, he really believed that Douglas's "popular sovereignty" would result in the fastening of slavery upon the territories, and was convinced that Congress had to prohibit the expansion of slavery, for the country's good.

His principles happened to coincide neatly with his ambition. But if he had been totally lacking in convictions and had been concerned with nothing but his political advancement, he still could have chosen no shrewder course than the one he actually followed.

By 1858 he was a far more careful, skillful politician than he had been in 1848. In a decade he learned much, and one of the things he learned was caution. His touch was far surer, as he drew every personal advantage he could from the political trends of the 1850s.

Douglas remained the most immediate, the most dangerous antagonist. He broke with his party head, President Buchanan, when Buchanan tried to force slavery upon Kansas, in violation of the popular-sovereignty principle of the Kansas-Nebraska Act. Some prominent Republicans in the East then hoped to win Douglas to the Republican fold—and with him his Democratic following of the Middle West. Horace Greeley, of the *New York Tribune,* took up the idea and played with it. "What does the New-York Tribune mean by its constant eulogizing, and admiring, and magnifying of Douglas?" Lincoln demanded of his friend, the Republican senator from Illinois, Lyman Trumbull. "Does it, in this, speak the sentiments of the Republicans at Washington? Have they concluded that the Republican cause, generally, can best be promoted by sacrificing us here in Illinois?" Lincoln would have none of it. He could have none of it if *he*—not Douglas—was to be the Republican leader of Illinois and the Midwest.

In his campaign to get Douglas's Senate seat, in 1858, Lincoln did his best to identify Douglas with slavery and thus to discredit him among Midwestern devotees of freedom and free soil. He even accused Douglas of conspiring with Buchanan to spread slavery and fix it permanently upon the nation. Actually, Buchanan at the moment was using the patronage of his administration to hinder Douglas and help Lincoln in the Illinois election. It would have been more apt to say that Lincoln was in league with Buchanan!

Lincoln lost in 1858—and yet he won. The Republicans got more votes than the Democrats did, and only the underrepresentation of the northern districts in the Legislature prevented the Republicans from controlling it and sending Lincoln to the United States Senate. He had compelled Douglas to state his popular-sovereignty views so forcefully that Douglas lost much of his following among Southerners who insisted that nobody, neither Congress nor the territorial governments, had the right to exclude slavery from the territories. Thus Lincoln weakened Douglas's chances for the Presidency in 1860. At the same time, he improved his own. At once, a few newspapers in Illinois and elsewhere began to mention him as a presidential possibility, and in the ensuing months the Lincoln-for-President talk steadily increased.

At what point Lincoln began to take his prospects seriously, he never said, and there is no way of knowing. No doubt every politician, however humble and obscure, has days when he thinks of the sudden rise of other undistinguished men and feels at least faint stirrings of hope within his own heart. Not every politician is fool enough to bray forth his aspiration the first time it occurs to him.

In December, 1858, Jesse W. Fell made a trip from Bloomington to Springfield and, in the cultured tones of the prosperous, well-educated man he was, told Lincoln he would make a formidable candidate. According to Fell's recollection, Lincoln replied casually: "Oh, Fell, what's the use of talking of me for the Presidency, whilst we have such men as Seward, Chase, and others, who are so much better known?" Fell urged: "What the Republican party wants, to insure success in 1860, is a man of popular origin, of acknowledged ability, committed against slavery aggressions, who has no record to defend, and no radicalism of an offensive character." Lincoln then said: "Fell, I admit the force of much that you say, and admit that I am ambitious, and would like to be President...but there is no such good luck in store for me as the Presidency."

The next April an enthusiastic Republican editor of Rock Island, Illinois, wrote to Springfield proposing a Lincoln-for-President movement. "I must, in candor, say I do not think myself fit for the Presidency," Lincoln wrote back. "I really think it best for our cause that no concerted effort, such as you suggest, should be made." As the months went by, Lincoln received other letters like the one from Rock Island, and he answered all of them in much the same spirit.

In December, 1859, he told Trumbull he "would rather have full term in the Senate than in the Presidency." Soon he gave his friends the impression that he was, indeed, interested in being considered for the presidential nomination—but only to improve his chances for eventual election to the Senate. "I am not in a position where it would hurt much for me not to be nominated on the national ticket," he informed Norman B. Judd in February, 1860, "but I am where it would hurt some for me not to get the Illinois delegates." Finally, in April, when the national convention was only two months away, he began to admit to a few of his correspondents that he did have presidential hopes. To one, he said it must be remembered that "when a not very great man begins to be mentioned for a very great position, his head is very likely to be a little turned." To Trumbull he confessed: "The taste *is* in my mouth a little...."

Whether or not Lincoln's coyness and hesitation reflected his modesty, he had been doing what any sensible aspirant would have done. Lincoln would have hurt his prospects if he had allowed a boom to get started prematurely. He would have made himself too conspicuous as a target for other contenders.

While Lincoln thus took care to keep himself from being knifed in the back, he was busy using the knife on his rivals for the nomination, and doing all he could to enhance his reputation as an outstanding Republican leader. During 1859 he was on the go much of the time, traveling a total of four thousand miles and speaking to twenty-three audiences, in such states as Ohio, Michigan, Wisconsin, and Kansas. In 1860 he spoke at Cooper Union in New York City, then toured New England to speak in several towns and cities. That same winter he wrote out an autobiographical sketch and sent it to Jesse W. Fell for publication. He also had his eloquent debates with Douglas published. And all the while he kept up a ceaseless correspondence with Republicans in Illinois and throughout the country.

He was ready with a reply for those who asked how Illinois would react to the nomination of various preconvention favorites: William H. Seward, Salmon P. Chase, Edward Bates, or John McLean. As for Seward, he "is the very best candidate we could have for the north of Illinois, and the very *worst* for the south of it," Lincoln wrote. Chase "is neither better nor worse" than Seward, "except that he is a newer man." Chase appeared to be "right-minded; but still he may not be the most suitable." Bates "would be the best man for the south of our state, and the worst for the north of it." "I think neither Seward nor Bates can carry Illinois if Douglas shall be on the track; and that either of them can, if he shall not be." McLean "could carry it with D. on or off." In fact, McLean would be a good man if only he were ten or fifteen years younger. "I hear no objection to Mr. McLean, except his age; but that objection seems to occur to every one."

The conclusion was unexpressed, but it was plain enough between the lines. Illinois could be carried by only one man—Abraham Lincoln. Indeed, the implication was that, for the North as a whole, he was the only truly *available* man the Republicans could pick.

After the nominating convention at last had met in Chicago, in June of 1860, a majority of the delegates—on the third ballot—appeared to agree with the conclusion which Lincoln so assiduously had been hinting. No doubt his nomination was furthered by the claque of Illinoisans who raised a din in the convention hall, the Wigwam, whenever his name was mentioned. No doubt the victory was clinched by the patronage promises which his managers made. But Lincoln himself had laid the groundwork and had done it well.

Once he had been chosen as the Republican candidate, Lincoln put aside his law practice and gave his full time to the direction of his campaign. He continued to keep the silence which—except for the speeches he had made to denounce Douglas and demand free soil—he had observed before the convention. Now he had absolutely nothing more to say, in public. For a presidential candidate to stump in his own behalf was not yet accepted as the best political etiquette. Besides, for Lincoln to do so would have been most risky.

To win, he needed the votes of all kinds of dissident groups in the North. He needed the votes of former Whigs and former Democrats, of men sworn to destroy slavery and men indifferent or favorable to it, of German and Irish immigrants and of native Americans prejudiced against the foreign-born, of high-tariffites and low-tariffites, of tipplers and temperance men. The issue of the Catholic foreigner was especially delicate. In the previous Presidential election, in 1856, the Native American or Know-Nothing party, with its anti-Catholic, antiforeigner platform, had taken many votes that Republicans desired. Lincoln still thought of those nativist votes.

He was not a Know-Nothing and never had been. Once (in 1855) he had written, privately: "As a nation, we began by declaring that 'all men are created equal.' We now practically read it 'all men are created equal, except Negroes.' When the Know-Nothings get control, it will read 'all men are created equal, except Negroes, and foreigners, and Catholics.' When it comes to this I should prefer emigrating to some country where they make no pretense of loving liberty—to Russia, for instance, where despotism can be taken pure, and without the base alloy of hypocrisy." Which was nobly said.

But Lincoln also observed (in 1855) that Know-Nothingism had "not yet entirely crumbled to pieces" and that it was important to "get the elements of this organization" for the Republican party. "I fear an open push by us now, may offend them, and prevent our ever getting them," he said, in confidence. "About us here, they are mostly my old political and personal friends; and I have hoped their organization would die out without the painful necessity of my taking an open stand against them."

He still refused, in 1860, to take an open stand against the Native Americans. When told that "Irishmen" were saying he had been seen coming out of a Know-Nothing lodge, he wrote a confidential letter stating that he had never been in such a place. "And now, a word of caution," he ended. "Our adversaries think they can gain a point, if they could force me to openly deny this charge, by which some degree of offence would be given to the Americans. For this reason, it must not publicly appear that I am paying any attention to the charge."

The candidate also declined to speak out on the tariff. He was an "old Henry Clay tariff Whig," he admitted confidentially. "Still, it is my opinion that, just now, the revival of that question will not advance the cause itself, or the man who revives it."

Though averring (in one of his many "Private & Confidential" letters) that he did not intend to serve liquor in the White House, he thought it "improper" for him to make a public statement in support of temperance.

He did not want to see the fugitive-slave law discussed. And of course he said nothing, publicly, in response to those who asked for some assurance about the future of slavery in Southern states.

He was carrying out the strategy of avoidance which he recommended for the party even before his nomination. His "main object" would be to "hedge against divisions in the Republican ranks," he had said. "The point of danger is the temptation in different localities to 'platform' for something which will be popular just there, but which, nevertheless, will be a firebrand elsewhere," he had warned. "In a word, in every locality we should look beyond our noses; and at least say *nothing* on points where it is probable we shall disagree."

In the circumstances of 1860, with the Democratic opposition split, the Lincoln strategy worked. And Douglas, running as the candidate of the Northern Democrats, was at last brought down in defeat.

Afterward many a Republican was given credit as the Warwick of the victorious party. People assumed there must have been a President-maker behind the scenes. It was one of Lincoln's Illinois friends and managers—Norman Judd, or David Davis, or Jesse W. Fell, or Leonard Swett. It was Horace Greeley of the *New York Tribune* or Charles Ray of the *Chicago Tribune,* and about Ray a book eventually was written with the title *The Man Who Elected Lincoln.* It was perhaps Stephen A. Douglas, an unwitting Warwick. Or it was someone else.

The most likely choice has been overlooked. It is Abraham Lincoln.

V

President Lincoln repaid the political debts his managers had contracted at the Chicago convention. He appointed to his Cabinet the men who had been his rivals: Seward, Chase, Bates, and Cameron. He found other places for his Illinois backers, a diplomatic post abroad for Norman Judd, a position on the Supreme Court for David Davis, and so on. Rewarding foes as well as friends, Lincoln was both generous and judicious with the patronage. Unquestionably he did this in order to hold the Republican party together. When the Confederates chose to fire upon the flag at Fort Sumter, the patriotic response gave additional strength and unity to the organization.

But divisions soon reappeared. While there rose many personal and factional rivalries, these generally were overshadowed by the two-way conflict between Radicals and conservatives. Between the two groups the main difference was this: the Radicals demanded a war to abolish slavery and remake the South; the conservatives desired only (or primarily) the reestablishment of the Union. The country, the Congress, and the Cabinet were divided on war aims. Throughout his presidency Lincoln had to concern himself with the "main object" he had defined even before his nomination—to overcome divisions within the Republican ranks. He had to cope with the problem of keeping his party in one piece and keeping himself at the head of it.

The supreme test came with the election of 1864. Lincoln craved a second term. "No man knows what *that gnawing* is till he has had it," he said, as if to apologize for his ambition to Provost Marshal-General James B. Fry.

For a time, Lincoln's chances to satisfy that gnawing appeared to be slim indeed. Before his own renomination, a splinter group of radicals held a separate convention and picked as their candidate the colorful, antislavery politician-general, John C. Frémont. After Lincoln's renomination, a number of prominent Republicans joined in a plot to set aside both Lincoln and Frémont and replace them with a single candidate upon whom the whole party presumably could unite. In August, with the election less than three months away, even the campaign manager, Henry J. Raymond, and the political wizard, Thurlow Weed, were convinced that the President could not be reelected.

Lincoln won, of course. Eventually the party was reunited behind him. He was able to win partly because of luck. The Democrats, while nominating the crowd-pleasing George B. McClellan, made the mistake of requiring their war hero to run on a peace platform. And news of Union victories, most notably of Sherman's victory at Atlanta, arrived just in time to refute the Democrats' plank declaring the war a hopeless failure. But, to bring about Lincoln's reelection, it took more than the errors of his opponents and the fortunes of the war. It took all his resourcefulness as an expert politician.

Just how he managed the election is in some respects not altogether clear. To this day, there remain at least two big puzzles. One of these has to do with his role in the nomination of Andrew Johnson as his running mate.

Alexander C. McClure released, some time after the fact, one very persuasive version of how Lincoln "chose" his Vice President. Though Lincoln was sure of his own place on the ticket when the regular Republican convention met in Baltimore, he feared that his candidacy might be a rather empty honor unless, on election day, he and the party could get the votes of many nominal Democrats in addition to the votes of confirmed Republicans. The better to appeal to Democratic voters, the Republican party was calling itself the "Union" party. Lincoln wanted to do more than merely change the name. He wanted to create an unbeatable bipartisan and bisectional combination which would bring together Republicans and War Democrats, Northerners and (in principle at least) Southerners. The way to do this was to have the Republicans produce a kind of coalition ticket, giving the second place to a Democrat who supported the war effort, a Southerner who remained loyal to the Union. Such a man was available in the person of North Carolina-born Andrew Johnson, currently military governor of Tennessee.

Of course, the country already had a Vice-president, Lincoln's running mate of 1860, Hannibal Hamlin of Maine. Lincoln had nothing against Hamlin himself, though the two did not always see eye to eye on issues of national policy. But Hamlin was expendable, since Maine was safely Republican. The problem was to ease him out with no embarrassment to him, to Lincoln, to the party as a whole. It would not do for the President to cut his colleague's throat in public. Therefore, during the sessions of the Baltimore convention, Lincoln pretended to leave the delegates entirely to their own devices. He even wrote a note to the effect that he would not interfere. Behind the scenes, however, he interfered indeed.

To McClure and other trusted emissaries he gave the word for the insiders at Baltimore: Johnson is the man. And Johnson was nominated on the first ballot.

Such, in essence, is the story that McClure released in his *Philadelphia Times* after Hannibal Hamlin died (in 1891). But the story did not go unchallenged. Promptly Lincoln's former private secretary, John G. Nicolay, sent a telegram to the recently bereaved Mrs. Hamlin and gave it to the press. In the telegram he said that the McClure report was wholly erroneous. "Mr. Lincoln's personal feelings, on the contrary were for Mr. Hamlin's renomination, as he confidentially expressed to me, but he persistently withheld any opinion calculated to influence the convention for or against any candidate, and I have written words to that effect." Nicolay referred the widow—and the public—to volume, chapter, and page of *Abraham*

Lincoln: A History, the monumental work which he had written in collaboration with John Hay.

Those pages tell how Nicolay, in Baltimore, was asked to get a statement from Lincoln on the matter of the vice-presidency. Some of the delegates were puzzled because Lincoln's close friend Leonard Swett was urging the nomination of Joseph Holt, a War Democrat from Kentucky. Nicolay wrote to Hay in Washington and requested him to find out whether Swett was "all right" and whether Lincoln had any instructions, confidential or otherwise. In reply Lincoln endorsed Nicolay's letter with this message: "Swett is unquestionably all right. Mr. Holt is a good man, but I had not heard or thought of him for V. P. Wish not to interfere about V. P."

The wording of this message, McClure asserted in rebuttal, really upheld his own contention (Swett's support of Holt being, McClure said, only a stratagem to prepare the way for Johnson's nomination). He repeated his story that Lincoln had called him to the White House and earnestly explained how the nomination of a "well-known Southern man like Andrew Johnson" would "nationalize the Republican party" and save the Union. McClure dismissed Nicolay by saying he had been a mere clerk who knew nothing of the confidential councils of the President and was not trusted by him. Naturally Lincoln "did not proclaim himself a fool by giving Nicolay an opportunity to herald Lincoln's sacredly private convictions as to the Vice-Presidency."

Answering in kind, Nicolay cited the Official proceedings of the convention to show that McClure himself had acted a very minor part at Baltimore. Did it stand to reason that the President had confided in McClure without confiding also in more important men? "You accuse President Lincoln of acting a low political deceit and with his own hand writing a deliberate lie," Nicolay expostulated. "That may be your conception of Abraham Lincoln, but it is not mine. That may be your system of politics, but it was not his."

Later, to clinch his case, Nicolay obtained a statement from the chairman of the Illinois delegation of 1864. Not satisfied with Lincoln's note to Nicolay, this Illinoisan had gone personally to the White House. He found Lincoln "particularly anxious not to make known his preferences" yet somehow gathered that Lincoln did have a preference. "After my interview with him I was as positive that Hannibal Hamlin was his favorite as I am that I am alive to-day."

McClure, for his last rebuttal, contented himself with presenting the reminiscences he collected from several of Lincoln's old acquaintances, including Ward Hill Lamon. On the main point—that Lincoln had desired the nomination of Johnson and had used his influence to bring it about—these reminiscences sustained McClure.

There the Nicolay-McClure controversy rested. There it still rests, unfortunately without a definite decision for either side.

The second big puzzle regarding Lincoln's tactics in 1864 has to do with a rumored deal by which he got rid of Frémont as a rival Republican candidate and at the same time won the reluctant Radicals to his own support. Many Radicals, such as Henry Winter Davis and Benjamin F. Wade, who in June had issued the "Wade-Davis manifesto" denouncing Lincoln, sulkily refused to campaign for him as late as September, though they were not Frémont men. The plot to supersede Lincoln had collapsed, but some of the former plotters demanded, as the price of their assistance, that he reform his Cabinet by dismissing the member most obnoxious to them, namely, Postmaster General Montgomery Blair. Lincoln, in return for sacrificing Blair, is supposed to have required the withdrawal of Frémont from the Presidential race. On September 22 Frémont withdrew. The next day Blair resigned. After that, Wade, Davis, and the rest of the Radicals, including former Frémont men, joined heartily in the campaign to reelect the President.

Had Lincoln actually made a bargain with Frémont? According to the biographer of the Blair family, he had. "To prevent almost certain defeat, he entered into a bargain with Frémont Radicals, they to support the Union National ticket in exchange for the decapitation of Postmaster-General Blair." But Frémont's biographer questions the bargain story, and one of Lincoln's biographers disposes of it as essentially "historical fiction."

The story first was told by Zachariah Chandler, a senator from Michigan, who was a fierce Radical and a friend of Wade, but who also was on good personal terms with Lincoln. According to his own account, Chandler undertook to heal the party breach. At the end of August he left his Michigan home to see Wade in Ohio and Lincoln and others in Washington. He found Wade willing to "give his earnest support" if Blair were removed. He found Lincoln willing to remove Blair "if harmony would follow." Then he proceeded to New York and "opened negotiations there with the managers of the Frémont movement." After putting him off for some time, they finally "agreed that, if Mr. Blair (whom General Frémont regarded as a bitter enemy) left the Cabinet," the general would withdraw.

In the light of other evidence, it seems uncertain whether Frémont himself entered into a bargain with Lincoln, no matter what Frémont's "managers" did. Frémont afterward denied that he had done so. Still, in his statement announcing his withdrawal, he hinted that he and his followers would show enthusiasm for Lincoln only if Lincoln reformed his administration.

On the other hand, it seems reasonably certain that Lincoln did agree to a bargain. There exist some scraps of contemporary correspondence which indicate as much. In letters of the time, Chandler is mentioned as seeing Lincoln to get his "ultimatum." Chandler himself writes that Lincoln "was most reluctant to come to terms *but came.*" Wade refers to Chandler's believing "it was essential that Frémont should withdraw." From such remarks as these, it seems safe to infer that Lincoln did promise to remove Blair if Frémont could be persuaded to quit. At least, Chandler so understood.

Whatever the truth about the Blair-Frémont deal—or about the choice of Andrew Johnson for the Union ticket—there can be no doubt that Lincoln himself was the chief strategist for his campaign in 1864, as he had been in 1860. He had advantages the second time that he did not have the first, and he made the most of them.

He did not always leave even the tactical details to his campaign manager or to the workers in the field. At times he took a hand in the management of the Republican speaker's bureau, selecting the men he thought most suitable for stumping in this area or that. He did not hesitate to step in to tell the state committees what to do when he felt they were functioning poorly.

Lincoln was especially active in hiring and firing government job-holders so as to meet the necessities of the campaign. At the New York Custom House he changed the top officials, removing men who were insufficiently enthusiastic themselves or incapable of arousing sufficient enthusiasm among New York voters. He approved the dismissal of Brooklyn Navy Yard workmen who would not swear they were loyal "Union" men.

As Commander in Chief of the Army and the Navy, Lincoln was in a position to utilize Republican sentiment among the Boys in Blue. Most of the states allowed their soldiers and sailors to vote in the field or on deck, or by proxy at home. Some states allowed the men to vote only if they personally cast their ballots in their own precincts.

On the advice of Pennsylvania politicians, Lincoln asked Meade and Sheridan each to furlough five thousand of the state's troops so that these men could be home on election day. (Pennsylvanians could cast their ballots in the field, but Lincoln wanted to increase the "home vote," lest it appear that he was overly dependent on the Army.) At the urgent and excited request of the Indiana governor, Lincoln sent a note to Sherman suggesting that the general let some of his Hoosiers go home to vote. In response to an appeal from the chairman of the New York State committee, who desired "facilities for taking the votes of Seamen & Sailors," Lincoln sent a note to Navy Secretary Welles: "Please do all for him in this respect which you consistently can."

In Pennsylvania, Indiana, and New York, and in Illinois, Maryland, and Connecticut, the citizens in uniform may have made the difference between victory and defeat. One cannot be sure, since the total of the soldier ballots, as well as the proportion which was Republican, cannot be exactly known. It has been estimated that three-fourths or more were Republican. On the whole it seems likely that without the Army's help in the six crucial states Lincoln would have lost them—and the election.

VI

"If Abraham Lincoln was not a master politician, I am entirely ignorant of the qualities which make up such a character," Alexander K. McClure declared in 1892. And McClure was not entirely ignorant of politics, or of Lincoln either. But he may not have been altogether accurate in his analysis of the qualities that made Lincoln a master.

Lincoln had a "peculiar faculty," McClure said, "of holding antagonistic elements to his own support, and maintaining close and apparently confidential relations with each without offense to the other."

He had a way with politicians. "You know I never was a contriver," McClure heard him say in his quaint, disarming manner to a group of Pennsylvanians he had summoned to the White House; "I don't know much about how things are done in politics, but I think you gentlemen understand the situation in your State, and I want to learn what may be done to insure the success we all desire." He proceeded to interrogate each man minutely about the campaign then in progress, about the weak points of the party and the strong points of the opposition, about the tactics to be used in this locality or that. Generalities, mere enthusiasm, did not interest him. He wanted facts. And he got them, along with the wholehearted cooperation of the gentlemen from Pennsylvania.

He understood the voters. "He had abiding faith in the people, in their intelligence and their patriotism," McClure thought; "and he estimated political results by ascertaining, as far as possible, the bearing of every vital question that was likely to arise, and he formed his conclusions by his keen intuitive perception as to how the people would be likely to deal with the issues."

Above all, he harnessed and used political power to get things done. "He was not a politician as the term is now commonly applied and understood," McClure believed; "he knew nothing about the countless methods which are employed in the details of political effort; but no man knew better—indeed, I think no man knew as well as he did—how to summon and dispose of political ability to attain great political results; and this work he performed with unfailing wisdom and discretion in every contest for himself and for the country."

Now, McClure undoubtedly was right in saying that Lincoln possessed a remarkable ability for holding together antagonistic elements. Undoubtedly, too, he had a knack of appealing to fellow politicians and talking to them in their own language.

But it is a little hard to see the kind of mystic partnership between Lincoln and the people which McClure believed existed. Direct, popular appeal does not appear to have been one of the strong points of Lincoln the political master. Rather, his strengths seem to have been those of a politician's politician, a manager of the party machine, a wire puller—in short, such a "contriver" as he professed not to be. Especially he relied upon the spoils system, spending a large proportion of his waking hours, down to the very day of his death, in the disposal of government jobs. Instead of appealing to the public for support on specific issues—as Andrew Jackson or Franklin D. Roosevelt did—Lincoln avoided issues as much as possible. He had a gift of noncommittalism.

And the statement that Lincoln knew how to "attain great political results" raises a question as to the meaning and allure of success in politics. Presumably this consists in gaining power, as a means, and using it toward some public end. If so, real success requires more than the mere winning of elections or the mere holding of elective office. It requires also the achievement of a set of governmental aims.

Of course, Lincoln was elected and reelected to the Presidency, yet he received no such popular majorities as a number of others have done— Dwight D. Eisenhower, Franklin D. Roosevelt, and Warren G. Harding, to name a few. In 1860 Lincoln was a minority winner, with only about 40 percent of the total popular vote. In 1864, though he got a seemingly comfortable majority, approximately 55 percent, the election was closer than that figure indicates. A shift of 2 percent, or a little more than 80,000 votes, in certain areas, would have resulted in his defeat.

As President, how well did he succeed in realizing a positive program of his own? If his aim was simply to save the Union, the answer would seem to be clear enough, for the war was won and the Union saved during his presidency. And the answer is enough to justify his high reputation for statesmanship.

He succeeded, then, in his great political objective. But to do this—to hold the party together, keep himself in power, and preserve the nation—he apparently had to sacrifice some of his lesser aims. At the start of the war he was, or at least he is supposed to have been, a conservative. Before the end of it he had many a fight with the Radicals of his party—the "Jacobins," as they were called by his secretary John Hay, who was familiar with the history of the French Revolution. These revolutionaries of the American

Civil War sought break up the social and political structure of the South. Lincoln presumably did not. Yet it seems that he gave in again and again to the Radicals.

"Against Lincoln and his conservative program the Jacobins waged a winning battle," T. Harry Williams contends. "The wily Lincoln surrendered to the conquering Jacobins in every controversy before they could publicly inflict upon him a damaging reverse. Like the fair Lucretia threatened with ravishment, he averted his fate by instant compliance."

And yet, perhaps, this seeming opposition between Lincoln and the Radicals did not really exist, or was in actuality much less sharp than it appears. Perhaps at heart he was a Radical himself in some respects, as earnest a friend of freedom as any of them. Perhaps he was only more understanding, more patient, more astute. Perhaps he only waited for the ideal moment when he could do most effectively what he had intended all along to do—that is, to free the slaves.

7

THE ORIGINS AND PURPOSE OF LINCOLN'S "HOUSE-DIVIDED" SPEECH

Don E. Fehrenbacher

The chronology of Abraham Lincoln's sudden rise from relative obscurity to a presidential nomination includes no more decisive date than June 16, 1858. At Springfield, Illinois, late that warm Wednesday afternoon, the Republican state convention unanimously designated him as its "first and only choice for the United States Senate," and he responded in the evening with his famous "House-Divided" speech. Either of these two events would have made the day significant; together they constituted a major turning point in Lincoln's career.

The resolution endorsing Lincoln for the Senate was more important than anyone realized at the time, for without it there probably would have been no Lincoln-Douglas debates. Douglas saw little profit for himself in joint discussions and rejected Lincoln's suggestion that they canvass the state together. He proposed instead—and Lincoln accepted—an alternative plan for just seven debates.[1] Only the fact that his rival had been specifically named as the Republican candidate induced the reluctant "Little Giant" to go even that far. So the convention's resolution, amounting to an informal nomination, proved to be the door of opportunity for Lincoln. Through it he stepped to the memorable contest with Douglas, and thus, at the age of forty-nine, to the stage of national politics.

• Events were equally important

This was not an ordinary door, however, but something strange and new, carpentered especially for the occasion. The nomination of a senatorial candidate by a state convention had no precedent in American politics. Even in the casual form of a resolution from the floor, the action represented an intrusion upon the vested authority of the legislature and a step toward the popular election of senators.[2] Yet the resolution was not offered as a constitutional experiment, but as a gesture of defiance. It was the angry response of Illinois Republicans to the praise and support which some of their eastern colleagues were thrusting upon Douglas as a result of his spectacular fight against the admission of Kansas under the Lecompton constitution.

The revolt of Douglas had thrown the political scene into confusion during the early months of 1858. Out of favor, now, in the South, and at swords' points with the Buchanan administration, he appeared to be cutting loose from his old Democratic moorings and drifting toward the Republican shore. The prospect of enlisting the author of the Kansas-Nebraska Act in the antislavery crusade stirred up considerable excitement in Republican circles and fairly intoxicated self-appointed strategists like Horace Greeley. Such a conspicuous accession to the cause of freedom, Greeley thought, would be worth some little sacrifice. In the columns of his New York *Tribune*, as well as in private correspondence, he argued that Douglas, by opposing the Lecompton iniquity, had earned another term in the Senate, that his re-election would be a severe rebuke to the slave power, and that the Republican party of Illinois ought to join cheerfully in making that re-election unanimous. Similar views were expressed by such sound antislavery publications as the New York *Times*, the Albany *Journal*, the Springfield *Republican*, and the *Atlantic Monthly*.[3] In Washington, furthermore, prominent Republicans like Schuyler Colfax, Anson Burlingame, and Henry Wilson had fallen under the Douglas spell; and even William H. Seward was apparently ready to lend him support.[4]

Thus the Illinois Republicans, who had expected to profit from the quarrel between Douglas and Buchanan, found themselves earnestly advised by leaders of their own party to abandon the field to the enemy. But this, as one of them protested, was "asking too much for human nature to bear."[5] After many rounds of bitter hand-to-hand combat with Douglas, they could not suddenly lift him to their shoulders and carry him back into the Senate. To do so, they believed, would only mean humiliation for themselves and disaster for their party. Angered as much by Greeley's patronizing tone as by his presumptuous advice, they warned the meddling editor and other "wiseacres down East" that they would "tolerate no interference from outsiders" in their local political affairs. Republicans elsewhere might sellout to Douglas if they wished, but in Illinois the party was "pledged to the support of the gallant Lincoln."[6]

• pledged to Lincoln in order to save face

The same sentiments were registered more formally at Republican county conventions held allover the state during late May and early June, 1858. In many—perhaps most—of these meetings, the delegates approved ringing declarations naming Lincoln as their one and only choice for the Senate.[7] The resolution passed at the state convention on June 16 was therefore actually the reiteration of an emphatic verdict already given at the grass-roots level. And it served not only to ratify the popular preference for Lincoln but also to rebuke those eastern Republicans who had been giving aid and comfort to Douglas.[8]

The unusual state of affairs which had produced the resolution did not escape Lincoln's attention when he spoke to the delegates on the evening of June 16. His carefully prepared address closed with a devastating criticism of the Greeley viewpoint and a solemn warning to Republicans against putting any faith in Douglas. How, he demanded, could the fight against slavery be led by a man who proclaimed his indifference to the evil? "Our cause...must be intrusted to, and conducted by its own undoubted friends—those whose hands are free, whose hearts are in the work." In a direct reference to the senatorial contest, and with more irony than modesty, he recited a pungent sentence from Ecclesiastes: "A *living dog* is better than a *dead lion*."[9]

But it was another scriptural quotation that gave the speech its name. The part that became famous was neither the conclusion nor the body of the speech, but the opening passage, in which Lincoln asserted his belief that the nation could not "endure, permanently half *slave* and half *free*." And here one meets a mystery that has never been satisfactorily resolved.

Why did Lincoln choose this moment for the most provocative utterance of his career? In the long run, to be sure, the speech added appreciably to his political stature. Widely read and acclaimed, it marked him out among party leaders in the nation and raised him to Seward's level as a Republican phrasemaker. But whether the house-divided metaphor suited the immediate needs of the day in Illinois is another question. Many of Lincoln's friends considered it more eloquent than wise. A group of them, given an advance reading of the manuscript just before the convention, registered almost unanimous disapproval.[10] And there were others, like the Chicago editor, John L. Scripps, who admired the speech when it appeared in print, but feared that it would be misinterpreted as a promise to make war upon slavery in the southern states.[11] Leonard Swett, an old companion on the judicial circuit, never departed from his belief that Lincoln invited certain defeat in 1858 with the "unfortunate" and "inappropriate" doctrine which he enunciated at the beginning of the campaign.[12]

The speech caused such misgivings because it seemed likely to alienate the very votes that Lincoln needed in order to unseat Douglas.

With Illinois divided, like the nation, into Republican north and Democratic south, the senatorial contest would actually be decided in a belt of doubtful counties stretching across the middle of the state. The crucial zone was a stronghold of old-line Whig elements whose traditional hostility to Locofoco Democracy was balanced by a deep aversion for the excesses of abolitionism. Sound political strategy seemed to require that the Republicans court the favor of this important group by striking a note of moderation and restraint as they opened the campaign. Instead, Lincoln pitched his first words to a Garrisonian key and thus exposed himself to the persistent Democratic charge that he was a dangerous radical.

The standard explanation for this apparent recklessness is the one distilled from memory and imagination by William H. Herndon. It pictures Lincoln as a man wrapped in passion like a Hebrew prophet, determined to speak his thoughts without concern for the consequences. "The time has come when these sentiments should be uttered," he is supposed to have told his faint-hearted friends, "and if it is decreed that I should go down because of this speech, then let me go down linked to the truth—let me die in the advocacy of what is just and right." As for the house-divided phrase itself, he allegedly declared: "I would rather be defeated with this expression in the speech, and uphold and discuss it before the people, than be victorious without it."[13]

It is hard to agree with the historian who detects a "ring of authenticity" in such words.[14] Direct quotations raked out of dim remembrance—a kind of retrospective ghostwriting—are questionable sources at best, and certainly less than conclusive as evidence of motivation. This pretentious talk does not sound at all like the flesh-and-blood Lincoln of 1858, but rather like the legendary figure subsequently evoked from the ashes of martyrdom by Herndon and others. The real Lincoln was a man of flexibility and discretion as well as conviction. A seat in the Senate had long been his fondest personal ambition, and he knew that the Republican cause would benefit immensely from the overthrow of Douglas. It is unlikely that the uttering of a few dramatic phrases could have seemed more important to him than victory at the polls—or than life itself.

Here another familiar interpretation of Lincoln's conduct may be noticed. It is often asserted or suggested that by 1858 he had already fixed his eyes upon the White House, and that more than once during the contest with Douglas he seemed ready to compromise his chances of becoming senator in order to improve his prospects of becoming president. This idea turns up frequently in accounts of the Freeport debate,[15] and the House-Divided speech—with its apparent disregard of urgent political realities—can also be explained as a gambler's throw for the highest stakes. "It was . . . his most important move in the game for the Presidency," says Albert J. Beveridge, "a game Lincoln meant to win."[16] Similarly, Richard Hofstadter believes he "was making the great gamble of his career at this point."[17]

And yet there is little in the contemporary record to support such theories. No one who follows Lincoln's campaign trail back and forth across the hot prairies of Illinois will find reason to doubt that he was concentrating all his attention upon the task immediately before him. Traveling 4,350 miles by train, carriage, and riverboat, he delivered sixty-three major speeches and many shorter ones, wrote scores of letters, conferred with hundreds of local party leaders, and exchanged thousands of greetings.[18] This was no left-handed gesture, but a maximum expenditure of physical and mental effort. Besides, even if vagrant thoughts of the presidency were also crossing his mind, they could only have strengthened his determination to carry the day against Douglas. Repeated failure in one's own state was not the customary path to national leadership. History would have combined with logic to counsel Lincoln that if he expected to be taken seriously in 1860, he must win, not lose, in 1858.

There is an eight-page manuscript in Lincoln's hand which clearly reveals the intensity of his concentration upon the senatorial contest. Using the election returns for 1856, he carefully estimated his chances in each of the doubtful counties, with particular attention to the critical problem of capturing the Whig-American vote.[19] These businesslike calculations were made in the early part of July, only a few weeks after the state convention. Did his outlook change in that short time? Or is it possible that the practical purposes which Lincoln had in mind when he delivered the House-Divided speech have been obscured by its historical consequences? A satisfactory answer must take into account the *full* text of the speech, the circumstances surrounding its composition, and the general background of Lincoln's thought on slavery and politics.

It was actually a rather short address, judged by the oratorical standards of the day, and the famous opening passage was crisply spoken in about two minutes. After only one prefatory sentence,[20] Lincoln plunged into an attack upon the Kansas-Nebraska policy, which instead of putting an end to sectional controversy had greatly intensified it. Agitation of the slavery question would not cease, he declared, until a crisis had been "reached and passed."

1. "A house divided against itself cannot stand."
2. I believe this government cannot endure, permanently half *slave* and half *free*.
3. I do not expect the Union to be *dissolved*—I do not expect the house to *fall*—but I *do* expect it will cease to be divided.

4. It will become *all* one thing, or *all* the other.
5. A) Either the *opponents* of slavery will arrest the further spread of it, B) and place it where the public mind shall rest in the belief that it is in course of ultimate extinction; C) or its *advocates* will push it forward, till it shall become alike lawful in *all* the States, *old* as well as *new—* *North* as well as *South*.
6. Have we no *tendency* to the latter condition?

Here, reproduced in its entirety, with Lincoln's own emphases and paragraphing, is the doctrine of the house divided.[21] These are the lines which Douglas denounced as a "revolutionary" effort to incite "warfare between the North and the South," which historians have often linked with Seward's Rochester speech as an expression of militant Republicanism, and which later generations have found "heavy with awful prophecies."[22] Yet when the passage is studied as a whole, with the more eloquent phrases confined to their context, it becomes apparent that much of the provocative quality inheres in the vigor of Lincoln's rhetoric, rather than in the substance of his argument. Nowhere in these sentences does he reproach the South or suggest a program of aggressive action against slavery. Like many of his countrymen, he sees another "crisis" approaching, but there is no mention here of "irrepressible conflict," no apocalyptic vision of the bloody years ahead.[23]

Instead, Lincoln considers four possible terminations of the sectional struggle, and in the process offers a series of predictions. It was, to be sure, disingenuous of him to protest a few weeks later: "I did not say that I was in favor of anything. . . . I only said what I expected would take place."[24] His expectations must have been based in part upon the assumption that the Republican party would pursue a certain course—one that he sanctioned and was helping to determine. What he favored was therefore an understood element of what he predicted, and it is not surprising that to southern ears such predictions should sound like threats. The house-divided passage was more than a prophecy. It must also be read as a declaration of purpose. But even then its total effect is less than incendiary, and certain qualifying words reveal the essential reasonableness of its author.

There is probably no better example of Lincoln's ability to order and compress his thoughts than these six sentences. The first two constituted a clear-cut rejection of the status quo as a final answer to the slavery question. This might be considered revolutionary doctrine if it were not for the insertion of the word "permanently," which lends special emphasis to the fact that the speaker was scanning a distant horizon, not just the proximate ground of sectional controversy. In the third sentence, he examined the alternatives to a divided house, dismissing one and accepting the other. Here his repetition of the verb "expect" was no doubt purely rhetorical, for on the subject of disunion his mind was already firmly set. Thus he curtly rejected partition of the nation as an ultimate arrangement, not because it seemed improbable, but because to him it was impermissible.[25] The house could not stand if it remained divided; yet it would not be allowed to fall; therefore it must—some day, somehow—cease to be divided.

This line of reasoning had merely led Lincoln to another pair of alternatives, stated in the fourth sentence and elaborated in the fifth. But now he was ready, it seems, for a final prediction. If he had indeed resolved, as Allan Nevins believes, to place the Republican party upon "more advanced ground," he needed only to brush aside as an absurdity any design to make slavery national, then clinch his case with "a statesmanlike examination of the necessity for facing all that was implied in 'ultimate extinction'."[26] Yet he did not take this last, obvious step. Perhaps his courage had momentarily failed him, as Professor Nevins implies; but a more reasonable explanation is that Lincoln's entire argument had simply been directed toward a different conclusion. Beginning with the sixth and final sentence of the house-divided passage, he devoted the major portion of his address to the contention that there was a real and imminent danger of slavery's being forced into the free states.

"Ultimate extinction," although it would ever afterwards be singled out as one of the main points of the speech, actually received only the briefest mention. In the first half of the long fifth sentence, Lincoln presented his own definition of Republican objectives: (A) The further spread of slavery was to be prevented, and (B) the institution was to be placed where the public could rest assured that it would eventually disappear. The clause marked "A" obviously amounts to nothing more than a reiteration of the most familiar and basic tenet of Republicanism. Part B, taken by itself, seems to go further; for by introducing the concept of "ultimate extinction," Lincoln was presumably stepping across the line that divided freesoil principles from the "more advanced ground" of abolitionism.

But the point is that B *cannot* be taken by itself without distorting its meaning, because it was not offered as a separate proposition, requiring separate implementation. The bright promise of ultimate extinction was one of the consequences expected to flow naturally from a settled policy of restriction. The achievement of B required nothing beyond the achievement of A—or so Lincoln believed, and quickly affirmed when his words were misinterpreted. Writing to John L. Scripps only a week after the speech, he denied having any wish to interfere with slavery in the southern states, and then added: "I believe that whenever the effort to spread slavery...shall be fairly headed off, the institution will then be in course of ultimate extinction; and by the language used I meant only this."[27] He made the same assertion in five of the seven debates with Douglas. Here, for example, is what he said at Ottawa: "Now, I believe if we could arrest the spread, and place it where Washington, and Jefferson, and Madison placed it, it *would be* in the course of ultimate extinction, and the public mind *would*, as for eighty years past, believe that it was in the course of ultimate extinction."[28]

And Lincoln maintained that once this belief had become firmly implanted "the crisis would be past." Slavery might continue to exist in the South for "a hundred years at least," because abolition would come only "in God's own good time," but the northern conscience would be satisfied without invading southern constitutional rights, and the Union would be safe.[29] These benefits were all to accrue from the simple act of confining slavery to the area where it already existed. Moreover, Lincoln continually insisted that the goal of ultimate extinction, far from being new and radical, had been established by the Founding Fathers. Openly disapproving of slavery, they had "restricted its spread and stopped the importation of importation, with the hope that it would remain in a dormant condition till the people saw fit to emancipate the negroes."[30]

These subsequent amplifications, which are consistent with the entire record of Lincoln's public and private observations upon the slavery issue, make it clear that he did not intend by his introduction of the phrase "ultimate extinction" to propose any course of action going beyond the exclusion of slavery from the territories. He did deliberately affirm, however, that exclusion was more than an end in itself, that it implied a moral judgment against slavery and a commitment to freedom. Republicanism, as Lincoln defined it, embraced a belief (that slavery was wrong), a program of action (federal legislation preventing its extension), and an ultimate objective or hope (complete extinction of the institution at some distant date and by some peaceful means not yet discovered). Such a definition was bound to invite trouble; yet Lincoln returned to it again and again, with mounting emphasis, as the campaign progressed.[31] His reasons for doing so were not quixotic but practical, and can be understood only against the background of unusual circumstances which had already produced his nomination for the Senate.

Remote as it may seem in retrospect, the possibility that the Republican party—or a considerable portion of it—might become a tail fastened to the Douglas kite loomed up before Lincoln's eyes as a real and imminent danger in the spring of 1858. The Lecompton controversy, besides making Douglas a hero to many antislavery leaders, had also softened their opposition to his "great principle." Popular sovereignty now wore a more benign aspect. Recent events in Kansas tended to support the argument that a policy of nonintervention, if honestly applied, would be sufficient (along with the iron necessities of climate) to prevent the extension of slavery into the remaining western territory. No less a Republican than William H. Seward had recently announced on the Senate floor that the battle for freedom in the territories was already substantially won.[32] Why then, it was asked, should the South be antagonized and the Union endangered by insistence upon a superfluous policy of congressional restriction?

Such arguments were especially persuasive as long as attention was narrowly centered upon the Kansas crisis and the issue of slavery in the territories.[33] But Lincoln regarded the territorial problem as just the point of contact in a larger and more fundamental struggle.[34] To him, the Douglas-Republican convergence on the Lecompton question seemed superficial and transient because it had not resulted from agreement on basic principles. It was also dangerous because it threatened the unity and purpose of the Republican party. In response to this threat, Lincoln laid down, in the House-Divided speech, a definition of Republicanism which, while merely articulating what everyone knew, served to emphasize the doctrinal gulf that still yawned between Douglas and the Republicans. The concept of "ultimate extinction" could thus be used as a touchstone for separating the true from the casual or pretended opponents of slavery. His object, it appears, was not to lead a Republican advance to higher, more radical ground, but rather to check an ill-considered retreat to the lower ground of popular sovereignty.

The brevity with which he treated the subject in the House-Divided address was not necessarily a mark of diffidence. A convention composed exclusively of party leaders needed no elaborate instruction in the meaning of Republicanism. Later, for the mixed political audiences attending the debates, he would explain, qualify, and vigorously defend the proposition that slavery should be restricted *because* it was wrong, and *in order to* anchor national policy upon the expectation of its ultimate demise. Now, however, he proposed to consider the sinister alternative: progressive legalization of slavery everywhere in the United States. This was the major theme to which his historic opening sentences had led. He proceeded to spend nearly three fourths of the entire speech detailing a solemn charge that the Kansas-Nebraska Act and the Dred Scott decision were part of a maturing Democratic plot to nationalize slavery. The leading conspirators, he said, were Douglas, Pierce, Taney, and Buchanan. Having first repealed the Missouri Compromise restriction upon slavery in the territories, and then denied the power of Congress to impose such a restriction, they needed only one more victory, namely: "another Supreme Court decision, declaring that the Constitution of the United States does not permit a *state* to exclude slavery from its limits." That decision was soon coming, Lincoln predicted. "We shall lie down pleasantly dreaming that the people of Missouri are on the verge of making their State free; and we shall awake to the reality, instead, that the Supreme Court has made Illinois a slave State."[35]

Modern scholars, however much they may admire Lincoln, are inclined to see in this sweeping accusation and somber warning only the extravagance of partisanship.[36] There is, it appears, no evidence of any organized movement in 1858 to push slavery into the free states, or of any disposition among members of the Supreme Court to attempt such folly. In short, the conspiracy that Lincoln described did not exist; the danger that he professed to fear was extremely remote. And so this, the major part of the House-Divided speech, is commonly dismissed as "an absurd bogey," unworthy of intensive scrutiny.[37] But political rhetoric is a response to historical developments, not a record of them, and circumstances can sometimes make the most erroneous statement credible, even justifiable, thus giving it a kind of temporary validity. The conspiracy charge may have been absurd, but the real problem is to explain why Lincoln, certainly a reasonable man, insisted that it was true.

In the setting of 1858, the charge carried conviction. It is not surprising that even reasonable men should have seen an ominous pattern in the sequence of events which had begun four years earlier with the Kansas-Nebraska Act. Nor was it hard for them to believe that behind such a pattern there must be some kind of concert. Lincoln, to be sure, was exercising the politician's privilege of overstating his case. In subsequent speeches he admitted that the existence of a plot could only be inferred, not proved, and he conceded that Douglas might have been playing the role of dupe instead of conspirator. But the effects were what mattered, he argued, not the motives. A trend toward the nationalization of slavery had become manifest; it was more than mere accident; and the advocates of Popular sovereignty, whether intentionally or not, were contributing to it.[38]

Still, even if there was some basis for suspecting a design to make slavery national, how could a reasonable man, knowing the strength of the antislavery forces in the North, have had any fear of its success? It is precisely at this point that the argument contained in Lincoln's June 16 declaration is often misconstrued. The error usually stems from a failure to observe the close connection between the "conspiracy" section of the speech and the "house-divided" passage which preceded it. In that passage Lincoln had asserted that one of two opposing policies must eventually prevail. The triumph of either would obviously have to begin with the disablement of the other. Just as the first step toward ultimate extinction of slavery was the thwarting of efforts to extend it, so the first step toward nationalization of slavery was the blunting of the moral opposition to it. Lincoln thought he detected signs of the latter. His warning that slavery might become lawful everywhere was therefore not absolute but conditional, and, within its context, far from absurd. He was describing what could happen *if* the existence of slavery should become a matter of general indifference—*if*, in other words, the Republicans should allow themselves to be deflected from their purpose.

And this was where Douglas fitted into the picture with his enunciated philosophy of not caring whether slavery was "voted down or voted up."[39] Douglas' function, Lincoln maintained, was to instill a complaisant attitude toward slavery in the minds of northerners and thus prepare the way for new advances, new court decisions which would make the institution universal and permanent. Here was the burden of Lincoln's case against Douglas and popular sovereignty, and to no other argument did he return more persistently and eloquently in his later speeches. He repeated it in ever stronger terms to the crowds attending the debates, to Ohio audiences in 1859, and to New Englanders in 1860. The proslavery conspiracy, he said, could not succeed without Douglas, its indispensable advance agent—its "miner and sapper." The "don't-care" policy was "just as certain to nationalize slavery as the doctrine of Jeff Davis himself." They were "two roads to the same goal," and the Douglas road, if somewhat less direct, was "more dangerous."[40] These and similar amplifications reinforce the conclusion that Lincoln aimed the conspiracy charge of the House-Divided speech primarily at Douglas and those who imitated him in "groping for some middle ground between the right and the wrong."[41]

The third—or "living-dog"—section of the speech followed logically. Here Lincoln considered and firmly rejected the Greeley proposition that Douglas, by his stand against the Lecompton constitution, had qualified himself as a leader of the antislavery forces. If not quite a dead lion, Douglas was "at least a caged and toothless one" as far as the battle for freedom was concerned. "Clearly," Lincoln declared, "he is not *now* with us—he does not *pretend* to be—he does not *promise* to *ever* be." The Republican cause, therefore, should be "intrusted to, and conducted by its own undoubted friends." With these remarks, justifying the decision to fight Douglas in Illinois, Lincoln had brought his argument down to the business immediately at hand. He then concluded with a brief plea for Republican perseverance and this final prediction:

The result is not doubtful. We shall not fail—if we stand firm, we shall not fail.

> *Wise councils* may *accelerate* or *mistakes delay* it, but, sooner or later
> the victory is *sure* to come.

The House-Divided address, which probably required about, thirty or thirty-five minutes to deliver, can thus be divided into three main parts: the introductory "house-divided" section (constituting approximately 7 percent of the entire speech), the "conspiracy" section (72 percent), and the "living-dog" section (21 percent). It is the fashion to treat everything that Lincoln said after the first two or three minutes as anticlimax, to look upon his argument as running downhill from high principles to low partisanship. Yet the careful reader will discover that from beginning to end the speech is dominated by a single, coherent theme. It opens with an attack upon Douglas' Kansas-Nebraska policy. The house-divided doctrine has the effect of eliminating the middle ground upon which Douglas stands. The concept of "ultimate extinction" defines Republicanism in terms that exclude Douglas. The conspiracy theory links Douglasism with the onward march of slavery. And the last part of the address demolishes the image of Douglas as an antislavery champion. Whatever judgment may be passed upon Lincoln's rhetorical effectiveness, or upon the soundness of his reasoning, or upon the accuracy of his particulars, the immediate *purpose* of the House-Divided speech seems abundantly clear. As a matter of practical politics, it may be viewed as an attempt to minimize the significance and impact of Douglas' anti-Lecompton heroics and to demonstrate the folly of diluting Republican convictions with the watery futility of popular sovereignty—in short, an attempt to vindicate the nomination of a Republican candidate for the Senate in Illinois.

There is, however, another way of probing for the meaning of the House-Divided address which ought not to be neglected. Herndon's assertion that Lincoln spent about one month preparing it is probably true as far as the final draft is concerned,[42] but the basic ideas were formulated over a longer period. Rudiments of the speech appear in some of Lincoln's earlier writings and utterances. An examination of the circumstances which produced them should throw light upon the progress of his thought.

Such a study was made a number of years ago by the historian Arthur C. Cole, who reported his findings in an address entitled "Lincoln's 'House Divided' Speech: Did It Reflect a Doctrine of Class Struggle?"[43] Cole's point of departure is his reluctance to take at face value Lincoln's warning that slavery might spread to all the states. That danger, Cole argues, was simply not serious enough in itself to arouse such apprehension in Lincoln. "Another factor was present, lurking in the background, perhaps, but influencing Lincoln, consciously or subconsciously, in his presentation of the struggle between slavery and freedom."[44] Cole thus undertakes to rationalize the warning by uncovering a deeper meaning beneath the literal one. His explanation, briefly put, is as follows: Lincoln had come to believe that the theories of proslavery extremists like George Fitzhugh endangered the "white man's charter of freedom." In their idealizing of slave society without regard to race, in their contempt for the doctrine that all men are created equal, in their advocacy of a "defensive and offensive alliance of the forces of capitalism, North and South," Lincoln read the beginnings of an assault upon the entire working class. The evil that he feared was therefore more monstrous than the mere expansion of Negro servitude; it was the progressive degradation of all white men who earned their living by toil.[45]

This line of reasoning, although it hardly tends to absolve Lincoln of raising up an "absurd bogey," has a certain limited validity. That is, Lincoln did assert more than once that the defense of slavery in the abstract posed a threat to the theoretical foundations of human liberty.[46] He did not, however, present it as a pressing problem demanding attention in the realm of political action. His concern for the white man's "charter of freedom" served to reinforce his belief that slavery was wrong, but that belief was the assumption with which most of his arguments began, not the conclusion toward which they were directed. The central problem to which he addressed himself in his speeches was *how* the widespread belief that slavery was wrong could be implemented within the framework of the American constitutional system. Convinced that the program of the Republican party offered the best solution, he regarded the Douglases, rather than the Fitzhughs, as the major obstacle to its success. Cole's elaborate inquiry consequently ends more or less in frustration. He is forced to concede that the class-struggle theme does not manifest itself either in the House-Divided address or in Lincoln's other recorded speeches of the campaign.[47] He acknowledges that most of the address was "directed, in its formal logic, against the leadership of Douglas." But, adhering to the view that the house-divided passage stands in "comparative isolation" from the rest of the text, Cole suggests that "a sense of the larger conflict between slavery and freedom served as a subconscious factor in Lincoln's historic statement."[48] This cautious conclusion scarcely constitutes an affirmative answer to the question posed in his title. Not without value, perhaps, as an insight into the general course of Lincoln's thought, it nevertheless adds little to our understanding of what he said on June 16, 1858.

The search for the origins of the House-Divided speech leads back to the year of the Kansas-Nebraska Act and even beyond. Before 1854, according to Lincoln's own testimony, he had been opposed to slavery, but had believed that it was in the course of ultimate extinction, and had therefore looked upon it as "a minor question."[49] Thus the expectation that the "house" would some day "cease to be divided" was virtually native to his thinking. The Kansas-Nebraska Act, from his viewpoint, amounted to a revolution. It impaired the hope for ultimate extinction, opened the way for slavery's unlimited expansion, and made this corrosive issue paramount in American politics. From the beginning, too, Lincoln objected to the doctrine of popular sovereignty as one of moral evasion. The germ of the conspiracy theory can be detected in a sentence from his famous Peoria speech of October 16, 1854: "This *declared* indifference, but as I must think, covert *real* zeal for the spread of slavery, I can not but hate."[50] The disruptive effects of the Kansas-Nebraska policy soon confirmed his fears and inspired the analogy of the divided house.

The surprising strength of the anti-Nebraska coalition in the elections of 1854 heartened Lincoln and, indeed, almost carried him into the Senate, but he still saw only uncertainty in the future. Writing to George Robertson, a Kentuckian, on August 15, 1855, he declared that there was no prospect of a peaceful extinction of slavery. Then he added: "Our political problem now is 'Can we, as a nation, continue together *permanently—forever—*half slave, and half free?' The problem is too mighty for me. May God, in his mercy, superintend the solution."[51] Other men, North and South, were of course asking the same question, and Lincoln himself later disclaimed credit for originating the concept of the absolute incompatibility of slave and free society.[52] But in other hands the concept tended to be merely descriptive, or, in the case of southern radicals, to point toward dissolution of the Union. Lincoln's unique contribution was not the invention of, but the use to which he put, the house-divided doctrine. He was the first to couple it with an adamant rejection of disunion, thus formulating the major premise of a disjunctive syllogism which presented a choice between uniform freedom and uniform slavery, but eliminated all mediative positions, all obscuring evasions, in between.

The obscuring force in 1858 was Douglas and the anti-Lecompton Democrats. During the middle years of the decade, however, it was primarily the Know-Nothing movement that stood in the way of the emerging Republican party and a clear-cut decision on the slavery question. In the presidential campaign of 1856, much of Lincoln's energy was expended in efforts to convince the followers of Fillmore in Illinois that by deflecting votes from Fremont they were actually aiding Buchanan and the cause of slavery.[53] Here, it would seem, was a situation which might have invited use of the house-divided doctrine. Did Lincoln give utterance to it that year? There is a tradition that he did, perhaps several times, but especially in a speech at Bloomington on September 12. Lincoln shared the platform that evening with his friend T. Lyle Dickey, a moderate antislavery Whig. It was Dickey's story, written down only a number of years later, that Lincoln on this occasion "proclaimed it as his opinion that our government could not last—part slave and part free." Dickey further recalled that in their hotel room after the meeting he remonstrated with Lincoln, and that the latter, while defending the truth of his statement, admitted it might have a harmful effect and promised not to use it again during the campaign.[54]

Since there is no precise corroboration of Dickey's assertion, it must be viewed with appropriate caution. Nevertheless, his veracity is to some extent endorsed by testimony from Lincoln's own pen. Before this can be demonstrated, however, it is necessary to examine the brief summary of Lincoln's remarks which appeared in the local newspaper. Bloomington, it should be noted, was in strong Whig territory where the Know-Nothing appeal met with a favorable response. Lincoln therefore centered part of his attack upon the American ticket:

> He showed up the position of the Fillmore party in fine style, both as to its prospects of success, and as to the propriety of supporting a candidate whose greatest recommendation, as urged by his supporters themselves, is that he is *neutral* upon the one only great political question of the times. He pointed out in regular succession, the several steps taken by the Administration in regard to slavery in the Territories, from the repeal of the Missouri Compromise down to the latest Border Ruffian invasion of Kansas, and the inevitable tendency of each and all of them to effect the spread of slavery over that country...contrasting all this with the assertion of our Northern Democratic speakers, that they are not in favor of the extension of slavery.[55]

Here, beyond any doubt, was a framework suitable for the introduction of the house-divided doctrine; for in it one finds not only rudimentary traces of the conspiracy theory, but also condemnation of that same moral neutralism (here represented by both the northern Democrats and the Fillmore party) which was to be the primary target of Lincoln's historic address in 1858.[56]

But it was not until a decision had been rendered in the Dred Scott case that the house-divided argument could be used with full force. The Supreme Court's pronouncement, coming only two days after the inauguration of Buchanan, supplied the materials which had been lacking for manufacture of the conspiracy charge. Now, for the first time, Lincoln could specify the means by which slavery might be extended into the free states—a "second Dred Scott decision"—and thus confront his listeners with a categorical choice between policies leading toward ultimate extinction and policies promoting nationalization of the institution. Yet, with all the pieces of his argument ready for assembling by March, 1857, he waited another fifteen months before enunciating the house-divided doctrine. Opportunities to introduce it earlier were admittedly few, because this was a relatively fallow period in local politics. Nevertheless, he did discuss the Dred Scott decision at length in a major address at Springfield on June 26, 1857. Rejecting the Court's assumptions, Lincoln ridiculed its logic and defended the Republican refusal to accept its judgment as final. But at the same time, he said nothing about the possibility of a second decision legalizing slavery everywhere. He did not allege a conspiracy to accomplish that purpose; nor did he advance the proposition that the nation could not endure permanently half slave and half free. The speech, in short, contained scarcely a hint of the one that he would make on the same spot one year later.[57]

These interesting omissions may mean nothing more than that Lincoln's thinking along house-divided lines had not yet fully crystallized in the summer of 1857. It is equally likely, however, that they reflect the current political situation, which was to change so abruptly before the end of the year. With the Democratic party ostensibly united behind a new president, with Douglas defending the Dred Scott decision, with the lines of battle clearly drawn, there was less need for the house-divided doctrine, as Lincoln used it. Only when the Lecompton controversy blurred the political picture, exalted Douglas, and confused many Republicans, did Lincoln decide to advance his provocative argument as a means of clearing the air and preserving the integrity of his party. There is no escaping the simple chronological fact that it was the revolt of Douglas, not the Dred Scott decision, which called forth the House-Divided speech.

This explanation would carry more weight if it could be shown that Lincoln actually began to compose the speech soon after Douglas first announced his opposition to the Lecompton constitution—that is, in December, 1857, rather than in May, 1858 (as Herndon leads us to believe). There is good evidence that Lincoln did just this, but it has long been obscured by the persistent misdating of an important document. In the first edition of their *Complete Works* of Lincoln, Nicolay and Hay grouped several undated manuscripts together and marked them "October 1, 1858?" One of these, obviously a draft of a speech, is about three quarters the length of the House-Divided address and contains the basic ideas, as well as some of the phraseology, of the latter document.[58] For convenience, it may be labeled the "House-Divided fragment." The editors of the *Collected Works of Abraham Lincoln*, pointing out that the fragment must have been written considerably earlier than October 1, chose to date it "c. May 18, 1858." But their reasons for doing so are unpersuasive, and it seems almost certain that in this instance they have committed one of their rare mistakes.[59]

With a single reading it becomes clear that the fragment was written while certain events of December, 1857, were still fresh. For example, referring to Buchanan, Lincoln says: "And now, in his first annual message, he urges the acceptance of the Lecompton constitution." The annual message was read to Congress on December 8. But it was Buchanan's special message of February 2, 1858, submitting the constitution for approval, which set off the real legislative battle, and Lincoln does not mention it at all. Then there is the attention that Lincoln devotes to a bill sponsored by Douglas in the Senate. This measure, authorizing the people of Kansas to frame another constitution, was introduced on December 18 and quickly buried in committee. It remained a subject of public interest for no more than a few weeks. Yet Lincoln treats it as a live issue and gives it his endorsement. Furthermore, at one point he uses the words "last year" in what is obviously a discussion of the campaign of 1856. These and other clues lead to the conclusion that the House-Divided fragment was probably written during the last ten days of December, 1857.[60] And it was on December 28, significantly, that Lincoln sent off a fretful letter to Lyman Trumbull in Washington. "What does the New-York *Tribune* mean by it's constant eulogising, and admiring, and magnifying of Douglas?" he demanded. "Does it, in this, speak the sentiments of the republicans at Washington? Have they concluded that the republican cause, generally, can be best promoted by sacrificing us here in Illinois?"[61]

If Lincoln drafted the House-Divided fragment with the intention of using it immediately in a public address, there is no record of his doing so. Perhaps, in anticipation of a strenuous campaign, he was beginning to put thoughts down on paper—even as he was working hard to make money at his law practice for expenditure in the months ahead. In any case, there can be little doubt that his composition of the fragment was provoked by the signs of Republican infatuation with Douglas, and that it was a preliminary draft of the speech he delivered the following June.

The first and major part of the fragment is a vigorous argument against Republican coalition with Douglas on his terms. It is thus analogous to the third—or "living-dog"—section of the House-Divided speech. Lincoln warns that if the Republicans drop their own organization and "fall in" with Douglas, they may end up "haltered and harnessed," ready to be "handed over by him to the regular Democracy, to filibuster indefinitely for additional slave territory—to carry slavery into all the States, as well as Territories, under the Dred Scott decision, construed and enlarged from time to time." After several more pages of attack upon "Nebraskaism" and its author, he broadens the scope of his argument with the assertion that "Kansas is neither the whole nor a tithe of the real question." Then follows this passage:

> *A house divided against itself cannot stand.*[62]
>
> I believe the government cannot endure permanently half slave and half free. I expressed this belief a year ago; and subsequent developments have but confirmed me. I do not expect the Union to be dissolved. I do not expect the house to fall; but I do expect it will cease to be divided. It will become all one thing or all the other. Either the opponents of slavery will arrest the further spread of it, and put it in course of ultimate extinction; or its advocates will push it forward till it shall become alike lawful in all the States, old as well as new. Do you doubt it? Study the Dred Scott decision, and then see how little even now remains to be done.

The eye-catching clause, "I expressed this belief a year ago," loses most of its mystery when a proper date is assigned to the fragment. Lincoln is almost certainly referring to his use of the house-divided doctrine during the campaign of 1856, thereby lending support to Dickey's account of the Bloomington incident.[63]

In the final pages of the manuscript, Lincoln briefly discusses the ominous implications of the Dred Scott decision and the dangerous futility of a "don't-care" attitude. "Welcome, or unwelcome, agreeable or disagreeable," he declares, "whether this shall be an entire slave nation, *is* the issue before us. Every incident—every little shifting of scenes or of actors—only clears away the intervening trash, compacts and consolidates the opposing hosts, and brings them more and more distinctly face to face." The conflict, he concludes, will be severe, and it will be fought through by "those who *do* care for the result." But victory can be won, under the Constitution, with "peaceful ballots," rather than "bloody bullets."

Verbally, the House-Divided fragment bears only an occasional resemblance to the House-Divided speech, but in substance the two documents are remarkably similar. The fragment, like the finished speech, may be divided into three parts: the rejection of Douglas (constituting approximately 72 percent of the whole), the house-divided passage (5 percent), and a conclusion which contains the core of the conspiracy theory (23 percent). If, then, there was a continuity between the fragment and the House-Divided speech, it is obvious that between December and June, Lincoln shortened the first section and moved it to the end of the address. At the same time, he greatly expanded the conspiracy argument. Various reasons for these modifications might be suggested,[64] but fundamentally they appear to reflect the changing political situation. With each passing month, the possibility of a permanent alliance between Douglas and the Republican party became more remote, but the danger of losing potential

Republican votes to his magnetic leadership and plausible doctrine remained as serious as ever. Lincoln was shifting his emphasis to meet the needs of the hour. The draft prepared in December is highly revealing as a stage in the development of Lincoln's thought, and it tends to reinforce certain conclusions already advanced, namely, that the different parts of the House-Divided speech were intimately related to one another and constituted a cohesive whole; that the speech was a direct response to the peculiar political conditions created by the revolt of Douglas; and that it was written not only as a statement of principle, but with a practical purpose in mind.

The speech itself represents one of those moments of synthesis which embody the past and illumine the future. Lincoln, who revered his country's historical tradition, believed that the cause he embraced pointed the way to a fuller realization of the ideals upon which the republic had been founded. Enjoying an advantage which accrues especially to founders of new political movements, he experienced little difficulty in squaring his partisan commitments with his moral convictions. He was confronted with no painful choice between expediency and principle.

At the level of practical politics, Lincoln was defending his own candidacy for the Senate and trying to save his party from disintegration. He never doubted that the decision to oppose Douglas in Illinois had been absolutely crucial. Speaking in Chicago on March 1, 1859, he said: "If we, the Republicans of this State, had made Judge Douglas our candidate for the Senate of the United States last year and had elected him, there would to-day be no Republican party in this Union."[65] And he continued to issue warnings against "the temptation to lower the Republican Standard in order to gather recruits."[66]

But if Lincoln had satisfied himself that his personal ambition accorded with the welfare of his party, he seems to have been equally certain that nothing other than unadulterated Republicanism could rescue the nation from the peril into which it had fallen. Although his language in the House-Divided speech contained echoes of old-line abolitionism, he was adapting Garrisonian rhetoric to a more conservative purpose. In his view, the Republican program offered the only solution to the problems of slavery and sectionalism because it alone recognized the tension between moral conviction and constitutional guarantees, and yielded as much to either as the other would allow. Douglas insisted, to be sure, that the concept of ultimate extinction conflicted with the promise not to attack slavery in the southern states.[67] And so it did, from the viewpoint of 1858. To Lincoln, however, the two propositions were like lines extending into the future, seemingly parallel, but capable of being brought together gradually and gently. Convinced that slavery was wrong, yet willing to settle for a promise of ultimate extinction, he believed that an established policy of restriction would incorporate that promise and bring peace to the nation.

It is at this point that his argument becomes, in retrospect, especially vulnerable. The house-divided doctrine was essentially an effort to polarize public opinion and elicit a clear-cut decision upon the most critical aspects of the slavery issue. Lincoln maintained that such a decision would terminate controversy and terminate it peaceably. He assumed, in other words, that the South would acquiesce in a Republican accession to power. But events soon proved that he had misread the southern mind and seriously underestimated the threat of disunion.

Yet it is unlikely that even a revelation of the future would have changed Lincoln's thinking. Civil war was not, in his opinion, the worst disaster that could befall the American people. Behind his expectation that the South *would* submit to a verdict at the polls was a conviction that it *must* submit; for if majority rule, based on popular elections and bounded by constitutional restraints, could be set aside at the will of a dissatisfied minority, what remained of democratic government?[68] Furthermore, Lincoln had constructed his political philosophy upon the belief that public policy should reflect an ethical purpose which was not itself subject to the daily barter of politics. "Important principles," he said, in the last speech of his life, "may, and must, be inflexible."[69] These words were, in a sense, his final postscript to the House-Divided speech.

NOTES

1. Roy P. Basler (ed.), *The Collected Works of Abraham Lincoln* (9 vols., New Brunswick, 1953–1955), II, 522, 528–32.
2. George H. Haynes, *The Senate of the United States: Its History and Practice* (2 vols., Boston, 1935), I, 99. The uniqueness of the 1858 campaign in Illinois was noted by many contemporaries. Perhaps the most extravagant criticism came from the Philadelphia *Pennsylvanian,* which denounced the Lincoln-Douglas contest as a "revolutionary" invasion of state sovereignty and a "dangerous precedent." Quoted in Springfield *Illinois State Register,* November 13, 1858. See also Springfield (Mass.) *Republican,* September 7, 1858 and Boston *Daily Advertiser,* November 6, 1858 (quoted in Washington *National Intelligencer,* November 9, 1858).
3. Horace Greeley, *Recollections of a Busy Life* (New York, 1868), 357–58; New York *Tribune,* March 3, May 4, 11, 27, 1858; Greeley to Schuyler Colfax, March 15, May 6, 12, June 2, 14, 1858, Greeley-Colfax Correspondence (New York Public Library); New York *Times,* April 15, May 10, 1858; Albany *Journal,* May 15, 1858; Springfield *Republican,* April 30, 1858; "Mr. Buchanan's Administration," *Atlantic Monthly* (Boston), I (April, 1858), 756–57.
4. Lyman Trumbull to Lincoln, January 3, 1858, Robert Todd Lincoln Collection (Manuscript Division, Library of Congress); Ovando J. Hollister, *Life of Schuyler Colfax* (New York, 1886), 119, 121; Henry Wilson, *History of the Rise and Fall of the Slave Power in America* (3 vols., Boston, 1872–1877), II, 567. It was widely rumored and believed that Douglas and Seward had concluded a secret agreement looking toward

the former's re-election to the Senate and the latter's succession to the presidency in 1860. See, for example, New York *Herald*, April 6, 13, November 20, 1858.

5. Jesse K. Dubois to Trumbull, April 8, 1858, Lyman Trumbull Papers (Manuscript Division, Library of Congress).

6. Chicago *Journal*, April 15, 24, May 4, 19, 1858; Ottawa *Republican*, April 24, 1858; Springfield *Illinois State Journal*, May 17, 20, 1858. See also Chicago *Tribune*, April 21, June 15, 1858; *Bureau County Republican* (Princeton, 111), April 22, May 6, 1858; Dixon *Republican and Telegraph*, May 20, 27, 1858; Alton *Weekly Courier*, May 27, 1858; Norman B. Judd to Trumbull, March 7, 1858, Trumbull Papers; John H. Bryant to Lincoln, April 19, 1858, Robert Todd Lincoln Collection. The Chicago *Journal* of May 20 printed clippings from many Illinois newspapers denouncing eastern intervention on behalf of Douglas. Various letters in the Stephen A. Douglas Papers (University of Chicago), and in other contemporary correspondence, indicate that there was some movement toward Douglas among rank-and-file Republicans in the state. Party leaders, however, presented an almost solid front against him.

7. The Chicago *Tribune* of June 14, 1858, asserted that resolutions for Lincoln were passed in 95 out of 100 counties, but a sampling of convention proceedings as published in various newspapers indicates that this was something of an overstatement.

8. There was an added complication in the figure of John Wentworth, antislavery editor, former congressman, and recently mayor of Chicago. Various Democratic newspapers in the state had repeatedly asserted that Wentworth was using Lincoln as his stalking-horse and would eventually emerge as the real Republican candidate for the Senate. This story, although palpably untrue, was damaging to the Republican cause and offered a second reason for nominating Lincoln. See, Don E. Fehrenbacher, *Chicago Giant: A Biography of "Long John" Wentworth* (Madison, 1957), 157–59.

9. This and all other quotations from the speech are taken from Basler (ed.), *Collected Works of Lincoln*, II, 461–69.

10. Paul M. Angle (ed.), *Herndon's Life of Lincoln* (Cleveland, 1949), 326. Herndon's recollection that he was the only man to respond favorably is supported by the testimony of others who were present, but one may be permitted to doubt that he actually predicted: "Lincoln, deliver that speech as read and it will make you President." See David Donald, *Lincoln's Herndon* (New York, 1948), 118, 119n.

11. John L. Scripps to Lincoln, June 22, 1858, Robert Todd Lincoln Collection.

12. Leonard Swett to Herndon, July 17, 1866, published in Emanuel, Hertz (ed.), *The Hidden Lincoln* (2nd ed., New York, 1940), 295–302.

13. Angle (ed.), *Herndon's Lincoln*, 324–26. In reconstructing Lincoln's words, Herndon drew upon his own memory and upon that of John Armstrong, a local Republican leader in Springfield who was apparently present at the pre-convention reading of the speech. Herndon's interview with Armstrong in 1870 is in the Ward Hill Lamon Papers (Henry E. Huntington Library). In another account of the meeting written many years later by William Jayne (brother-in-law of Lyman Trumbull), Lincoln is made to appear even more dedicated and pompous. He responds to the protests against the speech by reciting six verses from a poem by Bryant, quoting the Apostle Paul, and pointing to the example of Martin Luther. William Jayne, *Abraham Lincoln: Personal Reminiscences of the Martyred President* (Chicago, 1908), 38–42.

14. Allan Nevins, *The Emergence of Lincoln* (2 vols., New York, 1950), 1,360.

15. Lincoln, when urged by advisers not to ask his celebrated second question, is quoted as replying: "I am after bigger game. The battle of 1860 is worth a hundred of this." The earliest source for this remark appears to be the campaign biography by John L. Scripps, *Life of Abraham Lincoln* (Chicago, 1860), 28.

16. Albert J. Beveridge, *Abraham Lincoln, 1809–1858* (2 vols., Boston, 1928), II, 585. On another page (II, 656), Beveridge takes a dim view of efforts to endow Lincoln with "superhuman foresight" in 1858, but here (II, 585 n.) he cites as his only authority a naked assertion by Henry Clay Whitney: "While...his political friends were train

him for the Senate, he was coaching himself for the Presidency, two years thereafter."

17. Richard Hofstadter, *The American Political Tradition and the Men Who Made It* (New York, 1948), 114 n. Hofstadter reinforces this particular statement with a yarn from the pen of Joseph Medill. In 1862, Medill allegedly asked Lincoln why he had delivered "that radical speech" back in 1858, and Lincoln allegedly replied: "Well, after you fellows had got me into that mess and begun tempting me with offers of the Presidency, I began to think and I made up my mind that the next President of the United States would need to have a stronger anti-slavery platform than mine. So I concluded to say something." Unless Lincoln uttered these words in jest, the whole story is absurd.

18. Harry E. Pratt, *The Great Debates* (Springfield, Ill., 1956), *passim*, reprinted from *Illinois Blue Book*, 1953–1954 (Springfield, 1955).

19. Basler (ed.), *Collected Works*, 11,476–81.

20. "If we could first know *where* we are, and *whither* we are tending," Lincoln began, "we could then better judge *what* to do, and *how* to do it." This was a terse paraphrase of the opening sentence in Webster's reply to Hayne. Near the end of his speech, Lincoln also borrowed from Webster's peroration when he described the Democrats as "wavering, disseuered and belligerent."

21. Numbers and letters are added to facilitate subsequent references to the passage.

22. Basler (ed.), *Collected Works*, III, 8, 111; Joseph Fort Newton, *Lincoln and Herndon* (Cedar Rapids, 1910), 173.

23. Several times during the debates with Douglas, Lincoln made it plain that he expected the slavery controversy to be settled peaceably. "There will be no war, no violence," he assured his audience at Alton. Basler (ed.), *Collected Works*, III, 316.

24. Ibid., II, 491.

25. "But the Union, in any event, won't be dissolved," Lincoln had declared in a speech at Galena during the campaign of 1856. "We don't want to dissolve it, and if you attempt it *we won't let you.*" Ibid., II, 355.

26. Nevins, *Emergence of Lincoln*, I, 359, 361.

27. Basler (ed.), *Collected Works*, II, 471.

28. Ibid., III, 18. See also his statements at Jonesboro, Charleston, Quincy, and Alton, *ibid.*, III, 117, 180–81,276,306–308.

29. Ibid., III, 18, 92–93, 181.

30. Ibid., III, 78. These words are from the newspaper report of a speech that Lincoln delivered at Carlinville, Illinois, on August 31, 1858, but he identified his own views with those of the "fathers of the republic" in his speech at Peoria in 1854, and many times thereafter. See *ibid.*, II, 274, 276, 501, 513, 520–21; III, 18, 87, 92–93, 117–18, 181, 76, 306–308, 333, 484, 488, 489, 496, 498, 535, 537–38, 550, 551, 553; IV, 17–18, 21–22.

31. Ibid., 11, 498; 111, 92–93, 254–55, 312–13.

32. Seward's remark, made on the floor of the Senate, is in *Congressional Globe, 35* Cong., 1 Sess., 521 (February 2,1858). The New York *Times,* March 1, 1858, said that the statement "substantially dissolved" the loose alliance constituting the Republican party. The Chicago *Democratic Press,* March 9, 1858, carried an angry reply to the *Times.* For the drift of an important Republican editor toward Douglas and popular sovereignty, see George S. Merriam, *The Life and Times of Samuel Bowles* (2 vols., New York, 1885), I, 242. Lincoln's apprehensions were greatly augmented by a report from his law partner. Herndon, after visiting Washington, New York, and Boston in the spring of 1858, returned home fully convinced that a group headed by Greeley was plotting to lower the party platform so that Douglas could climb onto it. See Donald, *Lincoln's Herndon,* 114–17; Newton, *Lincoln and Herndon,* 153, 203, 209, 215–16, 219, 241–42, 245–47.

33. The historical viewpoint which holds that slavery was actually a relatively minor problem, inflated to dangerous proportions by fanatical minorities in both sections, is

a product of this same concentration upon the territorial aspects of the issue. Douglas, not surprisingly, usually fares extremely well in such interpretations.

34. For Lincoln's opinion that Kansas constituted hardly "a tithe" of the whole problem, see discussion of the "House-Divided fragment" below. In a speech to Chicago Republicans on March 1, 1859, he said: "Never forget that we have before us this whole matter of the right or wrong of slavery in this Union, though the immediate question is as to its spreading out into new Territories and States." Basler (ed.), *Collected Works*, III, 369.

35. Lincoln was by no means the first person to voice this fear, which was a part of the general Republican reaction to the Dred Scott decision. On March 10, 1857, for example, the Bloomington *Pantagraph* warned: "One little step only remains, to decide all *State* prohibitions of Slavery to be void."

36. Nevins, *Emergence of Lincoln*, I, 361–63; James G. Randall, *Lincoln the President: Springfield to Gettysburg* (2 vols., New York, 1945.1946), I, 107–108.

37. Nevins, *Emergence of Lincoln*, I, 362.

38. Basler (ed.), *Collected Works*, II, 521; III, 20–22, 27–30, 232–33. For an elaborate and persuasive defense of Lincoln's argument that there was a legal and political tendency toward the nationalization of slavery, see Harry V. Jaffa, *Crisis of the House Divided: An Interpretation of the Issues in the Lincoln-Douglas Debates* (New York, 1959), Chapters XI and XII. Professor Jaffa's book appeared after this article was written and submitted.

39. *Cong. Globe*, 35 Cong., 1 Sess., 18 (December 9, 1857). This remark, which Republicans lifted from context and quoted repeatedly, was directed specifically at the slavery clause of the Lecompton constitution, due to be submitted to the voters of Kansas on December 21. Douglas was merely announcing his opposition to the constitution no matter which way the vote went on the clause. Nevertheless, Lincoln believed that the phrase was an accurate summary of popular sovereignty, which, he said, "acknowledges that slavery has equal rights with liberty." Basler (ed.), *Collected Works*, IV, 155.

40. Basler (ed.), *Collected Works*, III, 29–30, 233, 316, 369, 404–405, 442, 469; IV, 5, 20–21.

41. These words, which so crisply sum up Lincoln's view of the Douglas doctrine, are from the Cooper Institute address of February 27, 1860. Such "sophistical contrivances," Lincoln said, were as "vain as the search for a man who should be neither a living man nor a dead man." *Ibid.*, III, 550.

42. Herndon to Jesse W. Weik, October 29, 1885, Herndon-Weik Collection (Manuscript Division, Library of Congress).

43. Arthur C. Cole, *Lincoln's "House Divided" Speech: Did It Reflect a Doctrine of Class Struggle?* (Chicago, 1923), an address delivered before the Chicago Historical Society, March 15, 1923, and published as a pamphlet.

44. Cole, *Lincoln's "House Divided" Speech*, 11.

45. *Ibid.*, 11–30.

46. Notably, in his eulogy of Henry Clay on July 6, 1852, in his Peoria speech of October 16, 1854, and in his speech at a Republican banquet in Chicago on December 10, 1856. Also, the brief newspaper report of his famous "lost speech" at the Bloomington convention on May 29, 1856, reports him as saying: "The sentiment in favor of white slavery now prevailed in all the slave state papers, except those of Kentucky, Tennessee and Missouri and Maryland." Basler (ed.), *Collected Works*, II, 130, 255, 275–76, 341, 385.

47. Cole, *Lincoln's "House Divided" Speech*, 14, 34.

48. *Ibid.*, 15, 34. Cole's study obviously influenced Hofstadter, *American Political Tradition*, 109–19. Here Lincoln is presented as a man "never much troubled about the Negro," who exploited the race prejudice of his constituents and whose assertion that slavery might become national was "a clever dialectical inversion" of Fitzhugh's challenge to the freedom of the white man. Hofstadter's influence, in turn, has been extensive. It is acknowledged, for example, by Daniel J. Boorstin in *The Genius of American Politics* (Chicago, 1953), 113–14, where Lincoln's opposition to the extension of slavery is

attributed primarily to his concern for the welfare of the white workingman. For criticism of the Hofstadter interpretation, see Jaffa, *Crisis of the House Divided*, 363–81.

49. Basler (ed.), *Collected Works*, II, 514.

50. Ibid., II, 255.

51. Ibid., II, 318.

52. Ibid., III, 431, 451 ; IV, 6–7, 23. Lincoln repeatedly cited the Richmond *Enquirer*'s use of the concept in 1856, but he also asserted that "almost every good man" since the formation of the government had uttered the same sentiment, including Washington, Jefferson, Jay, and Monroe. Prudently, he neglected to add that the idea of the incompatibility of slavery and freedom, together with the theory of a great slave power conspiracy, had long been a stock-in-trade of the abolitionists. See Russel B. Nye, *Fettered Freedom: Civil Liberties and the Slavery Controversy, 1830–1860* (East Lansing, 1949), 217–49. But it was the logic of events, not the example of northern and southern extremists, which brought Lincoln to a similar belief

53. See especially his form letter to Fillmore men in Basler (ed.), *Collected Works*, II, 374. This letter, it should be noted, was dated September 8, 1856, only four days before the Bloomington speech discussed below.

54. T. Lyle Dickey to Herndon, December 8, 1866, Herndon-Weik Collection. Dickey told substantially the same story in a letter to Isaac N. Arnold, February 7, 1883, Isaac N. Arnold Papers (Chicago Historical Society). Herndon included the incident in his biography, but said only that it took place "at Bloomington in 1856." Angle (ed.), *Herndon's Lincoln*, 325–26. This may have led some of his readers to connect the incident with the Republican convention at Bloomington on May 29, 1856, thus contributing to the development of a tradition that Lincoln used the house-divided doctrine in his famous "lost speech." The error may have begun with Ward H. Lamon, *The Life of Abraham Lincoln* (Boston, 1872), 398. The manuscript of Dickey's letter to Herndon removes all doubt. It states that the speech was given at "a political meeting" held in the evening of "some day in September or October of 1856."

55. Basler (ed.), *Collected Works*, II, 375.

56. Henry B. Rankin, in his *Personal Recollections of Abraham Lincoln* (New York, 1916), 235–36, asserted that Lincoln used the house-divided doctrine in a speech at Petersburg on August 30, 1856. He, too, misinterpreted Dickey's story as a reference to the Bloomington convention of May 29 (See note 54 above), and thus concluded, mistakenly, that in uttering the doctrine at Petersburg, Lincoln broke his promise to Dickey. Rankin's statement, published sixty years after the event, is of dubious value but perhaps adds something to the credibility of Dickey's recollection. Petersburg, it may be noted, was also in the heart of old Whig territory, and the newspaper account of Lincoln's speech shows him making an appeal to the Fillmore supporters. Basler (ed.), *Collected Works*, II, 366–68.

57. The editors of the *Collected Works* maintain that Lincoln's belief in the house-divided doctrine was "implicit" in his 1857 Springfield speech (II, 452 n.), but this is true only in so far as the belief was implicit in everything he was saying and doing by that time. The striking thing about the 1857 speech is the absence of any *explicit* reference to the ideas and arguments that dominated the House-Divided address.

58. John G. Nicolay and John Hay (eds.), *Abraham Lincoln: Complete Works* (2 vols., New York, 1894), I, 422–27. It seems likely that Nicolay and Hay were influenced in their selection of this date by the location of the manuscript in Lincoln's files. Since they used it, the manuscript itself has disappeared, except for the final page, which is in the Pierpont Morgan Library, New York City. The Morgan Library associates two other pages of manuscript with this page, but there is apparently no convincing reason for doing so. See Basler (ed.), *Collected Works*, II, 552–53.

59. The fragment appears in Basler (ed.), *Collected Works*, II, 448–54. All quotations from the fragment are taken from this source. The editors followed Nicolay and Hay and the page of manuscript in the Pierpont Morgan Library. The date which they

assign obviously takes into account Herndon's statement that Lincoln spent about one month writing the House-Divided speech (See note 42 above). They suggest May 18 specifically because on that day Lincoln delivered a speech at Edwardsville; but there is apparently no evidence of any kind linking the fragment with that speech. On the other hand, the contents of the fragment indicate beyond any doubt that it was written much earlier. For instance, Lincoln discusses the question of "whether the Lecompton constitution should be accepted or rejected" by Congress. But the Lecompton bill was, in effect, defeated on April 1 in the House, and the chief topic of public discussion in the latter part of April was the substitute English bill. This measure, which is not mentioned in the fragment, became law several weeks before, May 18.

60. The early part of January, 1858, should perhaps be included as a possibility because Lincoln speaks of "having seen the noses counted, and actually knowing that a major-ity of the people of Kansas are against slavery." This could be a reference to the Kansas election of January 4. However, the first clear proof of a free-state majority in Kansas had been furnished by the territorial elections of October 5, 1857, and it was probably this event that Lincoln had in mind.

61. Basler (ed.), *Collected Works*, II, 430

62. This is Lincoln's first recorded use of the biblical quotation in connection with the sectional controversy. In 1843, he and two other Whig leaders had quoted it in a circular pleading for party unity. Basler (ed.), *Collected Works*, I, 315. By 1858, the sentence had been used so often in one context or another that it was almost a cliché. Beveridge, *Abraham Lincoln*, II, 575 n., gives several examples. Others will be found in *Northwestern Christian Advocate* (Chicago), March 29, 1854; G. D. Jaquess to John J. Crittenden, March 1, 1858, John J. Crittenden Papers (Manuscript Division, Library of Congress); Chicago *Tribune*, March 22, 1858; New York *Herald*, June 8, 1858.

63. This clause, which is the only clue to the date of the fragment in its later pages, tends to justify the belief that all parts of the manuscript were written at about the same time and that it is indeed to be regarded as a single document. The belief is strengthened by the logical coherence of Lincoln's argument and by the fact that Nicolay and Hay, who presumably had the entire manuscript in their hands, came to the same conclusion.

64. Cole, *Lincoln's "House Divided" Speech*, 33, suggests that Lincoln was influenced by editorials in the Mattoon *National Gazette* advocating the legalization of slavery in Illinois. He was probably even more impressed by the widely-discussed decision of the California Supreme Court on February 11, 1858, in the case of the slave Archy, who was held to be still the property of his master even though the latter had settled down to more or less permanent residence in the state (Sacramento *Union*, February 12, 1858). Also, since Lincoln usually kept a watchful eye upon proceedings in Congress, he may have drawn inspiration from a speech enunciating the conspiracy theory which was delivered in the Senate on February 8, 1858, by William Po Fessenden of Maine (*Congo Globe*, 35 Congo, 1 Sess., 617).

65. Basler (ed.), *Collected Works*, III, 367.

66. Ibid., III, 379.

67. Ibid., III, 265–66, 323.

68. This question, implicit in Lincoln's approach to the sectional controversy by 1858, was forcefully posed in his First Inaugural address. *Ibid.*, iv, 267–68.

69. Ibid., viii, 405.

8

WHY THE REPUBLICANS REJECTED BOTH COMPROMISE AND SECESSION

David M. Potter

Historians have a habit of explaining the important decisions of the past in terms of principles. On this basis, it is easy to say that the Republicans rejected compromise because they were committed to the principle of antislavery and that they rejected secession because they were committed to the principle of union. But in the realities of the historical past, principles frequently come into conflict with other principles, and those who make decisions have to choose which principle shall take precedence. When principles thus conflict, as they frequently do, it is meaningless to show merely that a person or a group favors a given principle: the operative question is what priority they give to it. For instance, before the secession crisis arose, there were many Northerners who believed in both the principle of antislavery and the principle of union, but who differed in the priority which they would give to one or the other: William Lloyd Garrison gave the priority to antislavery and proclaimed that there should be "no union with slaveholders." Abraham Lincoln gave, or seemed to give, the priority to union and during the war wrote the famous letter to Horace Greeley in which he said: "My paramount object is to save the

Union and it is not either to save or to destroy slavery. What I do about slavery and the colored race, I do because I believe it helps to save the Union, and what I forbear, I forbear because I do not believe it would help to save the Union." Lincoln was always precise to almost a unique degree in his statements, and it is interesting to note that he did not say that it was not his object to destroy slavery; what he said was that it was not his paramount object—he did not give it the highest priority.

To state this point in another way, if we made an analysis of the moderate Republicans and of the abolitionists solely in terms of their principles, we would hardly be able to distinguish between them, for both were committed to the principle of antislavery and to the principle of union. It was the diversity in the priorities which they gave to these two principles that made them distinctive from each other.

A recognition of the priorities, therefore, may in many cases serve a historian better than a recognition of principles. But while it is important to recognize which principle is, as Lincoln expressed it, paramount, it is no less important to take account of the fact that men do not like to sacrifice one principle for the sake of another and do not even like to recognize that a given situation may require a painful choice between principles. Thus, most Northern antislavery men wanted to solve the slavery question within the framework of union, rather than to reject the Union because it condoned slavery; correspondingly, most Northern Unionists wanted to save the Union while taking steps against slavery, rather than by closing their eyes to the slavery question.

In short, this means—and one could state it almost as an axiom—that men have a tendency to believe that their principles can be reconciled with one another, and that this belief is so strong that it inhibits their recognition of realistic alternatives in cases where the alternatives would involve a choice between cherished principles. This attitude has been clearly defined in the homely phrase that we all like to have our cake and eat it too.

Perhaps all this preliminary consideration of theory seems excessively abstract and you will feel that I ought to get on to the Republicans, the crisis, and the rejection of compromise and secession; but before I do, let me take one more step with my theory. If the participants in a historical situation tend to see the alternatives in that situation as less clear, less sharply focused than they really are, historians probably tend to see the alternatives as more clear, more evident, more sharply focused than they really were. We see the alternatives as clear because we have what we foolishly believe to be the advantage of hindsight—which is really a disadvantage in understanding how a situation seemed to the participants. We know, in short, that the Republicans did reject both compromise and secession (I will return to the details of this rejection later) and that the four-year conflict known as the Civil War eventuated. We therefore tend to think not only that conflict of some kind was the alternative to the acceptance of compromise or the acquiescence in secession, but actually that this particular war—with all its costs, its sacrifices, and its consequences—was the alternative. When men choose a course of action which had a given result, historians will tend to attribute to them not only the choice of the course, but even the choice of the result. Yet one needs only to state this tendency clearly in order to demonstrate the fallacy in it. Whatever choice anyone exercised in 1860–61, no one chose the American Civil War, because it lay behind the veil of the future; it did not exist as a choice.

Hindsight not only enables historians to define the alternatives in the deceptively clear terms of later events; it also gives them a deceptively clear criterion for evaluating the alternatives, which is in terms of later results. That is, we now know that the war did result in the preservation of the Union and in the abolition of chattel slavery. Accordingly, it is easy, with hindsight, to attribute to the participants not only a decision to accept the alternative of a war whose magnitude they could not know, but also to credit them with choosing results which they could not foresee. The war, as it developed, certainly might have ended in the quicker defeat of the Southern movement, in which case emancipation would apparently not have resulted; or it might have ended in the independence of the Southern Confederacy, in which case the Monday morning quarterbacks of the historical profession would have been in the position of saying that the rash choice of a violent and coercive course had destroyed the possibility of a harmonious, voluntary restoration of the Union—a restoration of the kind which William H. Seward was trying to bring about.

I suppose all this is only equivalent to saying that the supreme task of the historian, and the one of most superlative difficulty, is to see the past through the imperfect eyes of those who lived it and not with his own omniscient twenty-twenty vision. I am not suggesting that any of us can really do this, but only that it is what we must attempt.

What do we mean, specifically, by saying that the Republican party rejected compromise? Certain facts are reasonably familiar in this connection, and may be briefly recalled. In December, 1860, at the time when a number of secession conventions had been called in the Southern states but before any ordinances of secession had been adopted, various political leaders brought forward proposals to give assurances to the Southerners. The most prominent of these was the plan by Senator John J. Crittenden of Kentucky to place an amendment in the Constitution which would restore and extend the former Missouri Compromise line of

36° 30', prohibiting slavery in Federal territory north of the line and sanctioning it south of the line. In a Senate committee, this proposal was defeated with five Republicans voting against it and none in favor of it, while the non-Republicans favored it six to two. On January 16, after four states had adopted ordinances of secession, an effort was made to get the Crittenden measure out of committee and on to the floor of the Senate. This effort was defeated by 25 votes against to 23 in favor. This was done on a strict party vote, all 25 of the votes to defeat being cast by Republicans. None of those in favor were Republicans. On March 2, after the secession of the lower South was complete, the Crittenden proposal was permitted to come to a vote. In the Senate, it was defeated 19 to 20. All 20 of the negative votes were Republican, not one of the affirmative votes was so. In the House, it was defeated 80 to 113. Not one of the 80 was a Republican, but 110 of the 113 were Republicans.

Another significant measure of the secession winter was a proposal to amend the Constitution to guarantee the institution of slavery in the states. This proposed amendment—ironically designated by the same number as the one which later freed the slaves—was actually adopted by Congress, in the House by a vote of 128 to 65, but with 44 Republicans in favor and 62 opposed; in the Senate by a vote of 24 to 12, but with 8 Republicans in favor and 12 opposed.

While opposing these measures, certain Republicans, including Charles Francis Adams, brought forward a bill to admit New Mexico to statehood without restrictions on slavery, and they regarded this as a compromise proposal. But this measure was tabled in the House, 115 to 71, with Republicans casting 76 votes to table and 26 to keep the bill alive. Thus, it can be said, without qualification, that between December and March, no piece of compromise legislation was ever supported by a majority of Republican votes, either in the Senate or the House, either in committee or on the floor. This, of course, does not mean either that they ought to have supported the measures in question, or that such measures would have satisfied the Southern states. It is my own belief that the balance between the secessionist and the non-secessionist forces was fairly close in all of the seceding states except South Carolina, and that the support of Congress for a compromise would have been enough to tip the balance. But the Crittenden measure would possibly have opened the way for Southern filibustering activities to enlarge the territorial area south of 36° 30'—at least this was apparently what Lincoln feared—and the "thirteenth" amendment would have saddled the country with slavery more or less permanently. When we say, then, that the Republicans rejected compromise, we should take care to mean no more than we say. They did, by their votes, cause the defeat of measures which would otherwise have been adopted by Congress, which were intended and generally regarded as compromise measures. In this sense, they rejected compromise.

When we say the Republican party rejected secession, the case is so clear that it hardly needs a recital of proof. It is true that at one stage of the crisis, many Republicans did talk about letting the slave states go. Horace Greeley wrote his famous, ambiguous, oft quoted, and much misunderstood editorial saying that "if the cotton states shall become satisfied that they can do better out of the Union than in it, we insist on letting them go in peace." Later, when the situation at Fort Sumter had reached its highest tension, a number of Republicans, including Salmon P. Chase, Simon Cameron, Gideon Welles, and Caleb Smith, all in the cabinet, advised Lincoln to evacuate the fort rather than precipitate hostilities; but this hardly means that they would not have made the issue of union in some other way. Lincoln himself definitively rejected secession in his inaugural address when he declared: "No state upon its own mere motion can lawfully get out of the Union. . . . I . . . consider that in view of, the Constitution and the laws, the Union are unbroken; and to the extent of my ability I shall take care, as the Constitution itself expressly enjoins upon me, that the laws of the Union be faithfully executed in all the States." After the fall of Fort Sumter, he translated this affirmation into action by calling for 75,000 volunteers, and by preparing to use large-scale military measures to hold the South in the Union. The fact that no major figure in the North, either Republican or Democrat, ever proposed to acquiesce in the rending of the Union and that no proposal to do so was ever seriously advocated or voted upon in Congress, is evidence enough that the Republicans rejected secession even more decisively than they rejected compromise. They scarcely even felt the need to consider the question or to make an organized presentation of their reasons. It is true that some of them said that they would rather have disunion than compromise, but this was a way of saying how much they objected to compromise, and not how little they objected to separation. It was almost exactly equivalent to the expression, "Death rather than dishonor," which has never been understood to mean an acceptance of death, but rather an adamant rejection of dishonor.

Here, then, in briefest outline is the record of the Republican rejection of compromise and of secession. What we are concerned with, however, is not the mere fact of the rejection, but rather with its meaning. Why did the Republicans do this? What was their motivation? What did they think would follow from their decision? What did they believe the alternatives to be? Specifically, did this mean that the choice as they saw it was clear-cut, and that they conceived of themselves as opting in favor of war in a situation where they had a choice between secession and war? As I come to this question, I must revert to my comments earlier in this paper by pointing out again the tendency of historians to see the alternatives with preternatural clarity and the fallacy involved in attributing to the participants a capacity to define the alternatives in the same crystalline terms.

Peace or war? Compromise or conflict? Separation or coercion? These alternatives have such a plausible neatness, such a readiness in fitting the historian's pigeon holes, that it is vastly tempting to believe that they define the choices which people were actually making and not just the choices that we think they ought to have been making. We all know, today, that economists once fell into fallacies by postulating an economic man who behaved economically in the way economists thought he ought to behave. But even though we do know this, we are not as wary as we should be of the concept of what might be called an historical man who behaved historically in the way historians thought he ought to have behaved. It is very well for us, a hundred years later, to analyze the record and to say there were three alternatives, as distinct as the three sides of a triangle, namely compromise, voluntary separation, or war. Indeed this analysis may be correct. The error is not in our seeing it this way, but in our supposing that since we do see it in this way, the participants must have seen it in this way also.

Nothing can be more difficult—indeed impossible—than to reconstruct how a complex situation appeared to a varied lot of people, not one of whom saw or felt things in exactly the same way as any other one, a full century ago. But in the effort to approximate these realities as far as we can, it might be useful to begin by asking to what extent the choices of compromise, separation, or war had emerged as the possible alternatives in the minds of the citizens as they faced the crisis. Did they see the Crittenden proposals as embodying a possibility for compromise, and did a vote against these proposals mean an acceptance of the alternatives of war or separation? Did a policy which rejected both compromise and war indicate an acceptance of the alternative of voluntary separation? Did a decision to send food to Sumter and to keep the flag flying mean an acceptance of war? By hindsight, all of these indications appear plausible, and yet on close scrutiny, it may appear that not one of them is tenable in an unqualified way.

Did a vote against the Crittenden proposals indicate a rejection of the possibility of compromise? If Republicans voted against the Crittenden proposals, did this mean that they saw themselves as rejecting the principle of compromise and that they saw the possibilities thereby narrowed to a choice between voluntary separation or fierce, coercive war? If they repelled the idea of voluntary separation, did this imply that they were prepared to face a choice between political compromise or military coercion as the only means of saving the Union? If they urged the administration to send food to the besieged men in Sumter and to keep the flag flying there, did this mean that they had actually accepted the irrepressibility of the irrepressible conflict, and that they regarded peaceable alternatives as exhausted?

Although it makes the task of our analysis considerably more complex to say so, still it behooves us to face the music of confusion and to admit that not one of these acts was necessarily seen by the participants as narrowing the alternatives in the way which our after-the-fact analysis might indicate. To see the force of this reality, it is necessary to look at each of these contingencies in turn.

First, there is the case of those Republicans, including virtually all the Republican members in the Senate or the House, who refused to support the Crittenden proposals. To be sure, these men were accused of sacrificing the Union or of a callous indifference to the hazard of war; and to be sure, there were apparently some men like Zachariah Chandler who actually wanted war. (It was Chandler, you will recall, who said, "Without a little blood-letting, the Union will not be worth a rush.") But there were many who had grown to entertain sincere doubts as to whether the adoption of the Crittenden proposals, or the grant of any other concessions to the South, would actually bring permanent security to the Union. The danger to the Union lay, as they saw it, in the fact that powerful groups in many Southern states believed that any state had an unlimited right to withdraw from the Union and thus disrupt it. Southerners had fallen into the habit of asserting this right whenever they were much dissatisfied and declaring they would exercise it if their demands were not met. They had made such declarations between 1846 and 1850, when the Free-Soilers proposed to exclude slavery from the Mexican Cession. They had done so again in 1850 when they wanted a more stringent fugitive slave law. The threat of secession had been heard once more in 1856 when it appeared that the Republicans might elect a Free-Soiler to the presidency. On each occasion, concessions had been made: the Compromise of 1850 made it legally possible to take slaves to New Mexico; the Compromise also gave the slave owners a fugitive act that was too drastic for their own good; in 1856, timid Union loving Whigs rallied to Buchanan and thus helped to avert the crisis that Fremont's election might have brought. Each such concession, of course, confirmed the Southern fire-eaters in their habit of demanding further concessions, and it strengthened their position with their constituents in the South by enabling them to come home at periodic intervals with new tribute that they had extorted from the Yankees. From the standpoint of a sincere Unionist, there was something self-defeating about getting the Union temporarily past a crisis by making concessions which strengthened the disunionist faction and perpetuated the tendency toward periodic crises. This was a point on which Republicans sometimes expressed themselves very emphatically. For instance, Schuyler Colfax, in 1859, wrote to his mother about conditions in Congress: "We are still just where we started six months ago," he said, "except that our Southern friends have dissolved the Union forty or fifty times since then." In the same vein, Carl Schurz ridiculed the threat of secession, while campaigning for Lincoln in 1860: "There had been two overt attempts at secession already," Schurz was reported as saying, "one the secession of the Southern students from the medical school at Philadelphia... the second upon the election of Speaker Pennington, when the South seceded from Congress, went out, took a drink, and then came back. The third attempt would be," he prophesied, "when Old Abe would be elected. They would then again secede and this time would take two drinks, but would come back again." Schurz's analysis may have been good wit, but of course it was disastrously bad prophesy, and it had the fatal effect of preparing men systematically to misunderstand the signs of danger when these signs appeared. The first signs would be merely the first drink; confirmatory signs would be the second drink. James Buchanan recognized, as early as 1856, that men were beginning to underestimate the danger to the Union simply because it was chronic and they were too familiar with it: "We have so often cried wolf," he said, "that now, when the wolf is at the door it is difficult to make the people believe it." Abraham Lincoln provided a distinguished proof of Buchanan's point in August, 1860, when he wrote: "The people of the South have too much of good sense and good temper to attempt the ruin of the government rather than see it administered as it was administered by the men who made it. At least, so I hope and believe." As usual, Lincoln's statement was a gem of lucidity, even when it was unconsciously so. He hoped and believed. The wish was father to the thought.

The rejection of compromise, then, did not mean an acceptance of separation or war. On the contrary, to men who regarded the threat of secession as a form of political blackmail rather than a genuine indication of danger to the Union, it seemed that danger of disunion could be eliminated only by eliminating the disunionists, and this could never be accomplished by paying them off at regular intervals. The best hope of a peaceful union lay in a development of the strength of Southern Unionists, who would. never gain the ascendancy so long as the secessionists could always get what they demanded. Viewed in this light, compromise might be detrimental to the cause of union; and rejection of compromise might be the best way to avoid the dangers of separation or of having to fight the disunionists.

If the rejection of compromise did not mean the acceptance of either separation or war, did the rejection of separation mean an acceptance of a choice between compromise and coercion as the remaining alternatives? This was the choice which history has seemed to indicate as the real option open to the country. But, though the unfolding of events may subsequently have demonstrated that these were the basic alternatives, one of the dominating facts about the Republicans in the winter of 1860–61 is that they rejected the idea of voluntary disunion and also rejected the idea of compromise, without any feeling that this narrowing of the spectrum would lead them to war. At this juncture, what may be called the illusion of the Southern Unionists played a vital part. Both Lincoln and Seward and many another Republican were convinced that secessionism was a superficial phenomenon. They believed that it did not represent the most fundamental impulses of the South, and that although the Southern Unionists had been silenced by the clamor of the secessionists, a deep vein of Unionist feeling still survived in the South and could be rallied, once the Southern people realized that Lincoln was not an Illinois version of William Lloyd Garrison and that the secessionists had been misleading them. Lincoln and Seward became increasingly receptive to this view during the month before Lincoln's inauguration. Between December 20 and March 4, seven Southern states had held conventions, and each of these conventions had adopted an ordinance of secession. But on February 4, the secessionists were defeated in the election for the Virginia convention. Within four weeks thereafter, they were again defeated in Tennessee, where the people refused even to call a convention; in Arkansas, where the secessionist candidates for a state convention were defeated; in Missouri, where the people elected a convention so strongly anti-secessionist that it voted 89 to 1 against disunion; and in North Carolina, where anti-secessionist majorities were elected and it was voted that the convention should not meet.

It clearly looked as though the tide of secession had already turned. Certainly, at the time when Lincoln came to the presidency, the movement for a united South had failed. There were, altogether, fifteen slave states. Seven of these, from South Carolina, along the south Atlantic and Gulf coast to Texas, had seceded; but eight others, including Delaware, Kentucky, and Maryland, as well as the five that I have already named, were still in the Union and clearly intended to remain there. In these circumstances, the New York *Tribune* could speak of the Confederacy as a "heptarchy," and Seward could rejoice, as Henry Adams reported, that "this was only a temporary fever and now it has reached the climax and favorably passed it." The Southern Unionists were already asserting themselves, and faith in them was justified. Thus, on his way east from Springfield, Lincoln stated in a speech at Steubenville, Ohio, that "the devotion to the Constitution is equally great on both sides of the [Ohio] River." From this it seemed to follow that, as he also said on his trip, "there is no crisis but an artificial one.... Let it alone and it will go down of itself." Meanwhile, Seward had been saying, ever since December, that the Gulf states would try to secede, but that unless they received the backing of the border states, they would find their petty little combination untenable and would have to come back to the Union. Again we owe to Henry Adams the report that Seward said, "We shall keep the border states, and in three months or thereabouts, if we hold off, the Unionists and the disunionists will have their hands on each others throats in the cotton states."

Today, our hindsight makes it difficult for us to understand this reliance upon Southern Unionism, since most of the unionism which existed was destroyed by the four years of war; and it was never what Seward and Lincoln believed it to be in any case. But it seemed quite real when five slave states in rapid succession decided against secession. Thus, in terms of our alternatives of compromise, separation, or war, it is interesting to see that an editorial in the New York *Tribune* on March 27, 1861, specifically examined the alternatives and specifically said that there were only three; but the three which it named were not the three we tend to perceive today. The fact that this editorial, rather closely resembling one in the New York *Times,* was probably inspired by the administration, gives it additional interest.

The *Tribune* began by saying that there were but three possible ways in which to meet the secession movement. One was "by prompt, resolute, unflinching resistance"—what I have been calling the alternative of war; the second was "by complete acquiescence in...secession"—that is, separation. But instead of naming compromise as the third alternative, the *Tribune* numbered as three "a Fabian policy, which concedes nothing, yet employs no force in support of resisted Federal authority, hoping to wear out the insurgent spirit and in due time re-establish the authority of the union in the revolted or seceded states by virtue of the returning sanity and loyalty of their own people." As the editorial continued, it explained the reasoning which lay behind the advocacy of this policy.

> To war on the Seceders is to give to their yet vapory institutions the strong cement of blood—is to baptize their nationality in the mingled life-blood of friends and foes. But let them severely alone—allow them to wear out the military ardor of their adherents in fruitless drilling and marches, and to exhaust the patience of their fellow-citizens by the amount and frequency of their pecuniary exactions—and the fabric of their power will melt away like fog in the beams of a morning sun. Only give them rope, and they will speedily fulfill their destiny—the People, even of South Carolina, rejecting their sway as intolerable, and returning to the mild and paternal guardianship of the Union.

In behalf of this policy, it is urged that the Secessionists are a minority even in the seceded States; that they have grasped power by usurpation and retain it by terrorism; that they never dare submit the question of Union or Disunion fairly and squarely to the people, and always shun a popular vote when they can. In view of these facts, the Unionists of the South urge that the Government shall carry forbearance to the utmost, in the hope that the Nullifiers will soon be overwhelmed by the public sentiment of their own section, and driven with ignominy from power.

It seems reasonably clear that this editorial defined quite accurately the plan of action which Lincoln had announced in his inaugural. In that address, although affirming in general terms a claim of federal authority which, as the *Tribune* expressed it, conceded nothing, he made it quite clear that he would, as the *Tribune* also said, "employ no force" in the immediate situation. He specifically said he would not use force to deliver the mails—they would only be delivered unless repelled. He specifically said that federal marshals and judges would not be sent into areas where these functions had been vacated. "While the strict legal right may exist in the government to enforce the exercise of these offices, the attempt to do so would be so irritating that I deem it better to forego for the time the use of such offices." Without officials for enforcement, Lincoln's statement that he would uphold the law became purely a declaration of principle, with no operative or functional meaning. Finally, after having first written into his inaugural a statement that "all the power at my disposal will be used to reclaim the public property and places which have fallen," he struck this passage from the address as it was ultimately delivered. It was at about this time that Senator William P. Fessenden of Maine wrote that "Mr. Lincoln believed that gentleness and a conciliatory policy would prevent secession"—as if secession had not already occurred.

Finally, there is a question of whether even the decision to send supplies to Fort Sumter involved a clear acceptance of the alternative of war as well as a rejection of the alternatives of separation or compromise. Professor Stampp and Richard Current have both argued with considerable persuasiveness that Lincoln must have known that the Sumter expedition would bring war, since his informants from Charleston had warned him that such an expedition would be met with military force; and they have shown too that anyone with as much realism as Lincoln had in his makeup must have recognized that the chances for peace were slipping away. Yet I think their argument is more a reasoning from logic—that Lincoln must have seen the situation as we see it—and not an argument based primarily on expressions by Lincoln himself, showing that he had abandoned his belief in Southern Unionism and accepted the alternative of war. Indeed, insofar as we have expressions from him, he continued to believe in the strength of Southern Unionism. Even when he sent his war message to Congress on July 4, he said: "It may well be questioned whether there is today a majority of the legally qualified voters of any state, except per-haps South Carolina, in favor of disunion. There is much reason to believe that the Union men are in the majority in many, if not in everyone of the so-called seceded states."

The crisis at Fort Sumter has possibly had almost too sharp a focus placed upon it by historians, and I do not want to dissect that question all over again in this chapter. I will state briefly that, in my opinion, Lincoln pursued the most peaceful course that he believed was possible for him to pursue without openly abandoning the principle of union. That is, he assured the Confederates that food only would be sent into Fort Sumter, and nothing else would be done to strengthen the Union position unless the delivery of the food was resisted. While this may be construed, and has been construed, as a threat to make war if the food were not allowed, it can equally well be regarded as a promise that no reinforcement would be undertaken if the delivery of the food was permitted. Lincoln's critics, who accuse him of a covert policy to begin in an advantageous way a war which he now recognized to be inevitable, have never said what more peaceable course he could have followed that would have been consistent with his purpose to save the Union. Thus, they are in the anomalous position of saying that a man who followed the most peaceable course possible was still, somehow, a maker of war.

But as I suggested a moment ago, this focus upon Fort Sumter can perhaps be intensified too much. Even if Lincoln anticipated that there would be shooting at Sumter (and he must have known that there was a strong likelihood of it), what would this tell us about the choice of alternatives leading to the American Civil War? We may again revert to the somewhat arbitrary practice of answering this question in terms of the alternatives as they appear to us now. If the situation is viewed in this way, one would say we have three options neatly laid in a row: separation, compromise, war. If a man rejects any two of them, he is choosing the third; and since Lincoln and the Republicans rejected separation or compro-mise, this means that they exercised a choice for war. As a statement of the way in which the historical process narrows the field of possible action, this may be realistic; but for illumination of the behavior of men it seems to me very misleading. It assumes two things: first that choices are positive rather than negative; second that a choice of a course which leads to a particular result is in fact a choice of that result. Neither of these assumptions seems valid. What often happens is not that a given course is chosen because it is acceptable, but that given alternatives are rejected because they are regarded as totally unacceptable; thus one course remains which becomes the course followed, not because it was chosen, but because it was what was left.

When Lincoln ordered the Sumter expedition to sail, it was not because he wanted to do so; it was because he hated even worse the contingency of permitting the Sumter garrison to be starved into surrender. As he himself said, he had been committed to "the exhaustion of peaceful measures, before a resort to any stronger ones." But by mid-April at Sumter, the peaceful measures had all been exhausted; and the course that Lincoln followed was taken not because it was what he had chosen, but because it was what was left. That course resulted, as we now say, in the bombardment of Sumter, and the bombardment of Sumter was followed by four years of fighting which we call the Civil War. But even though the sending of the expedition led to events which in turn led on to war, it does not follow that the choice to send the expedition involved an acceptance of the alternative of war.

If deeds and consequences could be thus equated, our view of human nature would have to be more pessimistic than it is; and at the same time, our view of the future of humanity might perhaps be somewhat more optimistic. For it would imply that men have deliberately caused the succession of wars that have blotted the record of human history—certainly a harsh verdict to pronounce on humanity—and it would also imply that they have a certain measure of choice as to what forces of destruction they will release in the world—a proposition which would be comforting in the age of nuclear fission. But when we examine the situations of the past, how seldom does it appear that men defined the alternatives logically, chose the preferable alternative, and moved forward to the result that was intended? How often, on the other hand, do we find that they grope among the alternatives, avoiding whatever action is most positively or most immediately distasteful, and thus eliminate the alternatives until only one is left—at which point, as Lincoln said, it is necessary to have recourse to it since the other possibilities are exhausted or eliminated. In this sense, when the Republicans rejected both compromise and secession, thus narrowing the range of possibilities to include only the contingency of war, it was perhaps not because they really preferred the Civil War, with all its costs, to separation or to compromise, but because they could see the consequences of voting for compromise or the consequences of accepting separation more readily than they could see the consequences of following the rather indecisive course that ended in the bombardment of Fort Sumter. They did not know that it would end by leaving them with a war on their hands, any more than they knew it would cost the life of one soldier, either Rebel or Yank, for every six slaves who were freed and for every ten white Southerners who were held in the Union. When they rejected compromise, because they could not bear to make concessions to the fire-eaters, and rejected separation, because they could not bear to see the Union broken up, this does not mean that they accepted war or that they were able to bear the cost which this war would make them pay. It may really mean that they chose a course whose consequences they could not see in preference to courses whose consequences were easier to appraise.

Historians try to be rational beings and tend to write about history as if it were a rational process. Accordingly, they number the alternatives, and talk about choices and decisions, and equate decisions with what the decisions led to. But if we examine the record of modern wars, it would seem that the way people get into a war is seldom by choosing it; usually it is by choosing a course that leads to it—which is a different thing altogether. Although war seems terribly decisive, perhaps it requires less positive decision to get into wars than it does to avert them. For one can get into a war without in any way foreseeing it or imagining it, which is easy. But to avert war successfully, it has to be foreseen or imagined, which is quite difficult. If this is true, it means that the Republicans may have rejected separation and compromise not because they accepted the alternative, but precisely because they could not really visualize the alternative. When they took the steps that led them into a war, they did so not because they had decisively chosen the road to Appomattox or even the road to Manassas, in preference to the other paths; instead they did so precisely because they could not grasp the fearfully decisive consequences of the rather indecisive line of action which they followed in the months preceding their fateful rendezvous.

IV

LINCOLN, THE PRESIDENCY, AND THE CIVIL WAR

9

THE EMANCIPATION PROCLAMATION: THE DECISION AND THE WRITING

John Hope Franklin

The road that led to the issuing of the Preliminary Emancipation Proclamation was a long and difficult one. It was marked by an incredible amount of pressure on Abraham Lincoln, pressure that began the day Sumter fell and that did not relent until his decision was announced on September 22, 1862. It is not possible to weigh the effects of the pressures created by hardheaded generals who would set slaves free in order to break the back of the Confederacy. One cannot know what impressions the procession of the Charles Sumners, the Orestes Brownsons and the religious deputations made on the President as they came by day and by night to tell him what he should do about slavery. Did a Greeley editorial or a Douglass speech sway him? One cannot know the answers to these questions, for Lincoln, the only one who could do so, never gave the answers. He was doubtlessly impressed by all arguments that were advanced, and he took all of them "under advisement." But the final decision was his.

Lincoln needed no convincing that slavery was wrong, and he had been determined for many years to strike a blow for freedom if the opportunity ever came his way. As a young man he told a New Orleans group in 1831, "If I ever get a chance to hit that thing, I'll hit it hard."[1] He fully appreciated, moreover, the disastrous effect of slavery on national development and on the national character. He told a Cincinnati audience in 1842 that "Slavery and oppression must cease, or American liberty must perish."[2]

Lincoln was irritated by any suggestion that he was "soft" on the question of slavery. "I am naturally anti-slavery," he wrote a friend shortly after the beginning of his second term. "If slavery is not, nothing is wrong.... And yet I have never understood that the Presidency conferred upon me an unrestricted right to act officially on this judgment and feeling.... And I aver that to this day [April 4, 1864] I have done no official act in mere deference to my abstract judgment and feeling on slavery."[3]

Thus Lincoln was troubled by unanswered questions regarding the legality as well as the effect of emancipation on the course of the war and on the peace and well-being of the country. Who could know if the soldiers of Kentucky would lay down their arms if Lincoln set the slaves free? Greeley replied, "Let them do it. The cause of Union will be stronger, if Kentucky should secede with the rest, than it is now." It was not quite so simple, when one had the responsibility for shaping the course of the war and preserving the life of the Union. What would happen to the Negroes once they are free? Who would take care of them? These were questions that Lincoln asked over and over. Frederick Douglass, the runaway slave who had been a resounding success on two continents, had the answer. "Let them take care of themselves, as others do." If the black man could take care of his master and mistress, he could take care of himself. Should the freed Negroes be allowed to remain in the United States? "Yes," Douglass replied, "they wouldn't take up more room than they do now." Facile, even witty answers were not enough for the troubled Lincoln.

Since Lincoln was quite certain that sooner or later, in war or in peace, the slaves would be free, he gave much attention to what should be done with them. "You and we are different races," he told a group of Negroes in August 1862. "Whether it is right or wrong I need not discuss, but this physical difference is a great disadvantage to us both, as I think your race suffer very greatly, many of them by living among us, while ours suffer from your presence. In a word we suffer on each side. If this be admitted, it affords a reason at least why we should be separated."[4] Freedom called for colonization, Lincoln felt; and it seemed to occupy his attention about as much as any single matter during the first two years of the war.

As Lincoln moved toward a policy of emancipation, his interest in colonizing Negroes in some other parts of the world quickened. Indeed, it is almost possible to measure his approach to emancipation by studying the increasing intensity of his efforts to formulate a feasible program of colonization. In 1854 he said that his first impulse "would be to free all the slaves and send them back to Liberia, to their own native land." In his first annual message he proposed colonization for Negroes freed in the course of the war. He urged colonization for the slaves of the District of Columbia when they were freed in April 1862. He spearheaded the legislation in July 1862 that appropriated a half million dollars to colonize slaves of disloyal masters.

When Lincoln met the group of Negroes in August 1862, and talked to them about colonization, he had already decided to issue the Proclamation. This very decision seemed to make him all the more anxious about colonization. He asked them to give serious consideration to the idea of colonizing in Central America. The Negroes showed little enthusiasm for the proposal. In the following two weeks he discussed colonization in Chiriqui, a province in Panama, with several individuals and with members of the Cabinet. At the end of the month he decided to abandon the project because of lack of support. He was not altogether discouraged, and for the next several months he continued his vain attempts to gain support for colonization.

Early in 1862 Lincoln reached the decision that either he or Congress should emancipate the slaves. By March he had composed the draft of a special message to Congress recommending compensated emancipation. He read it to Senator Sumner, who was not enthusiastic about it because it called for gradual emancipation. Neither Congress nor the Delaware leaders upon whom he urged compensated emancipation were any more enthusiastic than Sumner. While Congress passed a resolution embodying the President's recommendations, it made no serious attempt to implement them.

Lincoln later admitted his awareness of pressures, but he never admitted the effect of them on his decision. He said that he forbade Fremont's and Hunter's attempts at military emancipation because he did not then think it an indispensable necessity. When the border states declined his appeal to accept compensated emancipation, he was driven to the "alternative of either surrendering the Union, and with it, the Constitution, or of laying a strong hand upon the colored element."[5] He chose the latter. In doing so he hoped for greater gain than loss, but of this he was not entirely confident.

The best evidence supports the view that it was in the late spring of 1862 that the President decided to issue a proclamation freeing the slaves. "Things had gone on from bad to worse," he said, "until I felt that we had reached the end of our rope on the plan of operations we had been pursuing; that we had about played our last card, and must change our tactics, or lose the game!" It was then that he "determined on the adoption of the emancipation policy; and without consultation with, or knowledge of the Cabinet, I prepared the original draft of the proclamation..."[6]

Lincoln was a frequent visitor to the telegraph room of the War Department. He went there almost daily to receive the reports of the progress of the war and to get away from the turmoil and distraction of the White House, where he had no privacy. Thomas T. Eckert, who was in charge of the telegraph office, was understanding and unobtrusive. Lincoln usually sat at Eckert's desk while at the telegraph office. Early one June morning, Lincoln dropped into the office and asked Eckert for some paper on which to write something special. He sat down and began to write. "He would look out of the window a while," Eckert later reported, "and then put his pen to paper, but he did not write much at once. He would study between times and when he had made up his mind he would put down a line or two, and then sit quiet for a few minutes. After a time he would resume his writing..."

On that first day Lincoln did not fill one sheet of the paper Eckert had given him. When he left he asked Eckert to keep what he had written and not to show it to anyone. On the following day when he returned, he asked for the paper, which Eckert kept in a locked desk; and he began to write. "This he did every day for several weeks." On some days he did not write more than a line or two, and Eckert observed that he had put question marks in the margin. Each day he would read over what he had written and revise it, "studying carefully each sentence." Eckert later said that he did not know what the President was writing until he had finished the draft. Then, for the first time, he told Eckert that he had been writing an order "giving freedom to the slaves in the South for the purpose of hastening the end of the war." He explained that he had been able to work more quietly and could better command his thoughts at the telegraph office than at the White House, where he was frequently interrupted.[7]

Within the next few weeks Lincoln widened the circle of confidants with whom he discussed the Proclamation. He had many talks with Stanton, his Secretary of War, about the possible use of Negroes as soldiers. Stanton had the distinct impression that Lincoln was planning to emancipate the slaves at an early date. On May 28 he predicted to Senator Sumner that a decree of emancipation would be issued within two months. Although Lincoln was as yet unwilling to arm the slaves, he began to discuss with his advisers the matter of their emancipation *and* their arming. Stanton, an ardent protagonist of both propositions, seemed to be more optimistic as spring gave way to summer in 1862.

On June 18, 1862, the President had a busy day. He received many visitors and, as usual, he fretted over reports of the activity or inactivity of Union troops. To General Henry W. Halleck at Corinth, Mississippi, he sent a message inquiring about the progress of the proposed expedition toward East Tennessee. To McClellan he sent a curt message saying that he could better dispose of things if he knew about what day McClellan could attack Richmond.[8] Things, indeed, seemed to be going from bad to worse. To get away from it all the President had his horse saddled and, with Vice President Hannibal Hamlin, rode out to the Soldiers' Home for his evening meal. After dinner the two men retired to the library and talked behind locked doors. According to Hamlin the President began the conversation by saying, "Mr. Hamlin, you have been repeatedly urging me to issue a proclamation of emancipation freeing the slaves, I have concluded to yield to your advice in the matter and that of other friends,—at the same time, as I may say, following my own judgment. Now listen to me as I read this paper. We will correct it together as I go on."

The President then opened a drawer in his desk and took out the draft of the Proclamation. He read it slowly, during which time the Vice President made no interruptions. When he had finished, Hamlin said that he had no criticism. Lincoln could hardly believe that Hamlin regarded the document as perfect. "At least you can make some suggestions," Lincoln urged. Finally, Hamlin reported, he did make "three suggestions, two of which Mr. Lincoln accepted." He declined to make known what his suggestions were, insisting that the Emancipation Proclamation was the President's "own act, and no one else can claim any credit whatever in connection with it."[9]

The death of young James Hutchison Stanton, Stanton's infant son, occurred at about the same time in July, 1862, as McClellan's retreat from Richmond. Lincoln was grieved by both events, and his depressed state was apparent to his associates. He invited the Secretary of the Navy, Gideon Welles, and the Secretary of State, William H. Seward, to accompany him in the Presidential carriage to the infant's funeral. It was during this ride, on July 13, that Lincoln first mentioned his proposed emancipation proclamation to these highly placed advisers. The President "dwelt earnestly on the gravity, importance, and delicacy of the movement, said he had given it much thought and had about come to the conclusion that it was a military necessity absolutely essential for the salvation of the Union, that we must free the slaves or be ourselves subdued...."

Welles recorded in his diary that Lincoln told them that this was the first time that he had mentioned the subject to anyone. The President invited the two men to state frankly how the proposition struck them. Seward, never lacking a response, said that the subject involved consequences so vast and momentous that he wished more time for mature reflection before giving a decisive answer. His offhand opinion, however, was that the measure was "perfectly justifiable" and perhaps might be expedient and necessary. Welles concurred in this view.

During the ride of some two or three miles beyond Georgetown the three men returned to the subject several times. When they returned to the city the President asked Seward and Welles, as they took their leave, to give the matter their "specific and deliberate attention." As for himself he was firm in his conviction that something must be done.[10]

It was hardly accurate to say that Lincoln had never discussed the matter with anyone. One wonders if Welles' memory was playing tricks on him or if the President's agitated state caused him to speak inaccurately. It was, however, accurate for Welles to declare that it was a new departure for the President to state categorically that he intended to emancipate the slaves. Heretofore, as Welles stated, whenever the matter arose, the President had been "prompt and emphatic in denouncing any interference by the General Government with the subject." The reverses before Richmond and the formidable power and dimensions of the rebellion were forcing the Administration to adopt extraordinary measures to preserve the Union. The proposed emancipation of the slaves fell into the category of extraordinary measures.

The formal solicitation of advice from the Cabinet came at the meeting on July 22, a scarce ten days after the momentous discussion during the funeral ride. When the meeting was called to order, all members were present except Montgomery Blair, the Postmaster General, who arrived during the meeting. The President informed the Cabinet that he had resolved to issue a proclamation emancipating the slaves. His decision in the matter was firm, he assured them. He therefore had called them together to inform them and to solicit their suggestions regarding language and timing.

The President then proceeded to read the following document:

> In pursuance of the sixth section of the act of Congress entitled "An act to suppress insurrection and to punish treason and rebellion, to seize and confiscate property of rebels, and for other purposes" Approved July 17, 1862, and which act, and the Joint Resolution explanatory thereof, are herewith published, I, Abraham Lincoln, President of the United States, do hereby proclaim to, and warn all persons within the contemplation of said sixth section to cease participating in, aiding, countenancing, or abetting the existing rebellion, or any rebellion against the government of the United States, and to return to their proper allegiance to the United States, on pain of the forfeitures and seizures, as within and by sixth section provided.
>
> And I hereby make known that it is my purpose, upon the next meeting of congress, to again recommend the adoption of a practical measure for tendering aid to the free choice or rejection, of any and all States which may then be recognizing and sustaining the authority of the United States, and which may then have voluntarily adopted, or thereafter may voluntarily adopt, gradual abolishment of slavery within such

State or States—that the object is to practically restore, thenceforward to be maintain[ed], the constitutional relation between the general government, and each, and all the states, wherein that relation is now suspended, or disturbed; and that, for this object, the war, as it has been, will be, prosecuted. And, as a fit and necessary military measure for effecting this object, I, as Commander-in-Chief of the Army and Navy of the United States, do order and declare that on the first day of January in the year of Our Lord one thousand eight hundred and sixty-three, all persons held as slaves within any state or states, wherein the constitutional authority of the United States shall not then be practically recognized, submitted to, and maintained, shall then, thenceforward, and forever, be free.[11]

There is no known copy of the Proclamation that Lincoln drafted in Eckert's office in the War Department. Perhaps it was similar to the second paragraph of the document the President read to his Cabinet on July 22. The latter document, however, rested largely on the authorization provided by the Confiscation Act of July 17, 1862. One can be certain, therefore, that this draft was written less than five days before the meeting of the Cabinet. It was on two pages of lined note paper, 12 $\frac{1}{2}$ by 7 $\frac{7}{8}$ inches and is now in the Library of Congress. The President endorsed the document as the "Emancipation Proclamation as first sketched and shown to the Cabinet in July, 1882."

Upon the completion of the reading a lively discussion ensued. Despite the prior knowledge of some members of the Cabinet that the President was drafting such a document, interest in the Proclamation was high. Doubtless some members could not believe their ears. Since the first paragraph had the backing of law, there was no extensive consideration of this portion of the proclamation.

Edward Bates, the Attorney General, gave unreserved concurrence. Salmon P. Chase, the Secretary of the Treasury, said that the measure went beyond anything he contemplated. He would prefer to permit the generals to arm the Negroes and proclaim emancipation locally, as they occupied portions of the Confederacy. Stanton, the Secretary of War, had long urged emancipation and arming of the slaves. He, therefore, favored the President's issuing the proclamation at once. The Postmaster General, Montgomery Blair, thought the proposed action was highly impolitic and would cost the administration the fall elections. This would, of course, have an adverse effect upon the conduct and course of the war, he argued.

The most significant observations were made by the Secretary of State. Seward made it clear that he approved the Proclamation, but he questioned the expediency of its issue "at this juncture." The repeated reverses of the Union army had depressed the public mind. An Emancipation Proclamation issued at this time may be viewed as a "last measure of an exhausted government, a cry for help, the government stretching forth its hands to Ethiopia, instead of Ethiopia stretching forth her hands to the government."[12] He suggested that the matter be postponed "until you can give it to the country supported by military success, attended by fife and drum and public spirit."[13]

Lincoln was impressed by Seward's argument, but he did not commit himself at the meeting. Later in the afternoon he had his second conference of the day with Francis B. Cutting, an ardent pro-slavery Democratic lawyer from New York. Despite his views on slavery Cutting was convinced of the necessity of emancipation in order to forestall diplomatic recognition of the Confederacy and to rally the antislavery element behind the war. He expressed these views fully to Lincoln during the first interview. When the two men met after the Cabinet meeting Lincoln told Cutting that he intended to issue the proclamation the following day, July 23.

On the same day Blair sent the President a lengthy statement reaffirming his objection to the Proclamation on political grounds. He insisted that there was no public sentiment in the North, "even among extreme men which now demands the proposed measure." He argued that it would endanger the Administration's power in Congress and hand to those opposed to the war the control of the next House of Representatives.[14]

That evening Thurlow Weed, the remarkably astute political leader from New York, met with the President. He argued for postponement, not to reinforce Blair's arguments, but in support of Seward's views. He told Lincoln that the Proclamation could not be enforced, and its issuance at that time would be folly. Apparently, Lincoln agreed. Two days later he issued the "Proclamation of the Act to Suppress Insurrection," which was the first paragraph of the document he had read to the Cabinet. Presidential emancipation would wait—not for the fall elections but for a Union victory.

Lincoln did not merely file away the Proclamation for "future use." It remained constantly in his thoughts; and if he was ever disposed to neglect the matter, the constant pressure by Greeley and the others would have made this impossible.

The next two months were difficult for Lincoln. The Proclamation was prepared, but the propitious moment for its issuance seemed never to come. The public unaware of his plans, continued to urge an emancipation policy upon him. Military leaders, including Stanton, wanted Lincoln to arm the slaves. If Stanton did not press the President with greater zeal, he could not forget the manner in which Lincoln countermanded the actions of Hunter, Fremont, and the others. Stanton was among those who believed that armed slaves would accelerate the arrival of the proper moment to issue the Emancipation Proclamation. Lincoln could not agree; and he waited.

In the meetings of the Cabinet in August emancipation remained a subject of interest and discussion. On August 3 Chase urged the President to assure freedom for the slaves in the seceded states on condition of loyalty.[15] During those days that seemed an eternity, unknowing men and women chastised Lincoln for not reaching a decision on emancipation. He was always gracious and patient with all armchair emancipators and military strategists. He continued to wait, but he was becoming more anxious.

At the end of August, Second Bull Run was fought; and the Union troops were repulsed almost as sharply as they had been at First Bull Run thirteen months earlier. After this disaster the Union cause was at a most critical juncture. Even the capital was once more in danger. Lee was determined to capitalize on the victory and take the fight to the enemy. Early in September he crossed the Potomac near Leesburg and, on the seventh of September, occupied Frederick, Maryland.

Panic struck the entire North as news of Lee's movements spread. Some feared that Washington, Baltimore, and Philadelphia would fall. Lincoln fretted, and spent more time than usual at the War Department telegraph office. He must keep in touch with McClellan, now in command of the forces destined to repel Lee. After a sleepless night on September 11 he wired McClellan at 4 A.M., "How does it look now?" Things never looked too good to McClellan, and he remained diffident about advancing against Lee. But he could have replied that things were looking better. A Union private had discovered Lee's orders revealing the disposition of his forces, and had turned them over to McClellan. But the wary, hesitant leader lost his chances of destroying Lee's army because, characteristically, he overestimated enemy strength and power.

Lee's forces were inferior to McClellan's, and Lee knew it. With inadequate forces to push his invasion to the North, Lee resolved to withdraw across the Potomac into Virginia. At long last, however, McClellan made the attack at Antietam Creek, near Sharpsburg, on September 17. For fourteen hours the armies fought, and at the close of the day more than twenty thousand Union and Confederate soldiers lay dead and wounded. It was the heaviest engagement in American history up to that time. McClellan's claim of victory was disputed, but it could not be denied that Lee's offensive had been checked. On the following day Lee recrossed the Potomac and escaped the crushing blow that McClellan could have delivered had he pursued the intrepid Confederate leader. It was this failure to pursue the enemy that caused Lincoln to refer to McClellan's army as "the general's bodyguard."

Although Lincoln was disappointed in the outcome of Antietam it gave him the success he had long sought. Even on the evening of September 17, sensing victory, he worked on the final draft of the preliminary Emancipation Proclamation in the quiet of Soldiers' Home. On Saturday, the twentieth, he returned to the White House, ready to summon the Cabinet on Monday and tell his official family of his decision to issue the Proclamation immediately. On Sunday morning he carefully rewrote the document that was the culmination of months of work and worry.[16]

Once Lincoln made up his mind to issue the Proclamation, he lost no time in informing his Cabinet of his decision. Early on Monday morning he summoned the members of the Cabinet to the White House. By this time Washington was rife with rumors of an impending Proclamation. Every member of the Cabinet had known since July that sooner or later Lincoln would summon them and tell them that the time had come. After the President had finished his reading from Artemus Ward's new book, they could hardly have been surprised when he began to read his Proclamation. They listened attentively, doubtless sensing the enormous significance of the step the President was taking not only for the course of the war but also for the character and composition of the American social order.

After the President had read the draft of the Proclamation, he invited comments, making it clear that the decision and the consequences were his. There ensued a "long and earnest" discussion in which the President participated. Seward suggested one or two unimportant emendations that were approved. The document was then given to Seward to publish on the following day. Blair, ever political-minded and lukewarm on the slavery question, said that while he approved the principle of emancipation he did not concur in the expediency of the measure. He was convinced that the Emancipation Proclamation would drive the border slave states into the Confederacy. He thought, too, that certain elements in the free states that were opposed to the Administration would use the measure as a club with which to fight the party in power.[17]

The entire Cabinet entered into a general discussion of the question of the authority that the government possessed to set the slaves free. Some thought the government did not have the authority and that special legislation should be enacted before the step was taken. The President was convinced that under his war powers he had the authority to emancipate the slaves, and he had no intention of seeking further Congressional approval. Stanton remained silent, but as a strong advocate of the use of Negro troops and as a vigorous opponent of compensated emancipation he was undoubtedly disappointed. Chase was willing to take the document as written, although he would have approached the matter somewhat differently. This was not the first or the last time that he and the President would differ in their approaches. As usual the President had his way.

The Proclamation of September 22, 1862, commonly referred to as the "Preliminary Emancipation Proclamation," was based firmly on legislative and executive authority. If referred to the act of Congress of March 13, 1862, that prohibited officers from aiding in the capture or return of runaway slaves of disloyal masters. And it invoked the well-known

Confiscation Act of July 17, 1862, that gave freedom to fugitive, captured, and abandoned slaves of rebels. Obedience to the provisions of these acts would itself result in the emancipation of numerous slaves. Proper construction and enforcement of these acts would result in a considerable amount of emancipation by act of Congress.

As Commander-in-Chief of the Army and Navy, Lincoln referred to his military powers as the source of *his* authority to emancipate the slaves. This power was used to prosecute the war in order to restore the Union. Setting the slaves free had become an important means of accomplishing this end. He hoped, finally, to bring about legislative and executive cooperation with a view to developing a plan of emancipation in states that were not in rebellion and to colonize Negroes in Africa or elsewhere.

The significant feature of the proclamation was the provision that called for the emancipation of the slaves of January 1, 1863, in those states or parts of states that were then in rebellion against the United States. The clear implication was that if states or portions of states were not in rebellion on January 1, 1863, the Proclamation would not apply to them. Apparently, in such areas the President would seek to develop some plan of voluntary immediate or gradual emancipation. It was this provision that was to provoke the greatest amount of reaction in the months that followed.

The body of the Preliminary Emancipation Proclamation is in Lincoln's own hand, the penciled additions in the hand of the Secretary of State, and the final beginning and ending in the hand of the chief clerk. The document was presented by the President to the Albany Army Relief Bazaar held in February and March, 1864. Gerrit Smith, the abolitionist leader, purchased it for $1,000 and gave it to the United States Sanitary Commission. In April 1865, the New York Legislature appropriated $1,000 for its purchase and it was placed in the State Library. It is still in the possession of the New York State Library. The text, with the Lincoln and Seward emendations, follows:

BY THE PRESIDENT OF THE UNITED STATES OF AMERICA

A Proclamation

I, Abraham Lincoln, President of the United States of America, and Commander-in-Chief of the Army and Navy thereof, do hereby proclaim and declare that hereafter, as heretofore, the war will be prosecuted for the object of practically restoring the constitutional relation between the United States, and each of the states, and the people thereof, in which states that relation is, or may be suspended, or disturbed.

That it is my purpose upon the next meeting of Congress to again recommend the adoption of a practical measure tendering pecuniary aid to the free acceptance or rejection of all slave-states, so called, the people whereof may not then be in rebellion against the United States, and which states may then have voluntarily adopted, or thereafter may voluntarily adopt, immediate or gradual abolishment of slavery within their respective limits; and that the effort to colonize persons of African descent [with their consent][a] upon this continent, or elsewhere, [with the previously obtained consent of the Governments existing there][b] will be continued.

That on the first day of January in the year of our Lord, one thousand eight hundred and sixty-three, all persons held as slaves within any state, or designated part of a state, the people whereof shall be in rebellion against the United States shall be then, thenceforward, and forever free; and the executive government of the United States [including the military and naval authority thereof][b] will recognize [and maintain the freedom of][b] such persons, and will do no act or acts to repress such persons, or any of them, in any efforts they may make for their actual freedom.

That the executive will, on the first day of January aforesaid, by proclamation, designate the States, and parts of states, if any, in which the people thereof respectively, shall then be in rebellion against the United States; and the fact that any state, or the people thereof shall, on that day be, in good faith represented in the Congress of the United States, by members chosen thereto, at elections wherein a majority of the qualified voters of such state shall have participated, shall, in the absence of strong countervailing testimony, be deemed conclusive evidence that such state and the people thereof, are not then in rebellion against the United States.

That attention is hereby called to an Act of Congress entitled "An act to make an additional Article of War" approved March 13, 1862, and which act is in the words and figure following:[c]

Be it enacted by the Senate and House of Representatives of the United States of America in Congress assembled, That hereafter the following shall be promulgated as an additional article of war for the government of the army of the United States, and shall be obeyed and observed as such:

Article—. All officers or persons in the military or naval service of the United States are prohibited from employing any of the forces under their respective commands for the purpose of returning fugitives from service or labor, who may have escaped from any persons to whom such service or labor is claimed to be due, and any officer who shall be found guilty by a court-martial of violating this article shall be dismissed from the service.

Sec. 2. *And be it further enacted,* That this act shall take effect from and after its passage.

Also to the ninth and tenth sections of an act entitled, "An Act to suppress Insurrection, to punish Treason and Rebellion, to seize and confiscate property of rebels, and for other purposes," approved July 17, 1862, and which sections are in the words and figures following:[d]

Sec. 9. *And be it further enacted,* That all slaves of persons who shall hereafter be engaged in rebellion against the government of the United States, or who shall in any way give aid or comfort thereto, escaping from such persons and taking refuge within the lines of the army; and all slaves captured from such persons or deserted by them and coming under the control of the government of the United States; and all slaves of such persons found on (or) being within any place occupied by rebel forces and afterwards occupied by the forces of the United States, shall be deemed captives of war, and shall be forever free of their servitude and not again held as slaves.

Sec. 10. *And be it further enacted,* That no slave escaping into any State, territory, or the District of Columbia, from any other State, shall be delivered up, or in any way impeded or hindered of his liberty, except for crime, or some offence against the laws, unless the person claiming such fugitive shall first make oath that the person to whom the labor or service of such fugitive is alleged to be due is his lawful owner, and has not borne arms against the United States in the present rebellion, nor in any way given aid and comfort thereto; and no person engaged in the military or naval service of the United States shall, under any pretence whatever, assume to decide on the validity of the claim of any person to the service or labor of any other person, or surrender up any such person to the claimant, on pain of being dismissed from the service.

And I do hereby enjoin upon and order all persons engaged in the military and naval service of the United States to observe, obey, and enforce within their respective spheres of service, the act, and sections above recited.

And the executive will in due time recommend that all citizens of the United States who shall have remained loyal thereto throughout the rebellion shall (upon the restoration of the constitutional relation between the United States, and their respective states, and people, if that relation shall have been suspended or disturbed) be compensated for all losses by acts of the United States, including the loss of slaves.

In witness whereof, I have hereunto set my hand, and caused the seal of the United States to be affixed.

Done at the City of Washington, this twenty second day of September, in the year of our Lord, one thousand, eight hundred and sixty two, and sixty two, [*sic*] and of the Independence of the United States, the eighty seventh.

ABRAHAM LINCOLN
By the President
WILLIAM H. SEWARD
Secretary of State

^a In Seward's hand
^b In Lincoln's hand
^c A clipping from the official printing was inserted at this point.
^d Another clipping from the official printing was inserted at this point.

This was, in a very real sense, the President's own Proclamation. The composition of it began in the War Department's telegraph office in June and continued down through those September days at Soldiers' Home and at the White House the day before the Cabinet meeting. Hamlin, Welles, and Seward gave him no substantive assistance in his private consultations with them. The assistance offered by the Cabinet was essentially of an editorial nature. Even if members of the Cabinet had ideas and approaches that were substantially different from those of Lincoln's, he tended to discourage them from expressing them. If the President claimed for himself the responsibility for making the decision and for reaping the consequences, there was little the Cabinet could do.

To be sure Chase said that he would have approached the matter somewhat differently, but he did not press the point with any vigor in the Cabinet. Meanwhile he had managed to convey the impression among his followers that his influence on the President's emancipation policy was greater than it actually was. In Ohio a group of Negroes passed a vote of thanks for the way in which Chase had fulfilled his duties toward the oppressed "as a member of President Lincoln's Cabinet."[18] Another supporter was even more enthusiastic. On October 1, 1862, John Livingston wrote Chase, "The government is now on your platform and it is right. Everything I have, even to life itself, is now at the disposal of the authorities if necessary to carry out the views expressed by you and adopted by the President."[19] Thus, some of the followers of Chase failed to give the President full credit for the decision and the writing of the Proclamation. In other quarters the credit and the blame were laid at the President's door.

NOTES

1. William H. Herndon, *History and Personal Recollections of Abraham Lincoln.* Springfield, n.d., p. 76.
2. Emanuel Hertz, *Abraham Lincoln.* New York, 1931, vol. II, p. 531.
3. Lincoln to Albert G. Hodges, Frankfort, Kentucky, April 4, 1864, *Collected Works,* vol. VII, p. 281.
4. Lincoln, *Collected Works,* vol. V, p. 371.
5. Ibid., vol. VII, p. 282.
6. F. B. Carpenter, *The Inner Life of Abraham Lincoln: Six Months at the White House.* New York, 1869, pp. 20–21.
7. David H. Bates, *Lincoln at the Telegraph Office.* New York, 1907, pp. 138–41.
8. Lincoln, *Collected Works,* vol. V, pp. 275–76.
9. Charles E. Hamlin, *The Life and Times of Hannibal Hamlin.* Cambridge, 1899, pp. 428–29.
10. Gideon Welles, *Diary.* Boston, 1911, vol. I, pp. 70–71.
11. Lincoln, *Collected Works,* vol. V, pp. 336–37.
12. Carpenter, op. cit., p. 20.
13. Benjamin Thomas and Harold Hyman, *Stanton: The Life and Times of Lincoln's Secretary of War.* New York, 1962, p. 239.

14. David Donald, ed., *Inside Lincoln's Cabinet: The Civil War Diaries of Salmon P. Chase.* New York, 1954, pp. 97–98.
15. Ibid., pp. 105–6.
16. Tyler Dennett, ed., *Lincoln and the Civil War in the Diaries and Letters of John Hay.* New York, 1939, p. 50.
17. Welles, op. cit., vol. I, pp. 142–43.
18. Joseph Emery to Chase, September 29, 1862, Ms. in the Chase Papers, Library of Congress.
19. John Livingston to Chase, October 1, 1862, Ms. in the Chase Papers, Library of Congress.

10

LINCOLN AND THE STRATEGY OF UNCONDITIONAL SURRENDER

James M. McPherson

It is ironic that one of the most oft-quoted passages from Lincoln's writings is the concluding paragraph of his second inaugural address. "With malice toward none," said Lincoln, "with charity for all," let us "bind up the nation's wounds" and strive to "achieve and cherish a just, and a lasting peace."[1] These words have helped shape Lincoln's image as a man of compassion and mercy who desired a magnanimous peace. This image is true enough; but it is only part of the truth. While Lincoln did want a soft peace, he had recognized long before 1865 that it could be achieved only by a hard war. And he insisted on the unconditional surrender of Confederate forces before he would even talk of peace.

The fact is, the overwhelming circumstance shaping Lincoln's presidency was war. He had been willing to risk war rather than let the nation perish. He was a war president. Indeed, he was the only president in our history whose entire administration was bounded by the parameters of war. The first official document that Lincoln saw as president—on the morning after the inaugural ball—was a letter from Major Robert Anderson at Fort Sumter stating that unless resupplied he could hold out

only a few more weeks. This news, in effect, struck the first blow of
the Civil War; the fatal shot fired by John Wilkes Booth on April 14,
1865, struck virtually the last blow of the war. During the intervening
one thousand, five hundred and three days there was scarcely one in
which Lincoln was not preoccupied with the war. Military matters took
up more of his time and attention than any other matter, as indicated by
the activities chronicled in that fascinating volume, *Lincoln Day by Day*.[2]
He spent more time in the War Department telegraph office than any-
where else except the White House itself. During times of crisis, Lincoln
frequently stayed at the telegraph office all night reading dispatches from
the front, sending dispatches of his own, holding emergency conferences
with Secretary of War Stanton, General-in-Chief Halleck, and other officials. He wrote the first draft of the Emancipation Proclamation in this
office while awaiting news from the army.[3] This was appropriate, for the
legal justification of the proclamation was its "military necessity" as a
war measure.

Lincoln took seriously his constitutional duty as commander in chief
of the army and navy. He borrowed books on military strategy from
the Library of Congress and burned the midnight oil reading them. No
fewer than eleven times he left Washington to visit the Army of the
Potomac at the fighting front in Virginia or Maryland, spending a total
of forty-two days with that army. Some of the most dramatic events in
Lincoln's presidency grew out of his direct intervention in strategic and
command decisions. In May 1862, along with Secretary of War Stanton
and Secretary of the Treasury Chase, he visited Union forces at Hampton
Roads in Virginia and personally issued orders that led to the occupation
of Norfolk. Later that same month, Lincoln haunted the War Department
telegraph room almost around the clock for more than a week and fired
off a total of fifty telegrams to half a dozen generals to coordinate an
attempt to trap and crush Stonewall Jackson's army in the Shenandoah
Valley—an attempt that failed partly because Jackson moved too fast
but mainly because Union generals, much to Lincoln's disgust, moved
too slowly. A couple of months later, Lincoln made the controversial decision to transfer the Army of the Potomac from the Virginia peninsula
southeast of Richmond to northern Virginia covering Washington. And
a couple of months later yet, Lincoln finally removed General George
B. McClellan from command of this army because McClellan seemed
reluctant to fight. A year later, in September 1863, Lincoln was roused
from bed at his summer residence in a Maryland suburb of Washington
for a dramatic midnight conference at the War Department where he
decided to send four divisions from the Army of the Potomac to reinforce

General William S. Rosecrans's besieged army in Chattanooga after it had lost the battle of Chickamauga.

Lincoln subsequently put Ulysses S. Grant in command at Chattanooga and then in the spring of 1864 brought him to Washington as the new general in chief. Thereafter, with a commander in charge who had Lincoln's full confidence, the president played a less direct role in command decisions than he had done before. Nevertheless, Lincoln continued to help shape crucial strategic plans and to sustain Grant against pressures from all sides during that dark summer of 1864. "It is the dogged pertinacity of Grant that wins," the president told his private secretary. Lincoln wired Grant in Virginia during the terrible fighting at Petersburg: "I begin to see it. You will succeed. God bless you all."[4] When Confederate General Jubal Early drove a small Union army out of the Shenandoah Valley in the summer of 1864, crossed the Potomac, and threatened Washington itself before being driven off, Lincoln went personally to Fort Stevens, part of the Washington defenses, to observe the fighting. It was on this occasion that a Union officer standing a few feet from Lincoln was hit by a Confederate bullet and that another officer—none other than Oliver Wendell Holmes, Jr.—noting without recognizing out of the corner of his eye this tall civilian standing on the parapet in the line of fire, said urgently: "Get down, you damn fool, before you get shot!" A chastened president got down.[5]

Grant subsequently sent several divisions from the Army of the Potomac with orders to go after Early's army in the Shenandoah Valley "and follow him to the death." When Lincoln saw these orders he telegraphed Grant: "This, I think, is exactly right." But "it will neither be done nor attempted unless you watch it every day, and hour, and force it."[6] In response to this telegram Grant came to Washington, conferred with Lincoln, and put his most trusted subordinate, Philip Sheridan, in command of the Union forces in the Shenandoah Valley where they did indeed follow Early to the death of his army. About the same time, Lincoln approved the plans for Sherman's march through Georgia. It was these three campaigns—Grant's chewing and choking of Lee's army at Petersburg, Sheridan's following of Early to the death in the Valley, and Sherman's march through Georgia and the Carolinas—that finally destroyed the Confederacy and brought about its unconditional surrender.

Commander-in-Chief Lincoln was mainly responsible for this unconditional victory of Union forces. But in the huge body of writing about Lincoln—there are said to be more titles in the English language about Lincoln than about anyone else except Jesus and Shakespeare—a relatively small number of books and articles focus primarily on Lincoln as a war leader. In 1982 Mark Neely, Jr., completed *The Abraham Lincoln Encyclopedia,* a valuable compendium of information and scholarship—which devotes less than 5 percent of its space to military and related matters. In September 1984, Gettysburg College hosted a conference on recent scholarship about the sixteenth president. This conference had three sessions on books of psychohistory about Lincoln, two sessions on books about his assassination, two sessions on Lincoln's image in photographs and popular prints, one on his economic ideas, one on Lincoln and civil religion, one on his humor, one on his Indian policy, and one on slavery and emancipation—but no session on Lincoln as commander in chief. In 1987 the outstanding Lincoln scholar of our time, Don E. Fehrenbacher, published a collection of essays, *Lincoln in Text and Context.* Of its seventeen essays on Lincoln, none dealt with the president as a military leader.[7] This is not intended as criticism of these enterprises, which are superb achievements in writings about Lincoln. Rather, it is a reflection on the nature and direction of modern Lincoln scholarship.

In the 1950s, fine studies by two historians named Williams—T. Harry and Kenneth P.—told us everything we might want to know about Lincoln's search for the right military strategy and for the right generals to carry it out.[8] A number of other books and articles have also explored Lincoln's relationships with his generals, the wisdom or lack thereof that the president demonstrated in certain strategic decisions, and a great deal more of a similar nature. Many of these are excellent studies. They provide important and fascinating insights on Lincoln as commander in chief. But as a portrait of Lincoln the strategist of Union victory, they are incomplete. The focus is too narrow; the larger picture is somehow blurred.

Most of these studies are based on too restricted a definition of strategy. On this matter we can consult with profit the writings of the most influential theorist of war, Carl von Clausewitz. One of Clausewitz's famous maxims defines war as the continuation of state policy by other means—that is, war is an instrument of last resort to achieve a nation's political goals. Using this insight, we can divide our definition of strategy into two parts: First, *national strategy* (or what the British call grand strategy); second, *military strategy* (or what the British call operational strategy). National strategy is the shaping and defining of a nation's political goals in time of war. Military strategy is the use of armed forces to achieve those goals.[9] Most studies of Lincoln and his generals focus mainly on this second kind of strategy—that is, military or operational strategy. And that is the problem. For it is impossible to understand military strategy without also comprehending national strategy—the political war aims—for which military strategy is merely the instrument. This is true to some degree in all wars; it was especially true of the American Civil War, which was pre-eminently a *political* war precipitated by a presidential election in the world's most politicized society, fought largely by volunteer soldiers who elected many of their officers and who also helped elect the political leadership that directed the war effort, and in which many of the commanders were appointed for political reasons.

Let us look at this matter of political generals, to illustrate the point that military strategy can be understood only within the larger context of national strategy. Both Abraham Lincoln and Jefferson Davis appointed generals who had little or no professional training: men like Benjamin Butler, Nathaniel Banks, Carl Schurz, Robert Toombs, Henry Wise, and so on. A good many of these generals proved to be incompetent; some battlefield disasters resulted from their presence in command. Professional army officers bemoaned the prominence of political generals: Henry W. Halleck, for example, commented that "it seems but little better than murder to give important commands to such men as Banks, Butler, McClernand, and Lew Wallace, but it seems impossible to prevent it."[10]

A good many military historians have similarly deplored the political generals. They often cite one anecdote to ridicule the process. To satisfy the large German ethnic constituency in the North, Lincoln felt it necessary to name a number of German-American generals. Poring over a list of eligible men one day in 1862, the president came across the name of Alexander Schimmelfennig. "The very man!" said Lincoln. When Secretary of War Stanton protested that better-qualified officers were available, the president insisted on Schimmelfennig. "His name," said Lincoln, "will make up for any difference there may be," and he walked away repeating the name Schimmelfennig with a chuckle.[11]

Historians who note that Schimmelfennig turned out to be a mediocre commander miss the point. Their criticism is grounded in a narrow concept of *military* strategy. But Lincoln made this and similar appointments for reasons of *national* strategy. Each of the political generals represented an important ethnic, regional, or political constituency in the North. The support of these constituencies for the war effort was crucial. Democrats, Irish-Americans, many German-Americans, and most residents of the watershed of the Ohio River had not voted for Lincoln in 1860 and were potential defectors from a war to crush the rebels and coerce the South back into the Union. To mobilize their support for this war, Lincoln had to give them political patronage; a general's commission was one of the highest patronage plums. From the viewpoint of military strategy this may have been inefficient; from the viewpoint of national strategy it was essential.

And even in the narrower military sense the political patronage system produced great benefits for the North, for without it Ulysses S. Grant and William T. Sherman might not have gotten their start up the chain of command. Although West Point graduates, both men had resigned from the pre-war army and neither was conspicuous at the outbreak of the war. But Sherman happened to be the brother of an influential Republican senator and Grant happened to be an acquaintance of an influential Republican congressman from Illinois. These fortuitous political connections helped get them their initial commissions in the army. The rest is history—but had it not been for the political dictates of national strategy, they might never have made their mark on the history of military strategy.

Clausewitz describes two kinds of national strategy in war. One is the conquest of a certain amount of the enemy's territory or the defense of one's own territory from conquest. The second is the overthrow of the enemy's political system. The first usually means a limited war ended by a negotiated peace. The second usually means a total war ending in unconditional surrender by the loser.[12] These are absolute or ideal types, of course; in the real world some wars are a mixture of both types. In American history most of our wars have been mainly of the first, limited type: the Revolution, which did seek the overthrow of British political power in the thirteen colonies but not elsewhere; the War of 1812; the Mexican War; the Spanish-American War; the Korean War. American goals in World War I were mixed: primarily they involved the limited aims of defending the territory and right of self-government of European nationalities, but in effect this required the overthrow of the German and Austro-Hungarian monarchies. In Vietnam the American goal was mainly the limited one of defending the territory and sovereignty of South Vietnam and its anti-Communist government, but this was mixed with the purpose of overthrowing the political system that prevailed in part of South Vietnam and involved attacks on that system in North Vietnam as well.

World War II and the Civil War were the two unalloyed examples in American history of Clausewitz's second type of war—total war ending in unconditional surrender and the overthrow of the enemy's political system. These wars were also "total" in the sense that they mobilized the society's whole population and resources for a prolonged conflict that ended only when the armed forces and resources of one side were totally destroyed or exhausted.

Common sense, not to mention Clausewitz, will tell us that there should be congruity between national and military strategy. That is, an all-out war to overthrow the enemy requires total mobilization plus a military strategy to destroy the enemy's armies, resources, and morale, while a limited war requires a limited strategy to gain or defend territory. When national and military strategy become inconsistent with each other—when the armed forces adopt or want to adopt an unlimited military strategy to fight a limited war, or vice versa—then a nation fights at cross purposes, with dissension or failure the likely outcome. This can happen when a war that is initially limited in purpose takes on a momentum, a life of its own that carries the participants beyond their original commitment without a proper redefinition of war aims—for example World War I, which became a total war in military strategy without a concomitant redefinition of national strategy and ended with an armistice rather than with unconditional surrender. But it produced a peace treaty that Germany resented as a *Diktat* because it treated the Germans as if they had surrendered unconditionally. This in turn generated a stab-in-the-back legend that facilitated the rise of Hitler.

One of the reasons the Allied powers in World War II insisted on unconditional surrender was their determination that this time there must be no armistice, no stab-in-the-back legend, no doubt on the part of the defeated peoples that they had been utterly beaten and their Fascist governments overthrown. The Allies won World War II because they had a clear national strategy and a military strategy in harmony with it-along with the resources to do the job. In the Korean War, disharmony between President Truman, who insisted on a limited war, and General MacArthur, who wanted to fight an unlimited one, resulted in MacArthur's dismissal and a sense of frustration among many Americans who wanted to overthrow the Communist government of North Korea and perhaps of China as well. In Vietnam, the controversy and failure resulted from an inability of the government to define clearly the American national strategy. This inability resulted in turn from deep and bitter divisions in American society over the national purpose in this conflict. Without a clear national strategy to guide them, the armed forces could not develop an effective military strategy.

The Civil War confronted the Union government with these same dangers of unclear national strategy and a consequent confusion of purpose between national and military strategy. like World War I, the Civil War started out as one kind of war and evolved into something quite different. But in contrast to World War I, the government of the victorious side in the Civil War developed a national strategy to give purpose to a military strategy of total war, and preserved a political majority in support of this national strategy through dark days of defeat, despair, and division. This was the real strategic contribution of Abraham Lincoln to Union victory. His role in shaping a national strategy of unconditional surrender by the Confederacy was more important to the war's outcome than his endless hours at the War Department sending telegrams to generals and devising strategic combinations to defeat Confederate armies.

In one sense, from the beginning the North fought Clausewitz's second type of war—to overthrow the enemy's government—for the northern war aim was to bring Confederate states back into the Union. But Lincoln waged this war on the legal theory that since secession was unconstitutional, southern states were still *in* the Union and the Confederate government was not a legitimate government. Lincoln's first war action, the proclamation of April 15, 1861, calling for 75,000 militia to serve for ninety days, declared that their purpose would be to "suppress... combinations too powerful to be suppressed by the ordinary course of judicial proceedings."[13] In other words this was a domestic insurrection, a rebellion by certain lawless citizens, not a war between nations. Throughout the war Lincoln maintained this legal fiction; he never referred to Confederate states or to Confederates, but to rebel states and rebels. Thus, the North fought the war not on the theory of overthrowing an enemy state or even conquering enemy territory, but of suppressing insurrection and restoring authority in its own territory. This national strategy was based on an assumption that a majority of the southern people were loyal to the Union and that eleven states had been swept into secession by the passions of the moment. Once the United States demonstrated its firmness by regaining control of its forts and other property in the South, those presumed legions of loyal Unionists would regain political control of their states and resume their normal allegiance to the United States. In his first message to Congress, nearly three months after the firing on Fort Sumter, Lincoln questioned "whether there is, to-day, a majority of the legally qualified voters of any State, except perhaps South Carolina, in favor of disunion." And to show that he would temper firmness with restraint, Lincoln promised that while suppressing insurrection the federalized militia would avoid "any devastation, any destruction of, or interference with, property, or any disturbance of peaceful citizens."[14]

This was a national strategy of limited war—very limited, indeed scarcely war at all, but a police action to quell a rather large riot. This limited national strategy required a limited military strategy. General-in-Chief Winfield Scott—himself a loyal Virginian who shared the government's faith in southern unionism—came up with such a strategy, which was soon labeled the Anaconda Plan. This plan called for a blockade of southern ports by the navy and a campaign down the Mississippi by a combined army and fresh-water naval task force to split the Confederacy and surround most of it with a blue cordon. Having thus sealed off the rebels from the world, Scott would squeeze them firmly—like an Anaconda snake—but with restraint until southerners came to their senses and returned to the Union.

Lincoln approved this plan, which remained a part of northern military strategy through the war. But he also yielded to public pressure to invade Virginia, attack the rebel force at Manassas, and capture Richmond before the Confederate Congress met there in July. This went beyond the Anaconda Plan, but was still part of a limited-war strategy to regain United States territory and disperse the illegitimate rebel Congress in order to put down the rebellion within ninety days. But this effort led to the humiliating Union defeat at Bull Run and to an agonizing reappraisal by the North of the war's scope and strategy. It was now clear that this might be a long, hard war requiring more fighting and a greater mobilization of resources than envisioned by the restrained squeezing of the Anaconda Plan. Congress authorized the enlistment of a million three-year volunteers; by early 1862 nearly 700,000 northerners as well as more than 300,000 southerners were under arms. This was no longer a police action to suppress rioters, but a full-scale war.

Its legal character had also changed, by actions of the Lincoln administration itself. The blockade, for example, called into question the "domestic insurrection" theory of the conflict, for a blockade was recognized by international law as an instrument of war between sovereign nations. Moreover, after first stating an intention to execute captured crewmen of southern privateers as pirates, the administration backed down when the Confederate government threatened to retaliate by executing Union prisoners of war. Captured privateer crews as well as soldiers became prisoners of war. In 1862 the Union government also agreed to a cartel for the exchange of war prisoners, another proceeding recognized by international law as a form of agreement between nations at war.

Thus, by 1862 the Lincoln administration had, in effect, conceded that this conflict was a war between belligerent governments each in control of a large amount of territory. Nevertheless, the northern war aim was still restoration of national authority over territory controlled by rebels but not the overthrow of their fundamental political or social institutions. This limited war aim called for a limited military strategy of conquering and occupying territory—Clausewitz's first type of war. From the fall of 1861 to the spring of 1862, Union forces enjoyed a great deal of success in this effort. With the help of local Unionists they gained control of western Virginia and detached it from the Confederacy to form the new Union state of West Virginia. The Union navy with army support gained footholds along the south Atlantic coast from Norfolk to St. Augustine. The navy achieved its most spectacular success with the capture of New Orleans in April 1862 while army troops occupied part of southern Louisiana. Meanwhile, two Union naval forces drove up and down the Mississippi until they gained control of all of it except a 200-mile stretch between Vicksburg, Mississippi and Port Hudson, Louisiana. Union armies under Ulysses S. Grant and Don Carlos Buell, supported by river gunboats, captured Forts Henry and Donelson, occupied Nashville and most of Tennessee, penetrated far up the Tennessee River into northern Alabama, and defeated a Confederate counterattack in the bloody battle of Shiloh. In May 1862, the large and well-trained Army of the Potomac under George B. McClellan drove Confederates all the way up the Virginia Peninsula to within five miles of Richmond while panic seized the southern capital and the Confederate government prepared to evacuate it. The war for southern independence seemed to be tottering to defeat. The *New York Tribune* proclaimed in May 1862 that "the rebels themselves are panic-stricken, or despondent. It now requires no very far-reaching prophet to predict the end of this struggle."[15]

But the *Tribune* proved to be a poor prophet. The Confederacy picked itself up from the floor and fought back. Guerrilla attacks and cavalry raids in Tennessee and Mississippi struck Union supply bases and transport networks. Stonewall Jackson drove the Federals out of the Shenandoah Valley. Robert E. Lee drove them away from Richmond and off the Peninsula. In the western theater Vicksburg foiled the initial Union efforts to capture it and open the Mississippi. Confederate generals Braxton Bragg and Kirby Smith maneuvered the Yankees out of Tennessee and invaded Kentucky at the same time that Lee smashed them at second Manassas and invaded Maryland. In four months Confederate armies had counterpunched so hard that they had Union forces on the ropes. The limited-war strategy of conquering southern territory clearly would not do the job so long as Confederate armies remained intact and strong.

General Grant was one of the first to recognize this. Before the battle of Shiloh, easy northern victories at Forts Henry and Donelson and elsewhere in the West had convinced him that the Confederacy was a hollow shell about to collapse. After the rebels had counterattacked and nearly ruined him at Shiloh, however, Grant said that he "gave up all idea of saving the Union except by complete conquest."[16] By complete conquest he meant not merely occupation of territory, but destruction of enemy armies, which thereafter became Grant's chief strategic goal. It became

Lincoln's goal too. "Destroy the rebel army," he instructed McClellan before the battle of Antietam. When McClellan proved unable or unwilling to do so, Lincoln removed him from command. In 1863, Lincoln told General Joseph Hooker that "Lee's *army*, and not *Richmond*, is your true objective point." When Lee again invaded the North, Lincoln instructed Hooker that this "gives you back the chance [to destroy the enemy far from his base] that I thought McClellan lost last fall." When Hooker hesitated and complained, Lincoln replaced him with George G. Meade who won the battle of Gettysburg but failed to pursue and attack Lee vigorously as Lincoln implored him to do. "Great God!" exclaimed the distraught president when he learned that Meade had let Lee get back across the Potomac without further damage. "Our Army held the war in the hollow of their hand and would not close it."[17] Lincoln did not remove Meade, but brought Grant east to oversee him while leaving Sherman in command in the West. By 1864, Lincoln finally had generals in top commands who believed in destroying enemy armies.

This was a large step toward total war, but it was not the final step. When Grant said that Shiloh convinced him that the rebellion could be crushed only by complete conquest, he added that this included the destruction of any property or other resources used to sustain Confederate armies as well as of those armies themselves. Before Shiloh, wrote Grant in his memoirs, he had been careful "to protect the property of the citizens whose territory was invaded"; afterwards his policy was to "consume everything that could be used to support or supply armies." Grant's principal subordinate in the western theater was Sherman, whose experiences in Tennessee and Mississippi, where guerrillas sheltered by the civilian population wreaked havoc behind Union lines, convinced him that "we are not only fighting hostile armies, but a hostile people, and must make [them] ... feel the hard hand of war."[18]

Confiscation of enemy property used in support of war was a recognized belligerent right under international law; by the summer of 1862, Union armies in the South had begun to do this on a large scale. The war had come a long way since Lincoln's initial promise "to avoid any devastation, any destruction of, or interference with, property." Now even civilian property such as crops in the field or livestock in the barn was fair game, since these things could be used to feed Confederate armies. Congress approved this policy with a limited confiscation act in August 1861 and a more sweeping act in July 1862. General-in-Chief Halleck gave shape to the policy in August 1862 with orders to Grant about treatment of Confederate sympathizers in Union occupied territory. "Handle that class without gloves," Halleck told Grant, and "take their property for public use....It is time that they should begin to feel the presence of the war."[19]

Lincoln also endorsed this bare-knuckle policy by the summer of 1862. He had come around slowly to such a position, for it did not conform to the original national strategy of slapping rebels on the wrist with one hand while gently beckoning the hosts of southern Unionists back into the fold with the other. In his message to Congress on December 3, 1861, Lincoln had deprecated radical action against southern property. "In considering the policy to be adopted for suppressing the insurrection," he said, "I have been anxious and careful that the inevitable conflict for this purpose shall not degenerate into a violent and remorseless revolutionary struggle."[20] But during the epic campaigns and battles of 1862, the war did become violent and remorseless, and it would soon become revolutionary.

Like Grant, Lincoln lost faith in those illusory southern Unionists and became convinced that the rebellion could be put down only by complete conquest. To a southern Unionist and a northern conservative who complained in July 1862 about the government's seizure of civilian property and suppression of civil liberties in occupied Louisiana, Lincoln replied angrily that those supposed Unionists had had their chance to overcome the rebel faction in Louisiana and had done nothing but grumble about the army's vigorous enforcement of Union authority. "The paralysis—the dead palsy—of the government in this whole struggle," said Lincoln, "is that this class of men will do nothing for the government, nothing for themselves, except demand that the government shall not strike its open enemies, lest they be struck by accident!" The administration could no longer pursue "a temporizing and forbearing" policy toward the South, said Lincoln. Conservatives and southerners who did not like the new policy should blame the rebels who started the war. They must understand, said Lincoln sternly, "that they cannot experiment for ten years trying to destroy the government, and if they fail still come back into the Union unhurt."[21]

This exchange concerned slavery as well as other kinds of southern property. Slaves were the South's most valuable and vulnerable form of property. Lincoln's policy toward slavery became a touchstone of the evolution of this conflict from a limited war to restore the old Union to a total war to destroy the southern social as well as political system.

During 1861, Lincoln reiterated his oft-repeated pledge that he had no intention of interfering with slavery in the states where it already existed. In July of that year Congress endorsed this position by passing the Crittenden-Johnson resolution affirming the purpose of the war to be preservation of the Union and not interference with the "established institutions"—that is, slavery—of the seceded states. Since those states, in the administration's theory, were still legally *in* the Union, they continued to enjoy all their constitutional rights, including slavery.

Abolitionists and radical Republicans who wanted to turn this conflict into a war to abolish slavery expressed a different theory. They maintained that by seceding and making war on the United States, southern states had forfeited their rights under the Constitution. Radicals pointed out that the blockade and the treatment of captured rebel soldiers as prisoners of war had established the belligerent status of the Confederacy as a power at war with the United States. Thus its slaves could be confiscated as enemy property. The confiscation act passed by Congress in August 1861 did authorize a limited degree of confiscation of slaves who had been employed directly in support of the Confederate war effort.

Two Union generals went even farther than this. In September 1861, John C. Fremont, commander of Union forces in the border slave state of Missouri, proclaimed martial law in the state and declared the slaves of all Confederate sympathizers free. General David Hunter did the same the following spring in the "Department of the South"—the states of South Carolina, Georgia, and Florida, where Union forces occupied a few beachheads along the coast.

Lincoln revoked both of these military edicts. He feared that they would alienate the border-state Unionists he was still cultivating. Lincoln considered the allegiance of these states crucial; he would like to have God on his side, he reportedly said, but he must have Kentucky, and Fremont's emancipation order would probably "ruin our rather fair prospect for Kentucky" if he let it stand.[22] Lincoln at this time was also trying to maintain a bipartisan coalition in the North on behalf of the war effort. Nearly half of the northern people had voted Democratic in 1860. They supported a war for the Union but many of them probably would not support a war against slavery. General McClellan, himself a Democrat as well as the North's most prominent general in 1862, warned Lincoln about this in an unsolicited letter of advice concerning national strategy in July 1862 (after the failure of his Peninsula campaign). "It should not be a war looking to the subjugation of the [southern] people," the general instructed his commander in chief. "Neither confiscation of property... [n]or forcible abolition of slavery should be contemplated for a moment.... A declaration of radical views, especially upon slavery, will rapidly disintegrate our present armies."[23]

But by this time Lincoln had begun to move precisely in the direction that McClellan advised against. He had concluded that McClellan's conservative counsel on national strategy was of a piece with the general's cautious and unsuccessful military strategy. The president had also become disillusioned with border-state Unionists. Three times in the spring and summer he had appealed to them for support of a plan of gradual, compensated emancipation in their states, to be paid for mostly by northern taxpayers. Lincoln hoped that border-state acceptance of such a plan would break the logjam on slavery and deprive the Confederacy of any hope for winning the allegiance of these states. But the border-state congressmen rejected Lincoln's appeal at about the same time that McClellan advised against an emancipation policy.

For Lincoln this was the last straw. A conservative, gradualist policy on slavery was clearly of a piece with the limited-war strategy that had governed Union policy during the first year of the war. The very evening that he learned of the border-state rejection of his gradual emancipation plan (July 12, 1862), the president made up his mind to issue an emancipation proclamation as a war measure to weaken the enemy. The next day he privately told Secretary of State Seward and Secretary of the Navy Welles of his decision. A week later he announced it formally to the cabinet. Lincoln now believed emancipation to be "a military necessity, absolutely essential to the preservation of the Union," he told them. "The slaves [are] undeniably an element of strength to those who had their service," he went on, "and we must decide whether that element should be with us or against us. . . . We must free the slaves or be ourselves subdued." Lincoln conceded that the loyal slaveholders of border states could not be expected to take the lead in a war measure against *disloyal* slaveholders. "The blow must fall first and foremost on . . . the rebels," he told the cabinet. "Having made war on the Government, they [are] subject to the incidents and calamities of war."[24]

All members of the cabinet agreed except Montgomery Blair, a former Democrat from Maryland. He protested that this radical measure would alienate the border states and northern Democrats. Lincoln replied that he had done his best to cajole the border states, but now "we must make the forward movement" without them. They would not like it but they would eventually accept it. As for the Democrats, Lincoln was done conciliating them. The best of them, like Secretary of War Stanton, had already come over to the Republicans while the rest formed an obstructive opposition whose "clubs would be used against us take what course we might." No, said Lincoln, it was time for "decisive and extensive measures. . . . We [want] the army to strike more vigorous blows. The Administration must set an example, and strike at the heart of the rebellion."[25]

We must strike at the heart of the rebellion to inspire the army to *strike more vigorous blows.* Here we have in a nutshell the rationale for emancipation as a military strategy of total war. It would weaken the enemy's war effort by disrupting its labor force and augment the Union war effort by converting part of that labor force to a northern asset. Lincoln adopted Seward's suggestion to postpone issuing the Proclamation until Union forces won a significant victory. After the battle of Antietam, Lincoln issued the preliminary Proclamation warning that on January 1, 1863, he would proclaim freedom for slaves in all states or portions of states then in rebellion against the United States. January 1 came, and with it the Proclamation applying to all or parts of ten southern states in which, by virtue of his war powers as commander in chief, Lincoln declared all slaves "forever free" as "a fit and necessary measure for suppressing said rebellion."[26]

Democrats bitterly opposed the Proclamation, and the war became thereafter primarily a Republican war. Some Democrats in the army also complained, and seemed ready to rally around McClellan as a symbol of the opposition. But by January 1863, McClellan was out of the army and several other Democratic generals were also soon removed or reassigned. Many other soldiers who had initially opposed emancipation also changed their minds as the scale of war continued to escalate. In January 1863 an Ohio colonel almost resigned his commission in protest against the Emancipation Proclamation; a year later he confessed that while "it goes hard" to admit he had been wrong, he now favored "doing away with the...accursed institution of Slavery....Never hereafter will I either speak or vote in favor of Slavery; this is no hasty conclusion but a deep conviction."[27] By that time most Union soldiers likewise accepted the policy announced in the Emancipation Proclamation of recruiting black soldiers to fight for the Union. In August 1863, Lincoln maintained that "the emancipation policy, and the use of colored troops, constitute the heaviest blow yet dealt to the rebellion."[28]

Emancipation, then, became a crucial part of northern military strategy, an important means of winning the war. But if it remained merely a means it would not be a part of national strategy—that is, of the *purpose* for which the war was being fought. Nor would it meet the criterion that military strategy should be consistent with national strategy, for it would be inconsistent to fight a war using the weapon of emancipation to restore a Union that still contained slaves. Lincoln recognized this. Although restoration of the Union remained his first priority, the abolition of slavery became an end as well as a means, a war aim virtually inseparable from Union itself. The first step in making it so came in the Emancipation Proclamation, which Lincoln pronounced "an act of justice" as well as a military necessity. Of course the border states, along with Tennessee and small enclaves elsewhere in the Confederate states, were not covered by the Proclamation because they were under Union control and not at war with the United States and thus exempt from an executive action that could legally be based only on the president's war powers. But Lincoln kept up his pressure on the border states to adopt emancipation themselves. With his support, leaders committed to the abolition of slavery gained political power in Maryland and Missouri. They pushed through constitutional reforms that abolished slavery in those states before the end of the war.

Lincoln's presidential reconstruction policy, announced in December 1863, offered pardon and amnesty to southerners who took an oath of allegiance to the Union *and* to all wartime policies concerning slavery and emancipation. Reconstructed governments sponsored by Lincoln in Louisiana, Arkansas, and Tennessee abolished slavery in those states—at least in the portions of them controlled by Union troops—before the war ended. West Virginia came in as a new state in 1863 with a constitution pledged to abolish slavery. And in 1864, Lincoln took the lead in getting the Republican national convention that renominated him to adopt a platform calling for a Thirteenth Amendment to the Constitution prohibiting slavery everywhere in the United States. Because slavery was "hostile to the principles of republican government, justice, and national safety," declared the platform, Republicans vowed to accomplish its "utter and complete extirpation from the soil of the republic." Emancipation had thus become an end as well as a means of Union victory. As Lincoln stated in the Gettysburg Address, the North fought from 1863 on for "a new birth of freedom."[29]

Most southerners agreed with Jefferson Davis that emancipation and the northern enlistment of black soldiers were "the most execrable measures in the history of guilty man." Davis and his Congress announced an intention to execute Union officers captured in states affected by the Emancipation Proclamation as "criminals engaged in inciting servile insurrection."[30] The Confederacy did not carry out this threat, but it did return many captured black soldiers to slavery. And southern military units did, on several occasions, murder captured black soldiers and their officers instead of taking them prisoners.

Emancipation and the enlistment of slaves as soldiers tremendously increased the stakes in this war, for the South as well as the North. Southerners vowed to fight "to the last ditch" before yielding to a Yankee nation that could commit such execrable deeds. Gone was any hope of an armistice or a negotiated peace so long as the Lincoln administration was in power. The alternatives were reduced starkly to southern independence on the one hand or unconditional surrender of the South on the other.

By midsummer 1864 it looked like the former alternative—southern independence—was likely to prevail. This was one of the darkest periods of the war for the North. Its people had watched the beginning of Grant's and Sherman's military campaigns in the spring with high hopes that they would finally crush the rebellion within a month or two. But by July, Grant was bogged down before Petersburg after his army had suffered enormous casualties in a vain effort to hammer Lee into submission, while Sherman seemed similarly stymied in his attempt to capture Atlanta and break up the Confederate army defending it. War weariness and defeatism corroded the morale of northerners as they contemplated the seemingly endless cost of this war in the lives of their young men. Informal peace negotiations between Horace Greeley and Confederate agents in Canada and between two northern citizens and Jefferson Davis in Richmond during July succeeded only in eliciting the uncompromising terms of both sides. Lincoln wrote down his terms for Greeley in these words: "The restoration of the Union and abandonment of slavery." Davis made his terms equally clear: "We are fighting for INDEPENDENCE and that, or extermination, we will have."[31] As Lincoln later commented on this exchange, Davis "does not attempt to deceive us. He affords us no excuse to deceive ourselves. He cannot voluntarily reaccept the Union; we cannot voluntarily yield it. Between him and us the issue is distinct, simple, and inflexible. It is an issue which can only be tried by war, and decided by victory."[32]

This was Lincoln's most direct affirmation of unconditional surrender as the *sine qua non* of his national strategy. In it he mentioned Union as the only inflexible issue between North and South, but events in the late summer of 1864 gave Lincoln ample opportunity to demonstrate that he now considered emancipation to be an integral part of that inflexible issue of Union. Northern morale dropped to its lowest point in August. "The people are wild for peace," reported Republican political leaders. Northern Democrats were calling the war a failure and preparing to nominate McClellan on a platform demanding an armistice and peace negotiations. Democratic propagandists had somehow managed to convince their party faithful, and a good many Republicans as well, that Lincoln's insistence on coupling emancipation with Union was the only stumbling block to peace negotiations, despite Jefferson Davis's insistence that Union itself was the stumbling block. Some Republican leaders put enormous pressure on Lincoln to smoke out Davis on this issue by offering peace with Union as the only condition. To do so would, of course, give the impression of backing down on emancipation as a war aim.

These pressures filled Lincoln with dismay. The "sole purpose" of the war *was* to restore the Union, he told wavering Republicans. "But no human power can subdue this rebellion without using the Emancipation lever as I have done." More than 100,000 black soldiers were fighting for the Union, and their efforts were crucial to northern victory. They would not continue fighting if they thought the North intended "to betray them.... If they stake their lives for us they must be prompted by the strongest motive...the promise of freedom. And the promise being made, must be kept....There have been men who proposed to me to return to slavery the black warriors" who had risked their lives for the Union. "I should be damned in time & in eternity for so doing. The world shall know that I will keep my faith to friends & enemies, come what will."[33]

Nevertheless, Lincoln did waver temporarily in the face of the overwhelming pressure to drop emancipation as a precondition of peace negotiations. He drafted a private letter to a northern Democrat that included this sentence: "If Jefferson Davis wishes to know what I would do if he were to offer peace and re-union, saying nothing about slavery, let him try me." And Lincoln also drafted instructions for Henry Raymond, editor of the *New York Times* and chairman of the Republican national committee, to go to Richmond as a special envoy to propose "that upon the restoration of the Union and the national authority, the war shall cease at once, all remaining questions to be left for adjustment by peaceful modes." But Lincoln did not send the letter and he decided against sending Raymond to Richmond. Even though the president was convinced in August 1864 that he would not be re-elected, he decided that to give the appearance of backing down on emancipation "would be worse than losing the Presidential contest."[34]

In the end, of course, Lincoln achieved a triumphant reelection because northern morale revived after Sherman's capture of Atlanta and Sheridan's smashing victories in the Shenandoah Valley during September and October. Soon after the election Sherman began his devastating march from Atlanta to the sea. George Thomas's Union army in Tennessee destroyed John Bell Hood's Confederate Army of Tennessee at the battles of Franklin and Nashville. One disaster followed another for the Confederates during the winter of 1864–65, while Lincoln reiterated his determination to accept no peace short of unconditional surrender. And he left the South in no doubt of that determination. In his message to Congress on December 6, Lincoln cited statistics showing that the Union army and navy were the largest in the world, northern population was growing, and northern war production increasing. Union resources, he announced, "are unexhausted, and...inexhaustible....We are gaining strength, and may, if need be, maintain the contest indefinitely."[35]

This was a chilling message to the South, whose resources were just about exhausted. Once more men of good will on both sides tried to set up peace negotiations to stop the killing. On February 3, 1865, Lincoln himself and Secretary of State Seward met with three high Confederate officials including Vice President Alexander H. Stephens on board a Union ship anchored at Hampton Roads, Virginia. During four hours of talks Lincoln budged not an inch from his minimum conditions for peace, which he described as: "1) The restoration of the National authority throughout all the states. 2) No receding by the Executive of the United States on the Slavery question. 3) No cessation of hostilities short of an end of the war, and the disbanding of all forces hostile to the government." The Confederate commissioners returned home empty-handed, angry because they considered these terms "nothing less than unconditional surrender."[36] Of course they were, but Lincoln had never during the past two years given the South reason to expect anything else.

Lincoln returned to Washington to prepare his second inaugural address, which ranks in its eloquence and its evocation of the meaning of this war with the Gettysburg Address itself. Reviewing the past four years, Lincoln admitted that neither side had "expected for the war, the magnitude, or the duration, which it has already achieved. Each looked for an easier triumph, and a result less fundamental and astounding." Back in the days when the North looked for an easier triumph, Lincoln might have added, he had pursued a national strategy of limited war to restore the *status quo ante bellum*. But when the chances of an easy triumph disappeared, Lincoln grasped the necessity for a strategy of total war to overthrow the enemy's social and political system.

Whatever flaws historians might find in Lincoln's military strategy, it is hard to find fault with his national strategy. His sense of timing and his sensitivity to the pulse of the northern people were superb. As he once told a visiting delegation of abolitionists, if he had issued the Emancipation Proclamation six months sooner than he did, "public sentiment would not have sustained it."[37] He might have added that if he had waited six months longer, it would have come too late. After skillfully steering a course between proslavery Democrats and antislavery Republicans during the first eighteen months of war, Lincoln guided a new majority coalition of Republicans and converted Democrats through the uncharted waters of total war and emancipation filled with sharp reefs and rocks, emerging triumphant into a second term on a platform of unconditional surrender that gave the nation a new birth of freedom.

NOTES

1. Roy P. Basler, ed., *The Collected Works of Abraham Lincoln*, 9 vols. (New Brunswick, N.J., 1953–55), VIII, 333.
2. Earl Schenck Miers, ed., *Lincoln Day by Day: A Chronology 1809-1865*, 3 vols. (Washington, 1960), Vol. Ill: 1861–1865, ed. by C. Percy Powell.
3. David Homer Bates, *Lincoln in the Telegraph Office* (New York, 1907).
4. Tyler Dennett, ed., *Lincoln and the Civil War in the Diaries and Letters of John Hay* (New York, 1939), 180; *Collected Works of Lincoln*, VII, 393.
5. John Henry Cramer, *Lincoln under Enemy Fire* (New York, 1948).
6. *Collected Works of Lincoln*, VII, 476.
7. Mark E. Neely, Jr., *The Abraham Lincoln Encyclopedia* (New York, 1982); Gabor S. Boritt, ed., *The Historian's Lincoln: Pseudohistory, Psychohistory and History* (Urbana, 1988), a publication containing the papers and comments thereon at the 1984 Gettysburg conference; Don E. Fehrenbacher, *Lincoln in Text and Context: Collected Essays* (Stanford, 1987).
8. T. Harry Williams, *Lincoln and His Generals* (New York, 1952); Kenneth P. Williams, *Lincoln Finds a General*, 5 vols. (New York, 1949–59).
9. Carl von Clausewitz, *On War*, translated by Col. James J. Graham, 3 vols. (London, 1911), 1, 23; 111, 121; Russell F. Weigley, *The American Way of War* (Bloomington, 1973), xvii; Alastair Buchan, *War in Modern Society: An Introduction* (New York, 1968), 81–82.
10. *War of the Rebellion: A Compilation of the Official Records of the Union and Confederate Armies* (Washington, 1880–1901), Series Vol. 34, pt. 3, pp. 332–33. Hereinafter cited as *O.R.*
11. T. Harry Williams, *Lincoln and His Generals*, 11.
12. Clausewitz, *On War*, I, xxiii.
13. *Collected Works of Lincoln*, IV, 332.
14. *Ibid.*, IV, 437, 332.
15. *New York Tribune*, May 23, 1862.
16. *Personal Memoirs* of *U. S. Grant*, 2 vols. (New York, 1885), 1,368.
17. *Collected Works of Lincoln*, V, 426; VI, 257, 281; *Diary of Gideon Welles*, ed. Howard K. Beale, 3 vols. (New York, 1960), I, 370; Dennett, ed., *Lincoln and the Civil War in the Diaries and Letters of John Hay*, 69.
18. *Memoirs of Grant*, 1, 368–69; Burke Davis, *Sherman's March* (New York, 1980), 109.
19. *O.R.*, Ser. I, *Vol.* 17, Pt. 2, p. 150.
20. *Collected Works of Lincoln*, V, 48–49.
21. *Ibid.*, V, 344–46, 350.
22. *Ibid.*, IV, 506.
23. George B. McClellan, *McClellan's Own Story* (New York, 1886), 487–89.
24. Gideon Welles, "The History of Emancipation," *The Galaxy* 14 (Dec. 1872); 842–43.
25. *Ibid.*; David Donald, ed., *Inside Lincoln's Cabinet: The Civil War Diaries of Salmon P. Chase* (New York, 1954), 149–52; *Diary of Gideon Welles*, 1,142–45; John G. Nicolay and John Hay, *Abraham Lincoln: A History*, 10 vols. (New York, 1890), VI, 158–63.
26. The texts of the preliminary and final proclamations are in *Collected Works of Lincoln*, V, 433–36; VI, 28–30.
27. Marcus Spiegel to Caroline Spiegel, Jan. 25, 1863, Jan. 22, 1864, in Frank L. Byrne and Jean Powers Soman, eds., *Your True Marcus: The Civil War Letters* of a *Jewish Colonel* (Kent, Ohio, 1985), 226, 315–16.
28. *Collected Works of Lincoln*, VI, 408–9. Lincoln was here repeating the words of General Grant (a prewar Democrat) who had written to him on August 23, 1863, in enthusiastic support of emancipation and black troops. (Robert Todd Lincoln Collection of Abraham Lincoln Papers, Library of Congress.)
29. Edward Stanwood, *A History of the Presidency* (Boston, 1903), 301–2; *Collected Works of Lincoln*, VII, 23.

30. Dunbar Rowland, ed., *Jefferson Davis, Constitutionalist: His Letters, Papers, and Speeches*, 10 vols. (Jackson, Miss., 1923), V, 409; *O.R.*, Ser. II, Vol. 5, pp. 797, 940–41.
31. *Collected Works of Lincoln*, VII, 435; Hudson Strode, *Jefferson Davis: Tragic Hero, 1864–1889* (New York, 1964), 77. For the abortive peace negotiations of 1864, see Edward C. Kirkland, *The Peacemakers of 1864* (New York, 1927), chaps. 2–3.
32. *Collected Works of Lincoln*, VI ii, 151.
33. Ibid., VII, 499–501, 506–7.
34. Ibid., V, 501, 517; Nicolay and Hay, *Abraham Lincoln*, IX, 221.
35. *Collected Works of Lincoln*, VIII, 151.
36. Ibid., VIII, 279; Strode, *Jefferson Davis*, 140–41.
37. Francis B. Carpenter, *Six Months at the White House with Abraham Lincoln* (New York, 1866), 77.

11

LINCOLN AND THE CONSTITUTION

Mark E. Neely, Jr.

The Democratic depiction of Lincoln as a tyrant was to have more influence on history than it merited, but like many political caricatures, it contained a certain element of truth. To be sure, there was nothing of the dictator in Lincoln, who stood for reelection in 1864 and, until General Sherman captured Atlanta, genuinely feared that he would lose the presidency. But he did not by habit think first of the constitutional aspect of most problems he faced. His impulse was to turn to the practical.

WHIG HERITAGE

Lincoln had been a Whig for most of the life of that political party—twice as long as he was a Republican. And the Whigs generally took a broad view of what the Constitution allowed the federal government to do (create a national bank and fund the building of canals, roads, and railroads, for example). As a victim of rural isolation and lack of economic opportunity in his youth, Abraham Lincoln proved eager as a politician to provide the country with those things that seemed wanting in his hardscrabble past. His desire to get on with economic development made him impatient with Democratic arguments that internal improvements funded by the federal government were unconstitutional.

After years of political struggle to implement improvement schemes, Lincoln, as a congressman in the late 1840s saw "the question of improvements...verging to a final crisis." The Democratic national platform in 1848 declared that "the constitution does not confer upon the general government the power to commence, and carry on a general system of internal improvements." Speaking on the subject in the House of Representatives, the 39-year-old Lincoln expressed plainly his mature judgment that "no man, who is clear on the questions of expediency, needs feel his conscience much pricked upon this."

Emphasis on the practical was characteristic of Lincoln, but his confidence in this instance stemmed in part from a belief that the constitutional arguments were also on his side. In the Civil War, Lincoln would again suggest practical reasons for action and then add assurances and proofs that the Constitution permitted it anyhow.

In his 1848 speech on the internal improvements crisis, Lincoln laid unusual emphasis on constitutional subject matter. Despite his assertion that practical demands for internal improvements should weigh heavily against constitutional doubt or controversy, Lincoln seemed preoccupied with constitutional questions in the speech, devoting eight of twenty-six paragraphs, almost a third of his time, to that issue. He began these arguments with a modest disclaimer:

> Mr. Chairman, on the...constitutional question, I have not much to say. Being the man I am, and speaking when I do, I feel, that in any attempt at an original constitutional argument, I should not be, and ought not to be, listened to patiently. The ablest, and the best of men, have gone over the whole ground long ago.

Lincoln followed this by quoting and summarizing at some length arguments from Kent's *Commentaries.*

The Democratic president, James K. Polk, had suggested that it would require a constitutional amendment to make such internal improvements possible. Lincoln did not much like this idea, in part no doubt because of its impracticability and time-consuming nature, but in the speech, he attacked it in the language of sweeping constitutional conservatism.

> I have already said that no one, who is satisfied of the expediency of making improvements, needs be much uneasy in his conscience about its constitutionality. I wish now to submit a few remarks on the general proposition of amending the constitution. As a general rule, I think, we would [do] much better [to] let it alone. No slight occasion should tempt us to touch it. Better not take the first step, which may lead to a habit of altering it. Better, rather, habituate ourselves to think of it, as unalterable. It can scarcely be made better than it is. New provisions, would introduce new difficulties, and thus create, and increase appetite for still further change. No sir, let it stand as it is. New hands have never touched it. The men who made it, have done their work, and have passed away. Who shall improve, on what *they* did?[1]

Often quoted in later years, this passage had ra'
meaning in context from what constitutional conservati'
have imagined. What Congressman Lincoln was really
no amendment was needed if a reasonably broad inte₁ₚ
existing document were accepted.

Before this unusual speech, Lincoln had in his sixteen-year career
in politics rarely gone on record on constitutional questions. In 1832,
when he wrote at length on internal improvements for the Sangamon
River in his first published political platform, young Lincoln had dwelled
exclusively on practical matters of cost and navigability. In 1836, when he
declared his candidacy for reelection to the state legislature, the 27-year-
old Whig again favored a plan to make internal improvements possible
and focused exclusively on financial questions: "Whether elected or not,
I go for distributing the proceeds of the sales of the public lands to the
several states, to enable our state, in common with others, to dig canals
and construct rail roads, without borrowing money and paying interest on
it." Except for a brief comment the next year on the legality of the Illinois
State Bank under the state constitution, Lincoln first spoke on a constitutional question in his speech on Martin Van Buren's subtreasury scheme
delivered December 26, 1839. He stressed the practical advantages of a
national bank-increased circulation of money as well as cheaper and safer
operation over the Democrats' proposal. Then he addressed the question
of constitutionality. Lincoln was satisfied that the U.S. Supreme Court had
declared a national bank constitutional, as had a majority of the country's
famous founders. Rather than go over that well-worn path again, however, he now wanted "to take a view of the question...not...taken by
anyone before. It is, that whatever objection ever has or ever can be made
to the constitutionality of a bank, will apply with equal force in its whole
length, breadth and proportions to the Sub-Treasury." If there were no
"express authority" in the Constitution to establish a bank, he quipped,
there was none to establish the subtreasury either.[2]

Lincoln thought them both constitutional, of course. After all, the
Constitution specified general authority "to make all laws necessary and
proper" for carrying into effect the powers expressly enumerated, and
among those enumerated was Congress's power to lay and collect taxes
and to pay the debts of the United States. To accomplish those things, the
government had to be able to collect, keep, transfer, and disburse revenues.
The arguments of his adversaries on this question made Lincoln so impatient that at one point he dismissed them as "too absurd to need further
comment." This was not the tone he customarily used when arguing about
matters of expediency. There he usually managed to find some sympathy
for those who held opposing beliefs, saying even of Southern slaveholders

1854 that they were "just what we would be in their situation." The practical legislator from Illinois was not comfortable on the high ground of inflexible constitutional principle.[3]

In the 1840s, Lincoln appeared to be marching steadily toward a position of gruff and belittling impatience with constitutional arguments against the beleaguered Whig program. A set of resolutions drafted by Lincoln and adopted at a Whig meeting in Springfield in 1843 reiterated his position on the proven constitutionality of a national bank and followed with this abrupt dismissal of Democratic arguments against distribution of the proceeds from the sale of the national lands: "Much incomprehensible jargon is often urged against the constitutionality of this measure. We forbear, in this place, attempting to answer it, simply because, in our opinion, those who urge it, are, through party zeal, resolved not to see or acknowledge the truth." But Lincoln's movement away from constitutional modes of thinking was halted abruptly by the presidency of James K. Polk.[4]

When Lincoln spoke against the subtreasury in 1839, he devoted three of fifty-nine paragraphs to the constitutional issue; when he made his last ditch defense of internal improvements (while Polk was president in 1848), he devoted eight of the twenty-six paragraphs to the constitutional question. What had changed was Lincoln's awareness of the importance of constitutional issues in general. And that heightened awareness was a result of the Mexican War.

Lincoln hated the war, which he considered "unconstitutional and unnecessary." He was not yet, if he ever became one, an internationally minded man. Lincoln did not worry much about Mexico for the sake of Mexicans. In fact, in a lecture on discoveries and inventions he gave years later, Lincoln celebrated the Yankee "*habit* of observation and reflection" which he thought responsible for the quick discovery of gold in California, "which had been trodden upon, and over-looked by indians and Mexican greasers, for centuries." The slavery issue was not the key to his opposition to the Mexican War either. While campaigning for Zachary Taylor in the summer of 1848, Lincoln stated that (as the press reported it) he "did not believe with many of his fellow citizens that this war was originated for the purpose of extending slave territory."[5]

Lincoln maintained instead that "it was a war of conquest brought into existence to catch votes." The war was unnecessary "inasmuch as Mexico was in no way molesting, or menacing the U.S." and unconstitutional "because the power of levying war is vested in Congress, and not in the President." Polk's motive for starting the war with Mexico "was to divert public attention from the surrender of 'Fifty-four forty or fight' to Great Brittain [*sic*], on the Oregon boundary question.[6]

When Lincoln's law partner, William H. Herndon, also an active Whig, disputed this interpretation of the origins of the Mexican War, Lincoln engaged in a rare exercise for him: a long letter, lecturing in tone, on a constitutional question. Herndon's letter, which has not survived, may have caused his partner to focus on the constitutional question, for Lincoln's letter begins, "Your letter of the 29th. Jany. was received last night. Being exclusively a constitutional argument, I wish to submit some reflections upon it." Whatever the cause, once focused, Lincoln's scrutiny proved close and intense:

> The provision of the Constitution giving the war-making power to Congress, was dictated, as I understand it, by the following reasons. Kings had always been involving and impoverishing their people in wars, pretending generally, if not always, that the good of the people was the object. This, our Convention understood to be the most oppressive of all Kingly oppressions; and they resolved to so frame the Constitution that *no one man* should hold the power of bringing this oppression upon us. But your view destroys the whole matter, and places our President where kings have always stood?[7]

SLAVERY AND THE CONSTITUTION

At the very time that Abraham Lincoln's awareness of constitutional questions was on the rise, the issue of slavery in the territories was injected into American politics. The Wilmot Proviso, which would have forbidden slavery in any territory acquired as a result of the Mexican War, came up several times while Lincoln was in Congress, and he consistently voted for it. But the slavery controversy did not make a constitutional thinker of Lincoln, any more than the old economic issues of the 1830s and 1840s had.

This sets Lincoln apart from his era. A leading historian of the political ideas of the Whig party, Daniel Walker Howe, has criticized this era for a tendency to make every political question into a constitutional question: "The tendency to debate the constitutionality of issues rather than their expediency did little to temper the discussion; if anything, it exacerbated differences." This volatile constitutionalism became even more a factor in the era that followed. The 1850s, as Don E. Fehrenbacher has pointed out, witnessed the increasing "fashion of constitutionalizing debate on slavery." When pressed, Lincoln voiced an antislavery interpretation of the Constitution, but he was not one to constitutionalize the debate over slavery or anything else.[8]

Lincoln did think more about the Constitution after 1848 than in previous decades, but his ideas were quite unoriginal. He viewed the document as most antislavery moderates did, shunning the anti-Constitution "covenant-with death" views of the abolitionists and their unconstitutional political positions as well. He embraced the interpretation of the Constitution as a reluctant guarantor of the slave interest existing at the time of the country's founding. The Constitution betrayed the basically antislavery sentiments of its authors by hiding slavery "away,... just as an afflicted man hides away a wen or a cancer, which he dares not cut out at once, lest he bleed to death; with the promise, nevertheless, that the cutting may begin at the end of a given time." Like many of his fellow Republicans, Lincoln attributed great importance to the absence of any explicit mention of slavery or the Negro race in the document. It seemed a sure sign that the founders looked forward to the day when, with slavery eradicated by time, there would be "nothing in the constitution to remind them of it."[9]

Lincoln was a lawyer, but antislavery sentiment and Whig tradition go farther than professional outlook to explain Lincoln's views of the Constitution. The influence of Lincoln's profession on his political ideas has been exaggerated in recent years: "the last Blackstone Lawyer to lead the nation," one writer calls him. Such views have been expressed especially by biographers and historians interested in what is widely regarded as "Lincoln's first speech of distinction," his address to the Young Men's Lyceum of Springfield, delivered January 27, 1838. This speech contained not so much constitutional views as cheerleading for the laws of the land and was widely quoted in later years:

Let reverence for the laws, be breathed by every American mother, to the lisping babe, that prattles on her lap—let it be taught in schools, in seminaries, and in colleges;—let it be written in Primmers, spelling books, and in Almanacs;—let it be preached from the pulpit, proclaimed in legislative halls, and enforced in courts of justice. And, in short, let it become the *political religion* of the nation; and let the old and the young, the rich and the poor, the grave and the gay, of all sexes and tongues, and colors and conditions, sacrifice unceasingly upon its altars.

Lincoln mentioned the Constitution itself at the end of the speech, when he invoked "Reason, cold calculating, unimpassioned reason" to "furnish all the materials for our future support and defense. Let those [materials] be moulded into *general intelligence,* [sound] *morality* and, in particular, *a reverence for the constitution and laws.*"[10]

Thus, Lincoln gave "eloquent expression to the developing ideology of his profession," according to historian George M. Fredrickson, who sees "Lincoln's early speeches as an aspiring young lawyer and Whig politician" as part of a " 'conservative' response to the unruly and aggressive democracy spawned by the age of Jackson." Indeed Fredrickson finds this conservative law-and-order strain in Lincoln's political thought substantially unshaken until the *Dred Scott* decision of 1857 undermined "Lincoln's faith in the bench and bar as the ultimate arbiters of constitutional issues." The problem with such an interpretation stems mainly from its approach, that of "intellectual history," for Abraham Lincoln was neither an intellectual nor a systematic political thinker. He was a politician, and historians ignore the instrumental side of his political thought only at great peril. He rarely thought abstractly about the Constitution and the laws. He usually thought about them when a particularly pressing political problem arose. At the time of the Lyceum speech in 1838, Lincoln's recent admission to the Illinois bar was surely a less important circumstance than the political situation. The purpose of the speech was to urge the protection of unpopular minorities. Lincoln mentioned recent headlines describing mob violence and vigilante justice that victimized Mississippi gamblers and unfortunate black people. Most other interpreters of Lincoln's speech in modern times have assumed that the real shadow hanging over it was that of the martyred Elijah Lovejoy, killed just prior to the address by an anti-abolition mob in Alton, Illinois. To say that Lincoln here was at odds with democracy in the age of Jackson is either unfair to Lincoln or paints a dark caricature of Jacksonian democracy.[11]

Lincoln was not searching so much for order and community as for usable arguments and instruments. That is not to say that his constitutional thinking was nakedly opportunistic or embarrassingly shallow, but only that he changed his mind from time to time and that he did not characteristically reach first for a copy of the U.S. Constitution when confronted with a political or social problem. Even to survey Lincoln's ideas on the Constitution is to run the risk of overemphasizing his constitutional concerns, because thinking in constitutional ways did not come naturally to him. It was more often forced on him—by a rigid Democratic president like Polk or by his own law partner's arguments against the articles of their party faith. Whatever the Lyceum address may seem to mean, it is, in fact, difficult to find any tough threads of legalistic, procedural, or constitutional conservatism woven into Lincoln's political thought of the 1850s, even before the *Dred Scott* decision. Lincoln quickly embraced a moralistic antislavery ideology that pointed to the Declaration of Independence and the political libertarianism of Thomas Jefferson as its fundamental source while relegating the Constitution and the laws to a rather pale secondary role. Shortly after the passage of the Kansas-Nebraska Act in 1854, Lincoln told an audience in Springfield on October 4 that the "theory of our government is Universal Freedom. 'All men are created free and equal,' says the Declaration of Independence. The word

'Slavery' is not found in the Constitution." His political message varied little from this until 1861.[12]

Jefferson and the Declaration of·Independence assumed a conspicuous place in Lincoln's political imagery in this period. Nevertheless, careful readers of the previous paragraph will have noted, perhaps a little impatiently, that the Declaration did *not* say that all men were created "free" and equal. Lincoln did not take his political ideas straight and by rote from any single printed source, but of their many sources, the slogans of Thomas Jefferson proved to be of greater importance than the words of the Constitution and of increasing importance to Lincoln after 1854. On October 16, 1854, he spoke of "Mr. Jefferson, the author of the Declaration of Independence," as "the most distinguished politician of our history." He justified his anti-Nebraska stand by saying that "the policy of prohibiting slavery in new territory originated" with Jefferson and the Northwest Ordinance. The policy began "away back of the constitution, in the pure fresh, free breath of the revolution." The hint in this statement that the Constitution may have smothered the free spirit of the revolutionary era never was carried further in Lincoln's thought. He was not a systematic thinker. He was a politician, and few mainstream political candidates wanted to be placed in opposition to the government's founding document.

Instead, antislavery Republicans like Lincoln embraced an antislavery interpretation of (or created an antislavery myth about) the Constitution. "This same generation of men," he said, "mostly the same individuals...who declared this principle [of self-government]—who declared independence—who fought the war of the revolution through—who afterwards made the constitution under which we still live—these same men passed the ordinance of '87, declaring that slavery should never go to the north-west territory." With such language as this, Lincoln made of the founders a single cohort of heroes who drafted the Declaration of Independence, won the Revolution, and wrote the Constitution.[13]

In truth, the Constitution stood as an embarrassment to the antislavery cause. It protected slavery in the states as surely as it did anything, and all politicians, Republican and Democrat alike, knew it. The best the antislavery politicians could do was to find antislavery tendencies in the document. In building a mythical past for his political platform, Lincoln preferred to state the antislavery interpretation of the Constitution and get on quickly past that document to the Declaration of Independence. In a speech in Chicago on July 10, 1858, for example, he said, "We had slavery among us, we could not get our constitution unless we permitted them to remain in slavery, we could not secure the good we did secure if we grasped for more, and having by necessity submitted to that much, it does not destroy the principle that is the charter of our liberties. Let that charter stand as our standard." The spirit of the Constitution, properly and carefully looked at, was antagonistic to the Kansas-Nebraska bill, Lincoln could say after elaborate argument, but it was easier to say that the "spirit of seventy-six" and "the spirit of Nebraska" were "utter antagonisms."[14]

After the *Dred Scott* decision, Lincoln's constitutional views changed little and his overall political thought, less. The Taney court's decision may have accelerated his rush to the Declaration of Independence. In a Springfield speech after the decision, Lincoln asked: "I should like to know if taking this old Declaration of Independence, which declares that all men are equal upon principle and making exceptions to it where will it stop....If that declaration is not the truth, let us get the Statute book, in which we find it and tear it out!" Of course, the Declaration of Independence was not law, as the Constitution was, and could not properly be located in a "statute book." Lincoln knew this and, when not on the stump, could write about it in more lawyerly fashion. In an 1858 letter to an Illinois politician named James N. Brown, Lincoln said more soberly: "I believe the declaration that 'all men are created equal' is the great fundamental principle upon which our free institutions rest; that negro slavery is violative of the principle; but that, by our frame of government, that principle has not been made one of legal obligation." The *Dred Scott* decision merely forced Lincoln to articulate his view of what makes a lasting Supreme Court decision, which he did with characteristic avoidance of Latinate distinctions. Speaking rhetorically to the Southern people early in 1860, Lincoln pointed out what he thought were good reasons for doubting the force of this Supreme Court decision:

> Perhaps you will say the Supreme Court has decided the disputed Constitutional question in your favor. Not quite so. But waiving the lawyer's distinction between dictum and decision, the Court have decided the question for you in a sort of way. The Court have substantially said, it is your Constitutional right to take slaves into the federal territories, and to hold them there as property. When I say the decision was made in a sort of way, I mean it was made in a divided Court, by a bare majority of the Judges, and they not quite agreeing with one another in the reasons for making it; that it is so made as that its avowed supporters disagree with one another about its meaning, and that it was mainly based upon a mistaken statement of fact—the statement in the opinion that the right of property in a slave is distinctly and expressly affirmed in the Constitution.[15]

Here, in challenging Taney's careless opinion, the Republicans' emphasis on the absence of the words "slave," "slavery," or "property" in connection with the idea of slavery, was all the constitutional doctrine Lincoln needed.

WAR AND THE CONSTITUTION

Once Lincoln became president and faced civil war, his clear record on the Constitution became paradoxical and unclear. To be sure, his constitutional outlook all along had left room for the argument of "Necessity." Lincoln demonstrated this years before the Civil War, and not only in recognition of the founders' necessary protection of slavery in the U.S. Constitution. In 1854, while reviewing the history of the slavery-expansion controversy in a speech in Bloomington, Illinois, Lincoln stated matter-of-factly: "Jefferson saw the necessity of our government possessing the whole valley of the Mississippi; and though he acknowledged that our Constitution made no provision for the purchasing of territory, yet he thought the exigency of the case would justify the measure, and the purchase was made." As a Whig and a critic of the Mexican War, Lincoln's record was not as pro-expansion as that of most western politicians, but he admired Jefferson and agreed that the Louisiana Purchase was too good an opportunity to miss, no matter what the Constitution said. The prompt development of an attitude of indifference to the niceties of constitutional interpretation involved in suspending the writ of habeas corpus might have been predicted from the unpricked constitutional conscience of Lincoln's pre-presidential career. He naturally responded vigorously to the exigency of civil war. But on the question of emancipation, Lincoln appeared to some antislavery advocates at the time and to many historians since to have been strangely stricken with a paralyzing constitutional scrupulousness. When it came to putting the spirit of seventy-six into action, Lincoln as president grew suspiciously reluctant.[16]

The most telling event was his revocation of Fremont's emancipation proclamation in Missouri in 1861. In a moment of pique reminiscent of his argument with fellow Whig Herndon over the Mexican War thirteen years earlier, President Lincoln now lectured fellow Republican Orville Hickman Browning on the constitutional issues involved. Lincoln had not bothered to mention the Constitution or to dwell on law in first reprimanding Fremont, but once Browning brought it up, the president waded in:

> Genl. Fremont's proclamation, as to confiscation of property, and the liberation of slaves, is *purely political* and not within the range of *military* law, or necessity. If a commanding General finds a necessity to seize the farm of a private owner, for a pasture, an encampment, or a fortification, he has the right to do so, and to so hold it, as long as the necessity lasts;

and this is within military law, because within military necessity. But to say the farm shall no longer belong to the owner, or his heirs forever; and this as well when the farm is not needed for military purposes as when it is, is purely political, without the savor of military law about it. And the same is true of slaves. If the General needs them, he can seize them, and use them; but when the need is past, it is not for him to fix their permanent future condition. That must be settled according to laws made by law-makers, and not by military proclamations. The proclamation in the point in question, is simply "dictatorship." It assumes that the general may do *anything* he pleases—confiscate the lands and free the slaves of *loyal* people, as well as of disloyal ones. I cannot assume this reckless position; nor allow others to assume it on my responsibility. You speak of it as being the only means of *saving* the government. On the contrary it is itself the surrender of the government. Can it be pretended that it is any longer the government of the U.S.—any government of Constitution and laws,—wherein a General, or a President, may make permanent rules of property by proclamation?

I do not say Congress might not with propriety pass a law, on the point, just such as General Fremont proclaimed. I do not say I might not, as a member of Congress, vote for it. What I object to, is, that I as President, shall expressly or impliedly seize and exercise the permanent legislative functions or the government.

When he finished that part of the letter, Lincoln wrote, "So much for principle. Now as to policy." And then he proceeded to talk about Kentucky. It seems striking that when delaying freedom for the slave, Lincoln thought first of constitutional principle, then of policy. But policy considerations came first with him in dealing with the crisis following the firing on Fort Sumter. Was he willing to go farther to save the Union than to free the slaves? Did he value the Union more than liberty after all?[17]

To answer those questions will require a quick review of American thinking on the subject of emancipation and war before Abraham Lincoln faced both as live subjects rather than abstract possibilities. The review can be brief because there had been little thought on the subject and because what little thought there was had been clearly and succinctly put by an intelligent politician, John Quincy Adams. After his return to Washington as a member of the House of Representatives, "Old Man Eloquent" attempted to avenge his loss of reelection to the presidency in 1828 by attacking Southerners and the "Slave Power." In a debate in Congress as early as 1836, Adams expressed the belief that from "the instant that our slaveholding states become the theater of war, civil, servile or foreign...the war powers of Congress extend to interference with the institution of slavery in every way by which it can be interfered with." During the early rounds of the Texas controversy in 1842, when war was much spoken of, Adams again warned Southerners that Congress would have "full and plenary power" over slavery in a state at war.[18] Finally, galvanized by the vigorous example of his old nemesis Andrew Jackson at New Orleans, Adams, in the congressional debate over refunding the general's fine, suddenly declared that the president and even his subordinate commander of the army have the power to abolish slavery:

> When your country is actually in war, whether it be war of invasion or a war of insurrection, Congress has power to carry on the war, and it must carry it on according to the laws of war; and, by the laws of war, an invaded country has all its laws and municipal regulations swept by the board, and martial law takes the place of them.
>
> This power in Congress has, perhaps, never been called into exercise under the present constitution. But when the laws of war are in force, what, I ask, is one of those laws? Is it this: that when a country is invaded, and two hostile armies are met in martial array, the commanders of both armies have power to emancipate all the slaves in the invaded territory.
>
> And here, I recur again to the example of General Jackson.... You are ... passing a law to refund to General Jackson the amount of a certain fine imposed upon him by a judge under the laws of Louisiana. You are going to refund him the money with interest, and this you are going to do because the imposition of the fine was unjust. And why was it unjust? Because General Jackson was acting under the laws of war, and because the moment you place a military commander in a district that is the theatre of war, the laws of war apply to that district.... I lay this down as the law of nations. I say the military authority takes for the time the place of all municipal institutions and of slavery among the rest, and that under that state of things, so far from its being true, that the States where slavery exists have the exclusive management of the subject, not only the President of the United States, but the commander of the army, has power to order the universal emancipation of slaves.[19]

Lincoln's constitutional journey was similar to Adams's.[20] When President Lincoln revoked the Missouri proclamation in September 1861, he had already abandoned any belief that slavery, because of the Constitution, could not be touched in the states where it then existed. Generals could not fix the "permanent future condition" of the slaves in Missouri but the slaves' status could "be settled according to laws made by law-makers." Such an idea, daring though it was, did not fully anticipate the constitutional grounds of Lincoln's actions a year later when he announced his own Emancipation Proclamation, because Lincoln was no "law-maker." He was head of the executive branch; Congress made the laws. Lincoln still thought in 1861 that if he did it himself, it would constitute "dictatorship," but Lincoln would "not say Congress might not with propriety pass a law...just such as General Fremont proclaimed." He even hinted that if he were in Congress as Browning was, he might vote for it. He simply did not think he should, "as President...expressly or impliedly seize and exercise the permanent legislative functions of the government." What has never been noticed in the furor over the Fremont proclamation is how far Lincoln already had traveled down John Quincy Adams's constitutional road in 1861. Although Lincoln would never reach the point where he believed a general could proclaim emancipation, within less than a year of the Fremont episode, he had reached Adams's view that the president could do so. What Lincoln learned, between September 1861 and the drafting of the Emancipation Proclamation in July 1862, was not Adams's view that war threatened slavery; Lincoln knew that already. He learned, perhaps from William Whiting's *War Powers of the President* published in 1862, that war gave the president and not law-makers only the power to abolish slavery in enemy territory.[21]

Lincoln moved faster in adjusting his prewar ideas about the Constitution and slavery than most historians have previously believed. What he said to Browning, admittedly, was said in private. In public, Lincoln's utterances sounded more skeptical, but his constitutional doubts had clearly been dispersed well before the public announcement of the Emancipation Proclamation on September 22, 1862, and he wanted the public to know it. His famous letter of August 22, 1862, to Horace Greeley, counseling patience on the slavery question, said nothing of constitutional obstacles to action and expressed a willingness to free slaves, if such action would save the Union. On September 13, he explicitly told a delegation of Chicago Christians urging emancipation: "I raise no objections against it on legal or constitutional grounds; for, as commander-in-chief of the army and navy, in time of war, I suppose I have a right to take any measure which may best subdue the enemy. Emancipation was for him "a practical war measure" and as soon as military circumstances at the front seemed to require it and political circumstances in the border states seemed to permit it, Lincoln acted to end slavery in the Confederacy.[22]

Lincoln did worry more about the consequences of emancipation than the consequences of suspending the writ of habeas corpus—and for good reason. Lincoln regarded the suspension of the writ as an exception for a temporary emergency, and he felt sure that the American people would never want to continue the condition when the emergency was over. He put it more vividly, of course, comparing such an unimaginable course to that of a man fed emetics in illness and then insisting on "feeding upon them the remainder of his heathful life." About this, Lincoln proved essentially correct. Emancipation was different. Though it might be adopted as a practical measure to end the war, it could not be reversed when the crisis was over. As Lincoln put it in his letter to Browning about the slaves in Missouri, "If the General needs them, he can seize them, and use them; but when the need is past, it is not for him to fix their permanent future condition. That must be settled according to laws." Emancipation, though perhaps a matter of situational ethics in the midst of war, would necessarily affect American society for all time to come. Lincoln was a practical man, all right, but he did occasionally think about the country's "permanent future condition." He saw no danger in the temporary suspension of habeas corpus during rebellion or invasion, but the case of black people was clearly different. Only rigid safeguards would protect freedmen from popular race prejudice and possible reenslavement. Black freedom might prove as temporary and situational as the whites' brief loss of customary liberties during the Civil War. So Lincoln's thoughts necessarily turned to a constitutional amendment to end slavery in the United States.

This was a major change in his constitutional thinking. The Constitution was last amended five years before Abraham Lincoln was born. He was on record in a speech in Congress recommending that the document be left alone and that the American people not get into the habit of changing it. In the desperate throes of the secession crisis, he did agree to a proposed amendment that would have explicitly guaranteed slavery where it already existed. But this was redundant in Lincoln's view, merely reassuring the South of what it already had. In 1864, he wanted an amendment to guarantee that there would be nothing temporary about emancipation.

This ability to balance short-term practicality and long-term ideals is perhaps the essence of statesmanship. In Lincoln's case, the one helped preserve the Constitution as the law of the land, and the other brought such changes as made it worth preserving "throughout the indefinite peaceful future."

NOTES

1. *Coll. Works of Lincoln,* I, 480–81, 485, 486, 488.
2. Ibid., I, 5–8, 48, 62–63, 170–71.
3. Ibid., I, 171–72, 11, 255.
4. Ibid., I, 312.
5. Ibid., III, 358; I, 347–48, 476.
6. Ibid., I, 476, IV, 66.
7. Ibid., I, 451–52.
8. Daniel Walker Howe, *The Political Culture of the American Whigs* (Chicago: Univ. of Chicago Press, 1979), 23; Don E. Fehrenbacher, *The Dred Scott Case: Its Significance in American Law and Politics* (New York: Oxford Univ. Press, 1978), 465.
9. *Coll. Works of Lincoln,* II, 274, IV, 11.

10. Robert A. Ferguson, *Law and Letters in American Culture* (Cambridge: Harvard Univ. Press, 1984), 305. *Coll. Works Lincoln,* I, 112, 115. For opinions of the Lyceum address see Albertt. Beveridge, *Abraham Lincoln, 1809-1858,* I (Boston: Houghton Mifflin, 1928), 227; James G. Randall, *Lincoln the President: Springfield to Gettysburg.* I, 20-23; Benjamin P. Thomas, *Abraham Lincoln—A Biography* (New York: Alfred A. Knopf, 1952), 71-73, and (quoted here) Reinhard H. Luthin, *The Real Abraham Lincoln: A Complete One Volume History of His Life and Times* (Englewood Cliffs: Prentice Hall, 1960), 49-50.

11. George M. Fredrickson, "The Search for Order and Community," in Cullom Davis et al, *The Public and Private Lincoln: Contemporary Perspectives* (Carbondale: Southern Illinois Univ. Press, 1979), 91-93, 96-97.

12. *Coll. Works of Lincoln,* II, 245. Like most of Lincoln's speeches in the prepresidential period, this one is known only from newspaper reports; the possibility of inaccuracy is, unfortunately, high.

13. Ibid., II, 249, 267.

14. Ibid., II, 274, 501.

15. Ibid., II, 276, 500-1; III, 327, 543-44.

16. Ibid., II n, 231.

17. Ibid., IV, 531-32. Perhaps the first historian to state the question as it is stated above was the Englishman, K. C. Wheare, in *Abraham Lincoln and the United States* (New York: Macmillan, 1949), 158.

18. Leonard L. Richards, *The Life and Times of Congressman John Quincy Adams* (New York: Oxford Univ. Press, 1986), 123, 164; Charles Francis Adams, Jr., "John Quincy Adams and Martial Law," *Massachusetts Historical Society, Proceedings,* 2 sec., XV (Jan. 1902), 437-78.

19. S.S. Nicholas, *Martial Law,* pp. 1-2.

20. David Donald was the first historian to sense the importance of Adams's precedent for the Emancipation Proclamation; see Donald, *Lincoln Reconsidered—Essays on the Civil War Era,* 2nd ed. (New York, Vintage Books, 1961), 204-5.

21. William Whiting, *The War Powers of the President, and the Legislative Powers of Congress in Relation to Rebellion, Treason and Slavery* (Boston: John L. Shorey, 1862).

22. *Coll. Works of Lincoln,* V, 421.

SELECTED BIBLIOGRAPHY

PRIMARY AND REFERENCE WORKS

Paul M. Angle, ed. *The Lincoln Reader.* New Brunswick: Rutgers University Press, 1947.

Roy P. Basler, ed. *The Collected Works of Abraham Lincoln.* 8 vols. New Brunswick: Rutgers University Press, 1953.

Don E. Fehrenbacher and Virginia Fehrenbacher. *Recollected Words of Abraham Lincoln.* Stanford: Stanford University Press, 1996.

Harold Holzer, ed. *Lincoln as I Knew Him: Gossip, Tributes, and Revelations from His Best Friends and Worst Enemies.* Chapel Hill: Algonquin, 1999.

———, ed. *The Lincoln-Douglas Debates: The First Complete, Unexpurgated Text.* New York: HarperCollins, 1993.

John G. Nicolay and John Hay. *Complete Works of Abraham Lincoln.* 2 vols. New York: The Century Company, 1894.

Mark E. Neely, Jr. *The Abraham Lincoln Encyclopedia.* New York: McGraw-Hill, 1982.

SECONDARY WORKS

Albert J. Beveridge. *Abraham Lincoln, 1809–1858.* 4 vols. New York and Boston: Houghton Mifflin Company, 1928.

Gabor S. Boritt, *Lincoln and the Economics of the American Dream.* Memphis: Memphis State University Press, 1978.

———. *The Lincoln Enigma: the Changing Faces of an American Icon.* New York: Oxford University Press, 2001.

D. W. Brogan. *Abraham Lincoln.* New York: Schocken, 1963.

Michael Burlingame. *The Inner World of Abraham Lincoln.* Urbana: University of Illinois Press, 1994; 1997.

David Herbert Donald. *Lincoln.* New York: Simon and Shuster, 1995.

Don Edward Fehrenbacher. *Prelude to Greatness: Lincoln in the 1850s.* Stanford: Stanford University Press, 1962.

———. *The Leadership of Abraham Lincoln.* New York: Wiley, 1970.

Eric Foner. *Free Soil, Free Labor, Free Men: The Ideology of the Republican Party before the Civil War.* New York: Oxford University Press, 1970.

John Hope Franklin. *The Emancipation Proclamation.* Garden City, N.Y.: Doubleday, 1963.

William E. Gienapp. *Abraham Lincoln and Civil War America.* New York: Oxford University Press, 2001.

Harry V. Jaffa, *Crisis of the House Divided: An Interpretation of the Issues in the Lincoln-Douglas Debates.* Chicago: University of Chicago Press, 1959; 1982.

James M. McPherson. *Battle Cry of Freedom: The Civil War Era.* New York: Oxford University Press, 1988.

James M. McPherson. *Abraham Lincoln and the Second American Revolution*. New York: Oxford University Press, 1991.

Mark E. Neely, Jr. *The Last Best Hope of Earth: Abraham Lincoln and the Promise of America.* Cambridge, Massachusetts: Harvard University Press, 1993.

Allan Nevins. *The Ordeal of the Union*. 8 vols. New York: Scribner, 1947–1971.

John G. Nicolay and John Hay. *Abraham Lincoln: A History.* 10 vols. New York: The Century Co., 1890.

Stephen B. Oates. *With Malice Toward None: The Life of Abraham Lincoln.* Harperperennial Library, 1994.

Phillip S. Paludan. *The Presidency of Abraham Lincoln.* Lawrence: University Press of Kansas, 1994.

Merrill D Peterson. *Lincoln in American Memory.* New York: Oxford University Press, 1994.

James G. Randall. *Lincoln the President: Springfield to Gettysburg.* 2 vols. New York: Dodd, Mead, and Company, 1945.

Carl Sandburg. *Abraham Lincoln: The Prairie Years.* 2 vols. New York: Harcourt, Brace and Co., 1926.

———. *Abraham Lincoln: The War Years.* 4 vols. New York: Harcourt, Brace and Co., 1939.

Benjamin Platt Thomas. *Abraham Lincoln: A Biography.* New York: Knopf, 1952.

Douglas L. Wilson. *Honor's Voice: The Transformation of Abraham Lincoln.* New York: Knopf, 1998.

CONTRIBUTORS

RICHARD HOFSTADTER (1916–1970) was DeWitt Clinton Professor of American History at Columbia University and one of the most influential American historians in the twentieth century. His works include *The American Political Tradition and the Men who Made It* (1948), perhaps his best known book, as well as *The Age of Reform: From Bryan to F.D.R.* (1955), and *Anti-Intellectualism in American Life* (1963), both of which won the Pulitzer Prize.

EDMUND WILSON (1895–1972), the preeminent American literary critic of his time, wrote several books as well as a torrent of essays and reviews, during a career that lasted more than half a century. His best-known works include *Axel's Castle* (1931), *To the Finland Station* (1940), *The Wound and the Bow* (1941), and *Patriotic Gore* (1962).

JAMES OLIVER HORTON is Benjamin Banneker Professor Emeritus of American Studies and History at The George Washington University, director of the African American communities project of the Smithsonian's National Museum of American History, and past president of the Organization of American Historians. He has published widely in U.S. social and African American history, and has served as historical advisor to museums, the National Park Service, film and television productions, the White House, and the Disney Corporation. His most recent books are *Slavery and the Making of America* (2004) and the two-volume *Hard Road to Freedom: The Story of African America* (2002).

DAVID HERBERT DONALD is Charles Warren Professor Emeritus of American History at Harvard University. A recipient of the Pulitzer Prize for *Charles Sumner and the Coming of the Civil War* (1961) and *Look Homeward: A Life of Thomas Wolfe* (1988), Donald has also published path-breaking books on the American Civil War and Abraham Lincoln, including *Lincoln Reconsidered: Essays on the Civil War Era* (1947), *Lincoln's Herndon* (1948), *Civil War and Reconstruction* (1961), *Politics of Reconstruction, 1863–1867* (1965), *Lincoln* (1995), and *We Are Lincoln Men: Abraham Lincoln and His Friends* (2003).

JEAN H. BAKER is Elizabeth Todd Professor of History at Goucher College. A Fellow of the American Council of Learned Societies and the National Endowment for the Humanities, Baker's works include *Sisters: The Lives of America's Suffragists* (2005), *Mary Todd Lincoln: A Biography* (1987), and *Affairs of Party: The Political Culture of Northern Democrats in Mid-Nineteenth Century America* (1983), which received the Berkshire Prize in history.

RICHARD N. CURRENT is Distinguished Professor of History Emeritus at the University of North Carolina, Greensboro, and has published more than twenty books on the Civil War era including *Lincoln the President: Last Full Measure* (1955), which was awarded the prestigious Bancroft Prize, as well as *The Lincoln Nobody Knows* (1958), *Lincoln and the First Shot* (1963), and *The Political Thought of Abraham Lincoln* (1985).

DONALD E. FEHRENBACHER (1920–1997) was William Robertson Coe Professor of History and American Studies Emeritus at Stanford University. Fehrenbacher wrote widely on politics, slavery, and Abraham Lincoln, and received the Pulitzer Prize for history in 1979 for *The Dred Scott Case: Its Significance in American Law and Politics*. A collection of Fehrenbacher's selected writings on Lincoln, *Lincoln in Text and Context*, was published in 1987.

DAVID M. POTTER (1910–1971) was professor of history at Yale University (1942–1961), and William Robertson Coe Professor of History and American Studies at Stanford University (1961–1971). His comprehensive narrative history, *The Impending Crisis: 1848–1861*, which was edited and finished by Donald Fehrenbacher in 1976, won the Pulitzer Prize. Potter's other books include *People of Plenty: Economic Abundance and the American Character* (1954), *Lincoln and His Party in the Secession Crisis* (1962), and *The South and the Sectional Conflict* (1968).

JOHN HOPE FRANKLIN is James B. Duke Professor Emeritus at Duke University and recipient of many honors, including the Charles Frankel Prize for outstanding contribution to the humanities (1993) and the Presidential Medal of Freedom (1995). In addition to his presidencies of the Organization of American Historians, the American Historical Association, and the Southern Historical Association, Franklin received many appointments to national commissions including the National Council of the Humanities, the President's Advisory Commission on Ambassadorial Appointments, and One America: The President's Initiative on Race. His most influential work, *From Slavery to Freedom: A History of African Americans* (1947), has sold millions of copies and is in its eighth edition. Franklin's many works include *The Free Negro in North Carolina* (1943), *The Militant South, 1800–1861* (1956), *Reconstruction after the Civil War* (1961), *The Emancipation Proclamation* (1965), *Equality in America* (1976), *The Color Line: Legacy for the 21st Century* (1993), and *Runaway Slaves: Rebels on the Plantation* (1999). Franklin received the Pulitzer Prize for biography for *George Washington Williams: A Biography* (1986).

JAMES M. MCPHERSON is George Henry Davis '86 Professor Emeritus of United States History at Princeton University, and received the Pulitzer Prize in history for his book, *Battle Cry of Freedom: The Civil War Era* (1988), which, in part, reignited national interest in the American Civil War. McPherson's other works include *The Struggle for Equality: Abolitionists and the Negro in the Civil War and Reconstruction* (1964), *Marching Toward Freedom: The Negro in the Civil War, 1861–1865* (1968); *For Cause and Comrades: Why Men Fought in the Civil War* (1997), *This Mighty Scourge* (2007), and, most recently, *Tried by War: Abraham Lincoln as Commander-in-Chief* (2008).

MARK E. NEELY, JR. is McCabe Greer Professor in the American Civil War Era at Pennsylvania State University. His book *The Fate of Liberty: Abraham Lincoln and Civil Liberties* won the 1992 Pulitzer Prize in history. Neely's other works include *The Last Best Hope of Earth: Abraham Lincoln and the Promise of America* (1993), *The Union Divided: Party Conflict in the Civil War North* (2002), and, most recently, *The Boundaries of American Political Culture in the Civil War Era* (2005).

INDEX